J. T. (John Thomas) Ball

Historical Review of the Legislative Systems Operative in Ireland

From the Invasion of Henry the Second to the Union (1172-1800)

J. T. (John Thomas) Ball

Historical Review of the Legislative Systems Operative in Ireland
From the Invasion of Henry the Second to the Union (1172-1800)

ISBN/EAN: 9783744721783

Printed in Europe, USA, Canada, Australia, Japan

Cover: Foto ©ninafisch / pixelio.de

More available books at **www.hansebooks.com**

HISTORICAL REVIEW

OF

THE LEGISLATIVE SYSTEMS

OPERATIVE IN IRELAND,

FROM THE

INVASION OF HENRY THE SECOND TO THE UNION

(1172—1800).

BY THE RIGHT HON.
J. T. BALL, LL.D., D.C.L.

NEW EDITION,
REVISED THROUGHOUT AND ENLARGED.

LONDON:
LONGMANS, GREEN, AND CO.,
AND NEW YORK: 13 EAST 16th STREET.
DUBLIN:
HODGES, FIGGIS, AND CO.
1889.

PREFACE.

RECENT political discussion has attracted attention to the legislative systems operative in Ireland prior to its Union with Great Britain. If, however, we desire to ascertain what is recorded of them, and to examine their respective characteristics, we must proceed to search for the requisite facts through the entire series of events with which the general history of the country is concerned. There is as yet wanting a consecutive narrative which shall trace the succession of these systems to each other, the forms they respectively assumed, and their distinctive peculiarities. In the following pages it is sought to supply the deficiency. At the same time, it is intended also to consider the controversies connected with the claim made by the English Parliament to legislate for Ireland, with the relinquishment of that claim in

1782, and with the Union of Great Britain and Ireland in 1800—excluding, however, from the last of these subjects questions which have been raised respecting the means employed to induce adoption of the policy of Union by the Irish Parliament, and also respecting the degree of support which, when proposed, this policy received outside Parliament, as such questions could not be satisfactorily investigated without a minute and lengthened examination of evidence, disproportioned to the limits proposed for this treatise.

April, 1888.

In the present edition I have endeavoured to correct errors, and supply omissions which have been observed in the former. Subjects also, and observations, which were then placed in the Appendix, have been introduced in the body of the treatise; and some matters formerly excluded receive consideration. The result has necessarily been considerable additions to, and alterations of, the original text; but in no instance has there consciously been any deviation from the original scope and design, which proposed merely a narrative of events, and a record of the opinions entertained respecting them at the time when they occurred, without passing upon them the judgment which a later and more enlightened political philosophy might form. This course has at least the authority of Bacon to defend it, who pronounces it 'the true office of history to represent the events themselves, together with the counsels, and to leave the observations and conclusions thereupon to the liberty and faculty of every man's judgment.'

J. T. B.

August, 1889.

CONTENTS.

CHAPTER I. (1172–1613.)

	PAGE
HENRY II. WITH AN ARMY LANDS IN IRELAND,	1
RECEIVES THE HOMAGE OF IRISH KINGS AND CHIEFTAINS,	1
SYNOD OF CASHEL AND COUNCIL OF LISMORE,	2
COUNCILS IN HENRY'S REIGN,	3
COUNCILS OF JOHN, A.D. 1204,	3
SUBSEQUENT COUNCILS,	4
ENGLISH LAW INTRODUCED,	5
PRIVY COUNCIL,	6
WOGAN'S PARLIAMENT, A.D. 1295,	7
BEGINNING OF ELECTIVE REPRESENTATION,	7
SUBSEQUENT PARLIAMENTS,	8
HOUSE OF LORDS AND HOUSE OF COMMONS,	11
THE IRISH ADMITTED INTO PARLIAMENT, 33 HEN. VIII.,	13
ELIZABETH'S FIRST PARLIAMENT, A.D. 1560,	13
POYNINGS' LAW,	14
PERROT'S PARLIAMENT, A.D. 1585,	15
PARLIAMENT OF JAMES I., A.D. 1613,	17
CONVOCATION, A.D. 1613,	20

CHAPTER II.

IRISH REPRESENTATIVES SUMMONED TO ENGLAND,	23
CLAIM OF ENGLISH PARLIAMENT TO LEGISLATE FOR IRELAND,	24
ACTS OF PARLIAMENT ASSERTING THIS CLAIM,	25
IRISH PARLIAMENT ASSERTS ITS OWN EXCLUSIVE JURISDICTION IN IRELAND,	26
DECISIONS OF THE ENGLISH COURTS ON THE AUTHORITY OF THE ENGLISH PARLIAMENT IN IRELAND,	28

CHAPTER III. (1613–1688.)

	PAGE
PARLIAMENT OF 1634,	34
PARLIAMENT OF 1640,	34
CLAIMS EXCLUSIVE LEGISLATIVE JURISDICTION,	36
BOLTON'S TREATISE,	37
'HEADS OF BILLS' DEBATED IN IRISH PARLIAMENT,	38
ADVENTURERS' ACT,	39
CONFISCATIONS ENFORCED BY THE COMMONWEALTH,	40
IRISH MEMBERS IN ENGLISH PARLIAMENT (1654),	41
IRISH PARLIAMENT OF RESTORATION,	42
ENGLISH ACTS OF CHARLES II. AFFECTING IRELAND,	43

CHAPTER IV. (1688–1700.)

IRISH PARLIAMENT OF JAMES II. (1689,)	45
ENGLISH PARLIAMENT ANNULS ITS PROCEEDINGS,	46
IRISH PARLIAMENT OF WILLIAM AND MARY (1692),	48
IRISH PARLIAMENT OF 1695,	49
MOLYNEUX'S 'CASE OF IRELAND',	50
EXPORT OF WOOL FROM IRELAND, EXCEPT TO ENGLAND, PROHIBITED BY ENGLISH PARLIAMENT,	52

CHAPTER V.

TREATISES OF BOLTON, MOLYNEUX, MAYART, EXAMINED,	54

CHAPTER VI.

CLAIM OF THE ENGLISH PARLIAMENT TO LEGISLATE FOR IRELAND CONSIDERED,	66

CHAPTER VII. (1700–1719.)

ALLEGED ANALOGY OF SCOTCH PARLIAMENT CONSIDERED,	77
ACT OF UNION OF SCOTLAND WITH ENGLAND,	83
EXAMPLE OF SCOTLAND INFLUENCES IRISH PARLIAMENT,	83

Contents.

PAGE

IRISH HOUSES OF LORDS AND COMMONS SUGGEST UNION OF IRELAND WITH GREAT BRITAIN IN 1703 AND 1707,	84
SUGGESTION NOT ENCOURAGED IN ENGLAND,	85
OUTSIDE PARLIAMENT UNION UNPOPULAR IN IRELAND,	86
APPELLATE JURISDICTION OF ENGLISH HOUSE OF LORDS IN IRISH SUITS DISPUTED,	86
ACT OF 6 GEORGE I. (ENGLISH),	88
CONVOCATION NOT SUMMONED AFTER 1711,	89

CHAPTER VIII. (1719–1760.)

EFFECT OF ENGLISH ACTS AFFECTING IRISH TRADE,	90
DISSATISFACTION WITH 6 GEORGE I. IN IRELAND,	91
SWIFT,	92
WOOD'S COINAGE,	93
THE DRAPIER'S LETTERS,	94
PROSECUTION OF THE DRAPIER'S LETTERS,	96
ITS FAILURE,	96
WOOD'S PATENT REVOKED,	97
CONSTITUTION AND CHARACTER OF THE IRISH HOUSE OF COMMONS AT THIS TIME,	97
MODE IN WHICH THE IRISH PARLIAMENT WAS THEN MANAGED,	98
COMMONS ACTED WITH INDEPENDENCE AS TO FINANCE,	99
LUCAS,	99
UNION THEN HAD NO ADVOCATES IN IRELAND,	101
AN OPPOSITION FORMED IN THE HOUSE OF COMMONS,	103

CHAPTER IX. (1760–1780.)

ACCESSION OF GEORGE III.,	104
OCTENNIAL ACT.	104
EFFECTS OF THIS ACT,	105
PARLIAMENT OF 1768,	106
PATRONAGE OF THE CROWN USED TO INFLUENCE VOTES IN PARLIAMENT,	106
FLOOD,	107
DISCONTENT OF THE HOUSE OF COMMONS WITH THE SUBORDINATE POSITION OF THE IRISH PARLIAMENT,	108
VOLUNTEERS,	109

	PAGE
VOLUNTEERS COMBINE WITH PARLIAMENT TO DEMAND FREE TRADE,	111
RESOLUTIONS OF COMMONS AS TO FREE TRADE,	111
SUBSEQUENT PROCEEDINGS,	112
FREE TRADE CONCEDED,	112

CHAPTER X. (1780.)

MOVEMENT IN IRELAND FOR LEGISLATIVE INDEPENDENCE,	113
GRATTAN,	115
MOVES IN THE HOUSE OF COMMONS A RESOLUTION DECLARING THE RIGHTS OF THE IRISH PARLIAMENT,	116
MOTION FAILS,	117
GRATTAN'S SPEECH WHEN PROPOSING RESOLUTION,	117

CHAPTER XI. (1780–1782.)

OBJECT AND EFFECT OF GRATTAN'S SPEECH,	124
THE VOLUNTEERS,	128
CONVENTION OF VOLUNTEERS AT DUNGANNON,	129
GRATTAN MOVES IN THE HOUSE OF COMMONS RESOLUTIONS AS TO THE RIGHTS OF PARLIAMENT,	130
MOTION ADJOURNED,	130
MESSAGE FROM THE KING, APRIL 16, 1782,	131
TERMS INSISTED UPON BY GRATTAN,	132

CHAPTER XII. (1782.)

REPEAL OF THE ACT OF 6 GEORGE I.,	133
RENUNCIATION ACT,	135
REPEAL OF POYNINGS' LAW,	136
NEW CONSTITUTION MAKES NO PROVISION FOR THE CASE OF THE BRITISH AND IRISH PARLIAMENTS DISAGREEING,	138
PROVISIONS TO AVERT THIS DANGER SUGGESTED BY THE DUKE OF PORTLAND,	139
REASONS WHY THESE WERE NEVER PROPOSED IN PARLIAMENT,	140

CHAPTER XIII. (1782-1786.)

	PAGE
EFFECT OF CONSTITUTION OF 1782,	143
PATRONAGE USED TO INFLUENCE THE IRISH PARLIAMENT,	144
IN 1785 DISAGREEMENT BETWEEN BRITISH AND IRISH PARLIAMENTS,	146
COMMERCIAL RESOLUTIONS, 1785,	150

CHAPTER XIV. (1785-1798.)

POLICY OF UNION REJECTED IN 1707 NOW AGAIN REVIVED,	155
CONSIDERATIONS WHICH LED TO ITS REVIVAL,	156
EFFECT OF EXAMPLE OF SCOTLAND,	156
LITERARY ADVOCACY OF UNION,	158
UNION UNPOPULAR IN IRELAND,	159
REGENCY QUESTION,	160
CATHOLIC QUESTION,	163
PITT BEGINS IN 1792 TO FAVOUR UNION,	164
POLICY OF UNION DELAYED,	165
EVENTS BRING IT FORWARD,	167

CHAPTER XV.

HINDRANCES TO THE POLICY OF UNION,	171
MOTIVES TO FAVOUR THIS POLICY,	177

CHAPTER XVI. (1799.)

MARQUIS CORNWALLIS APPOINTED LORD LIEUTENANT 1798,	181
COOKE'S PAMPHLET,	181
BILL FOR UNION IN PREPARATION (SEPTEMBER 1798),	183
LORD CLARE,	183
NO PROVISION IN THE BILL FOR UNION FOR REMOVAL OF CATHOLIC DISABILITIES,	185
MESSAGE FROM KING TO BRITISH PARLIAMENT, 1799,	185
SHERIDAN DISSENTS FROM ADDRESS,	186
PITT REPLIES,	188
AFTERWARDS INTRODUCES RESOLUTIONS DEFINING TERMS OF UNION,	189
SPEECH OF PITT, 31ST JANUARY, 1799,	189
RESOLUTIONS CARRIED BOTH IN LORDS AND COMMONS IN ENGLAND,	196

CHAPTER XVII. (1799.)

	PAGE
LORD LIEUTENANT'S SPEECH TO IRISH PARLIAMENT, JANUARY, 1799,	197
PROCEEDINGS IN COMMONS AND LORDS,	197
GOVERNMENT DEFEATED IN FORMER,	198
STATE OF PARTIES IN THE HOUSE OF COMMONS,	198
FOSTER,	200
LORD CASTLEREAGH,	200
REGENCY BILL PROPOSED,	201
SPEECH OF FOSTER AGAINST UNION,	202

CHAPTER XVIII.

DIFFICULTIES IN THE WAY OF THE MINISTERIAL POLICY,	206
PRIVATE INTERESTS UNION WOULD AFFECT,	207
POWER OF OWNERS OF BOROUGHS IN IRELAND,	208
COMPENSATION TO BE GIVEN TO THEM,	210
EXERTIONS TO GAIN EXTERNAL SUPPORT FOR UNION,	212
EFFECT OF THEM,	213

CHAPTER XIX. (1800.)

SESSION OF 1800,	215
LORD LIEUTENANT'S SPEECH,	215
AMENDMENT TO ADDRESS MOVED IN COMMONS DEFEATED,	216
RESOLUTIONS OF 1799 ARE SENT BY LORD LIEUTENANT TO BOTH HOUSES, AND ARE CARRIED,	216
ANALYSIS OF DIVISION LIST IN COMMONS,	217
SAURIN, BUSHE, GRATTAN,	218
SPEECH OF LORD CLARE,	219
MOTION IN COMMONS TO ADDRESS CROWN FOR A DISSOLUTION OF PARLIAMENT DEFEATED,	220
MOTION CONSIDERED,	220
MOTION MADE IN ENGLISH HOUSE OF COMMONS FOR SUSPENSION OF PROCEEDINGS FOR UNION DEFEATED,	222
ACTS OF UNION PASSED BY BRITISH AND IRISH PARLIAMENTS,	224
ACT COMPENSATING OWNERS OF DISFRANCHISED BOROUGHS,	224

CHAPTER XX.

	PAGE
ACTS OF UNION,	225
CONSTITUTION OF IMPERIAL PARLIAMENT,	226
CONSIDERED,	227
IRISH EXECUTIVE DEPARTMENT NOT ALTERED,	228
OBJECTION THAT IRISH ACT OF UNION EXTRA VIRES,	226
THE ANSWERS GIVEN TO THE OBJECTION,	229
NO INTERMEDIATE COURSE OR COMPROMISE PROPOSED,	233
SHERIDAN'S OBSERVATIONS ON THE PLAN OF A LIMITED IRISH PARLIAMENT,	235
CANNING'S OBSERVATIONS ON SUCH A MEASURE,	236
OBJECTIONS TO, FROM ENGLISH POINT OF VIEW,	238

CHAPTER XXI.

RETROSPECT,	240

APPENDIX—NOTES AND ILLUSTRATIONS,	258
INDEX,	279

CORRIGENDUM.—Page 65. In the second sentence of the last paragraph the words 'affirmative' and 'negative' have been accidentally exchanged. The sentence should be:—As Molyneux took the affirmative side, so those who answered him took the negative.

IRISH LEGISLATIVE SYSTEMS.

CHAPTER I.

COUNCILS AND PARLIAMENTS.

[1172—1613.]

THE authority of the Crown of England in Ireland dates from the winter of 1172-3, when Henry II.—who in the previous month of October had landed near Waterford at the head of an army formidable rather from its valour and discipline than its number—received the homage of the principal kings and chieftains. At this period in England the Council (as the national legislature was called) had attained considerable importance, and its advice and assistance were sought whenever taxation or other needs of the government rendered such a proceeding necessary or advisable. No institution of a similar character existed in Ireland from which Henry could ask a confirmation of the sovereignty that henceforward he assumed over the country: if he desired to refer to such an assembly, he

<small>Synod of Cashel.</small>

must himself devise its form and give it being. National synods of the Irish clergy had, however, on various occasions been held, the last of them about twenty years before he came to Ireland. These were the legislatures of the Church. To have a Synod of the bishops and clergy summoned, would be merely to follow precedents; and if it came in obedience to Henry's wishes, and afterwards acted upon the policy of adopting English views of the questions considered, it must, from the superior intelligence and education of its members and the reverence entertained for their offices, exercise immense influence upon public opinion. He therefore caused a Synod of the Irish Church to meet at Cashel. Over this assembly Christian, Bishop of Lismore, the Papal Legate in Ireland, presided. Several decrees were then made, of which one object was to bring the usages of the Irish Church more into harmony with those of the English Church than they had previously been.

Council of Lismore.
According to some contemporary historians, the Synod of Cashel was not the only assembly for legislative purposes which Henry, during his stay in Ireland, caused to be convened. Another, lay in character, although ecclesiastics may have been present, is by them narrated to have met at Lismore. The name of Council has been given to the meeting; but, if held (for this cannot be considered certain, since some writers of the highest authority in reference to the period make

no mention of such an event), it seems to have been rather a convention of Irish chieftains and of the leading English knights who, by the permission or command of Henry, came to Ireland. Those who were present upon this occasion are reported to have gratefully accepted the laws of England, and to have bound themselves by an oath to their observance.*

Henry remained in Ireland about six months. There is some reason to think that after his departure Councils were during his reign summoned in Ireland, which resembled the English Councils, and were called for similar purposes and with similar powers. Evidence exists of legislation at that time, difficult to explain or account for, unless it were enacted by some such authority, and in the proceedings of at least one subsequent Parliament it is distinctly asserted that there had been institutions similar to itself from the 'time of the conquest by Henry Fitz Empress.' Moreover, it is improbable that the King did not afford to his Deputy in another country the assistance which he was himself accustomed to rely upon in his own.† <small>Councils under Henry II.</small>

But the extant records of Councils in Ireland resembling the English National Councils do not begin until after John's accession to the <small>Council summoned in Ireland A.D. 1204.</small>

---

* See further as to the Council of Lismore, Note A of Appendix.

† For evidence that Councils were held under Henry II., see Note B of Appendix.

throne of England. The first is dated in the fifth year of his reign, A.D. 1204. Menaced by France, the King had obtained from the English Council an Aid (as supplies of money were then termed), and he now sought to procure a further Aid from an Irish Council. The writ or mandate for this Council is addressed to the Archbishops, Bishops, Abbots, Priors, Archdeacons, and the whole clergy in Ireland, and (as appears by a memorandum at foot of the record) also to the Earls, Barons, Justices, Sheriffs, Knights, Citizens, Merchants, Freeholders (*liberis tenentibus*), and all other the King's faithful in Ireland (*per Hiberniam constitutis*). It refers to the Aid obtained in England, and asks that those to whom it is addressed should give assistance (*non consuetudinarie sed amabiliter efficax nobis auxilium faciatis*), in such manner as the Justiciary (Walter de Lacy) and others who were then sent over should declare unto them.*

Subsequent Councils.

The constitution of this Council was imitated from the constitution of contemporary Councils in England. This will be seen by comparing the persons to whom writs requiring attendance were to be addressed with the persons attending

---

* This writ or mandate is contained in a Roll in the Tower of London. It is printed in full in Mr. Lynch's Treatise, entitled *A View of the Legal Institutions, Honorary Hereditary Offices, and Feudal Baronies of Ireland established during the reign of Henry II.*: it will be found at p. 289 of the treatise.

similar assemblies in England. During the remainder of the thirteenth century Councils continued to be summoned in Ireland, and they also follow the same models. The classes specified as those from which they were to be composed are, however, not always the same. Sometimes, too, the general terms *magnates, communitas*, are substituted for distinct enumeration of the persons whom the designation was intended to include.* It is not probable that more than a selection from the classes named in the mandate was on any occasion actually cited.

From the first the English who settled in Ireland seem, among and between themselves, to have adhered to the legal principles by which rights of person or property were determined in their own country. The gifts of land from the Crown were framed in conformity with the feudal system: they conferred upon the grantees the privileges, and required from them the duties, which according to that system were connected with the position of the chief tenants from the Crown. The legal consequences of such grants descended also to subordinate interests created under them. If questions arose which the principles of feudalism did not answer, there was nothing in the local customs and usages to induce the emigrants to abandon the rules of their own jurisprudence in reference to

English law introduced into Ireland.

---

* See Note C of Appendix.

them. But powerful as these circumstances were to establish the authority of the laws of England in Ireland, it was not left to rest merely upon this basis. Positive enactments declared it. Omitting the decree of the Council of Lismore as a controverted matter, we have undoubted acts of John directing that these laws should be obeyed, and as undoubted confirmations of John's acts by Henry III.*

<small>English law disregarded in Irish districts.</small>

The language of all these enactments is wide enough to include the entire island within its operation. No distinction was made in them between the native Irish and the persons of English race who had settled in the country. But their practical effect was very different from their apparent intention. Outside the districts inhabited by the English the old customs and usages continued: the laws sought to be imposed were not taken notice of, and the English Government made no attempt to enforce them.

<small>Connexion of Privy Council with legislation.</small>

As the English kings did not reside in Ireland, they placed over the people a chief governor deriving his authority from themselves. At first this governor was termed the Justiciary or Deputy;†

---

* See Note D of Appendix.

† Mr. Bagwell thinks that the first person who had the title of Lord Lieutenant (if we except an early case of de Courcy) was Lionel, Earl of Ulster and Duke of Clarence, one of the royal family, sent to Ireland in 1361. Deputy was originally applicable where there was an absent Governor, and another acted for him. (See Bagwell's *Ireland under the Tudors*, vol. i., p. 100.)

afterwards, but (except in rare instances) not until a later date, he was described as Lord Lieutenant. From about the reign of Henry III. the Governor was surrounded by advisers or counsellors, who in process of time came to be known as the Privy Council. When this body was first formed is not clear. It, no doubt, soon followed the establishment of the corresponding institution in England, which can be traced under Henry III., although it was not developed until the reign of the two first Edwards. Imitating the functions of its model in relation to the King, the Irish Privy Council would, we may assume, advise the Deputy in respect of his legislative acts.*

In 1295 the principle of elective representation of the Commons was introduced into the Councils. Henceforward we may fairly dignify the Irish legislative assemblies with the title of Parliaments—a name which about this time began to come into general use in England. The representation, however, of the Commons in the assembly of 1295 was of a limited character, extending only to the counties of Dublin, Louth, Kildare, Waterford, Tipperary, Cork, Limerick, Kerry, Roscommon, and the liberties (as counties palatine were called) of Meath, Kilkenny, and Ulster.† Each sheriff of a county and

In 1295 elective representation of the Commons.

---

* See Note E of Appendix.

† A 'Liberty' or 'County Palatine' lay under the rule of some great nobleman, who nominated the sheriffs and administered justice, much like an absolute prince.

seneschal of a liberty was directed—the former in full court of his county (*pleno comitatu*), and the latter in full court of his liberty (*in plenâ curiâ libertatis suæ*)—to cause two of the better and more discreet knights of the county or liberty to be elected as representatives to the assembly of Bishops, Abbots, Priors, Barons, and other persons of high station (*optimates*) then summoned.

Parliament of 1295 called by Sir John Wogan.

The Parliament of 1295 is known as Wogan's Parliament,* because convened by Sir John Wogan, upon whom about that time the government of Ireland was conferred by Edward I. The basis of representation then adopted was enlarged in subsequent Parliaments, so as to give elective rights to towns as well as counties—citizens and burgesses being, in 1311 and afterwards, directed to be returned from cities and boroughs. In 1360, separate representation was given in some counties to portions under ecclesiastical jurisdiction called crosses (*croceæ*).†

Representation of the Commons previously in England.

The introduction of elective representation of the Commons in Ireland followed the introduction of a similar procedure in England. Thus, in 1254, for an English Parliament, the election of knights from the shires was directed; in 1264, at Simon de Montfort's Parliament, representatives from cities and boroughs were added;

---

* In the *Liber Niger* of Christ Church Cathedral there is an account of Wogan's Parliament. See Note F of Appendix.

† Compare chaps. III. and XI. of Lynch's *Treatise on Dignities*, already cited, and the writs there extracted.

and in 1295 the summons of two knights from each shire, two citizens from each city, and two burgesses from each borough, may be regarded as having fixed a final plan of representation for English shires and towns.*

The representative constitution of the House of Commons which commenced in Ireland under Wogan was always afterwards continued; but the number of constituencies to return members varied, as writs were not always sent to the same counties or towns. In like manner the number of bishops, peers, and superiors of religious houses who were summoned was not constant; there were sometimes but few of a class, and in at least one instance, while some peers were omitted, a few knights were cited by name.† {Representation of the Commons continued.}

The importance of the early Councils and Parliaments of Ireland is disputed. Some depreciate it so much as to hold that there were no assemblies within the first one hundred and forty years from the Invasion of Henry II. worthy of these titles. The true view appears to be that many were summoned for petty purposes, but that others were of a much more elevated character.‡ No doubt all deserve the reproach of {Early Councils and Parliaments.}

---

* See Stubbs' *Constitutional History*, 4th ed., vol. ii., pp. 132–3, 230–2.

† In 1360, 33 Edw. III. See statement of the writs then issued, printed from the original records by Lynch, *ut supra*, p. 315.

‡ See Note G of Appendix.

being exclusive, and from only a portion of the inhabitants of the island. The native Irish, unless it may be in very rare instances, were never invited to attend them; nor, if they had been, is it probable that they would have come. The profession of allegiance made by the chieftains had never been followed by any genuine reconcilement with English rule; and if they were to acknowledge the jurisdiction of Parliament and attend its meetings, they must have ceased to be (what they had been) princes, and become subjects.

<small>Natives unwilling to attend.</small>

For similar reasons, in process of time, the Norman nobles and knights, to whom territories had been assigned in Irish districts, were found unwilling to obey the summonses directed to them. Assimilating their habits to those of the people by whom they were surrounded, they became, like them, disinclined to meet the adherents of English policy and usages. To check their tendency to absence, fines were from an early period imposed for non-attendance.*

<small>Nobles and knights from Irish districts unwilling to attend.</small>

After the regular legislative assemblies had developed into Parliaments, there still seem to have been others of less importance (probably upon emergencies or for local affairs) held, which retained the old name of Councils. An ordinance of Edward III. (*Ordinatio de Statu Hiberniæ*, 31 Edw. III.) assumes both modes of legislating to

<small>Councils continue after there were Parliaments.</small>

---

* See Note H of Appendix.

exist, and in enumerating the persons to attend either Councils or Parliaments includes Privy Councillors.*

At first all the members of a Parliament, whether ecclesiastical or lay, whether peers or commoners, sat together; afterwards there were two Houses. The date of separation does not appear, but was certainly after a similar arrangement was made in the English Parliament.† Separation into two Houses.

When the distinction of the Houses in the Irish Parliament becomes apparent, the House of Lords is found to consist of lords spiritual and temporal, the former including the heads of some religious houses, along with the bishops;‡ in the House of Commons, besides knights from counties, and citizens and burgesses from cities and boroughs; some of the clergy, elected to represent their order—termed Proctors—attended. It is probable that as the sitting of Parliament was not accompanied by the sitting of any ecclesiastical convocation or synod, the Proctors originally voted in the proceedings, at least when they concerned the Church; but in the reign of Henry VIII. a statute was passed which How the separate Houses constituted.

28 Henry VIII., ch. 12.

---

* See Note I of Appendix.

† Stubbs seems to date the separation of the two Houses of Parliament in England about 1332 (*Const. Hist.*, 4th ed., vol. ii., chap. 16, p. 393).

‡ According to Ware, 24 in number—14 Abbots and 10 Priors. He gives the names of their Monasteries. *Antiq.*, chap. 26.

declared that they were mere counsellors and assistants.

Constitution of House of Commons variable.
Writs for the election of representatives to the House of Commons were not, as a rule, sent outside the limits of the counties that had been formed before the time of their being issued; but sometimes Connaught and Ulster were treated as each in itself a county. Down to the accession of Elizabeth, the only counties which appear in the writs are Dublin, Kildare, Meath, Uriel or Louth, Catherlough or Carlow, Kilkenny, Wexford, Cork, Limerick, Kerry, and Tipperary—reputed to have been constituted by John; two small ones, Ards and Down, of later date; Westmeath, made by dividing Meath, under Henry VIII.; King's County and Queen's County, constituted by Philip and Mary; and in a few instances Roscommon.

Members in House of Commons.
Sir John Davis asserts that until the 34th year of the reign of Henry VIII., when Meath was divided, the number of members of the House of Commons could not have amounted to over a hundred. The counties previously were, he says, twelve besides the liberty of Tipperary, the cities four, and the boroughs not above thirty.* Any addition to these numbers before the reign of

---

* See Address of Sir John Davis, as Speaker of the House of Commons, to Sir Arthur Chichester, then Deputy, afterwards referred to. Davis treats Tipperary as two counties: this is because there was the liberty of Tipperary, and the cross of Tipperary.

Queen Elizabeth could have been only from the subdivision of Meath and the formation of the King's and Queen's Counties. Her first House of Commons, called immediately on her accession to the crown (A.D. 1560), seems to have numbered only 76; twenty members from ten counties, and fifty-six from twenty-eight cities and boroughs.*

To a Parliament held in the 33rd year of Henry VIII. Sir John Davis attributes the admission of persons of Irish race to sit in Parliament. It was attended by some of the chieftains, who gave their approval to the Act then passed, by which it was provided that the kings of England should thenceforth be kings of Ireland, and not merely lords of Ireland, as they had until then been called. But these chieftains seem to have been rather assenting parties to the proceedings than actual members of the assembly.† 33 Hen. VIII., Irish admitted to Parliament.

From the reign of Elizabeth Parliaments were held always in Dublin; previously they met also at other places, which were selected from motives of temporary convenience; in some instances, with the object of establishing by their presence the authority of the English Government in a particular locality.‡ Members appear to have had, at least during some periods, an allowance Where Parliament met.

---

* Writs appear to have been sent to ten more counties and one more borough. See Note K of Appendix.

† See Note L of Appendix.

‡ See Lord Mountmorres's *Treatise*, vol. ii., p. 98.

for their attendance—a practice imitated from the English Parliaments.

Poynings' Law, 10 Hen. VII., ch. 4.

Before leaving this epoch, it is proper to notice that the action of the Irish Parliament was from the tenth year of Henry VII. subject to restrictions then imposed by an Act of its own. Poynings' Law, as the statute was called, because passed under the rule of a Deputy of that name, enacted that Parliaments should not be holden in Ireland until the king's lieutenant and council had notified to the king, under the Great Seal of that land, the causes and considerations, and all such Acts as to them seemeth should pass in the same Parliament, nor until such causes, and acts, and considerations had been affirmed by the king and his council to be good and expedient, and licence to summon Parliament had been given under the Great Seal of England.

Why desired.

These provisions were desired, by the king's ministers because enabling them to direct the course of legislation, and by Parliament because protecting it against the governors sent over from time to time, who, until that period, could summon a meeting when and for what purposes they might please *—a power which had been abused in the troubled reign of Henry VI.

---

* Sir John Davis says the statute was made at the prayer of Parliament (Discovery, ed. 1704, p. 49). See also Flood's Speech in the Irish House of Commons, 11th December, 1781.

Under Henry VIII. and Elizabeth, Poynings' Law was, by statutes of the Irish Parliament, on some occasions temporarily repealed or rather suspended; and an Act of the latter (15 Elizabeth, ch. 3) provided that this should not be done, except by the greater part of both the Lords and Commons, meaning probably not merely by a majority of those present, but by a number equal to what would constitute in each House a majority if every member were present.*

<small>Poynings' Law sometimes suspended.</small>

The reign of Queen Elizabeth brought a great increase to the counties, and a consequent enlargement of the representative element in the House of Commons. Sir Henry Sidney, in 1565, formed the counties of Longford, Galway, Sligo, Mayo, and defined Clare and Roscommon. Sir John Perrot formed, in 1583, the county of Leitrim; in 1584, the counties of Armagh, Monaghan, Tyrone, Coleraine or Derry, Donegal, Fermanagh, and Cavan. He also finally constituted Antrim and Down. Wicklow, too, appears in a parliamentary record before the Queen's death.

<small>Counties added by Elizabeth.</small>

In 1585 a Parliament was called by Sir John Perrot, from whom it has been named Perrot's Parliament. The number of members of the House of Commons attending it were, 54 from 27 counties, and 72 from 36 cities and boroughs —126 in all, of whom 18 seem (to judge by their names) to have been of Irish race.

<small>Perrot's Parliament, A.D. 1585.</small>

---

* See Lord Mountmorres, vol. i., pp. 49–52.

House of Lords in 1585.

At this time the House of Lords was composed of bishops and temporal lords; and such had been its constitution from the time when the monasteries were suppressed by Henry VIII., and when, as a consequence, abbots and priors ceased to be summoned. The temporal peers were nobles either by virtue of patents conferring titles on themselves or by hereditary right derived from those on whom titles had been before conferred; and so it had been for about two centuries. In Perrot's Parliament the number of spiritual peers was 26; of temporal, also 26. Of the latter, 4 were of Irish race, among whom was O'Neill.

Irish chieftains attend Perrot's Parliament.

In addition to Peers and members returned by the counties, cities, and boroughs to the House of Commons, a considerable number of Irish chieftains attended Perrot's Parliament, but not as forming part of it. They were required to come in order that they might thus give evidence of their allegiance to the Queen, and, by assenting to the proceedings, be the more bound to carry into effect whatever might be enacted.*

Perrot's Parliament not obedient.

Until Perrot's Parliament the English Governments seem to have obtained from the Irish Parliaments such measures as were requisite to carry into effect their policy, even when these were not in harmony with the sentiments of either Lords or Commons. Thus, in 1536, Henry VIII., and in 1560, Queen Elizabeth, succeeded in hav-

---

* See, as to Perrot's Parliament, Note M of Appendix.

ing their Supremacy Acts and the other statutes intended to alter the ecclesiastical system passed. But under Perrot a spirit of opposition developed itself in the House of Commons. It refused to suspend Poynings' Law, as previous Parliaments had done for other deputies, and rejected a bill for a subsidy and another to vest in the Queen without inquisition the lands of attainted persons.*

For twenty-seven years after the Parliament of 1585 no Parliament was called in Ireland. In the interval James I. had succeeded to the throne of England, and brought with him a policy which, as regards Ireland, was in many respects more enlarged than that of his predecessors. His object was to establish his own authority over its people, whether native or Anglo-Irish, and in return to treat all as subjects. He therefore desired that in the House of Commons the Irish districts should be represented, and that a much increased proportion of the members should be Irish. Accordingly, in 1613 he convened a Parliament for which no qualification of race or of religion was required. To counterbalance the effect which this might have in weakening the English interest, he created about forty new boroughs, situate for the most part in Ulster where the Scottish and English colonists of the Plantation had settled. These boroughs had then very few inhabitants.

Parliament of James I., A.D. 1613.

---

* Leland, *History*, 3rd ed., vol ii., p. 296.

C

Constitution of Parliament of 1613.

When Parliament assembled, the House of Commons consisted of 232 members, about a hundred more than Perrot's Parliament of 1585 (the last preceding) contained. Of those returned 226 attended. At this time distinctions founded on religious differences had taken the place of former distinctions of race or nationality, and the House was divided into two parties representing these differences. The Recusants (as those who adhered to the Church of Rome were at that time termed) are said to have numbered 101.

Address of Sir John Davis, Speaker, to Sir Arthur Chichester

Sir John Davis, who, after much resistance from the minority, became Speaker of the House of Commons, delivered an address to Sir Arthur Chichester, then the Deputy, the object of which was to extol the importance of the Parliament and the wisdom which had called it together. He contrasts it with its predecessors as regards its number, enlargement of the character of its representation, and the purposes for which it was called. Some abatement must be made from his panegyric, delivered not without a design to please James; but, after every proper abatement is made, there will remain sufficient to establish the superiority of the House of Commons he presided over in the several points which he has selected for praise. The addition of forty boroughs, then much objected to by the Parliamentary Opposition, he defends, upon the ground that Queen Elizabeth had made no boroughs, and that forty boroughs did not bear a greater proportion to the seventeen counties formed in her reign, than the thirty cities and boroughs which had been constituted representative in the original twelve counties did to them.*

But whatever may be thought as to the superiority over its predecessors claimed for this Parliament in respect of its constitution, there can be little controversy as to its superiority in policy. Legislation before this period had drawn a broad line of separation between the Anglo-Irish and the natives. Acts of Parliament, of which the Statute of Kilkenny passed in the reign of Edward III. was the earliest, and an Act of Henry VIII. the latest, were as yet in force, under whose provisions intermarriage, fostering, gossipred with the Irish, rendered any of the English race subject to the penalties of high treason. To adopt Irish customs, to imitate their usages and manners, even in such trifling matters as having long hair, not shaving the upper lip, wearing linen dyed with saffron, were offences.†

Legislation of Parliament of 1613.

---

* See Note N of Appendix.

† Statute of Kilkenny and 28 Henry VIII., chap. 15. The statute of Kilkenny is not in the printed collections of statutes. A very perfect edition of it, by Mr. Hardiman, has been published by the Irish Archæological Society. Other statutes, in the several collections of Irish statutes, also relating to the natives, are—5 Edward IV., chap. 3; 25 Henry VI., chap. 4; 28 Henry VI., chap. 1; 10 Henry VII., chap. 8. See, besides, an Act prohibiting the English attending Irish fairs, 7 Henry VI., and also an Act, 25 Henry VI., and another,

<small>13 James I., ch. 5.</small>

The Parliament of 1613 at once repealed this whole code, and introduced in the Act passed for the purpose a declaration—more important even than the repeal thereby enacted—that the cause of these laws did then cease, since the inhabitants of the kingdom, without distinction, were taken into his Majesty's gracious protection; and that there were no better means to settle peace than to allow them to commerce and match together, that so they might grow into one nation, and former differences be forgotten.

<small>Convocation summoned.</small>

James, desirous of completing his Irish legislative arrangements as near English example as possible, convened, along with the Parliament of 1613, a Convocation of the clergy. There had before been, as has been already mentioned, national synods, but no assembly in the nature of an English Convocation. The present was modelled upon the precedent of the Convocation of Canterbury, except that it was for all Ireland, while the latter was for a province. The Convocation of 1613 voted the king a subsidy, and established the precedent that it was by an ecclesiastical body the clergy in Ireland were to be taxed.

---

19 Edward IV. (none of them in the printed collections), which are cited by Hardiman, *ut supra*, p. 115. 13. 11.

CHAPTER II.

THE CLAIM OF THE ENGLISH PARLIAMENT TO LEGISLATE FOR IRELAND.

THE last chapter traces the growth of the legislative systems existing in Ireland through a period of more than four hundred years. They took the shape at first of Councils, afterwards of Parliaments with a representative element, and finally with two separate Houses. The extent of their authority, the subjects in respect of which they might exercise legislative jurisdiction, had not, when they were originally called into existence, been defined by any treaty, ordinance, or statute. They were modelled upon contemporary English precedents, and when the originals grew in importance so did the copies along with them. As far as depended upon their constitution, whatever jurisdiction was inherent in the nature of such institutions was possessed by these Irish Parliaments, subject necessarily to the limitation that, as they were created by the kings of England, the character of the jurisdiction and the subjects on which it might operate should not be inconsistent with such other relations as were held to

<small>Authority of councils and Parliaments.</small>

subsist between the Irish people and the crown and kingdom of England.

Poynings' Law. It was, of course, in the power of the Irish Parliaments to impose restrictions upon themselves by positive enactments for the purpose, and this had been done, as we have seen, long previous to the time at which we have arrived, in relation to the procedure requisite for the purpose of legislation. Before any valid statute could be passed, Poynings' law obliged the consent of the Irish Privy Council and of the English Privy Council to be procured.

New principle of legislation introduced by James I. There has been occasion already to notice that although the legislation of the Irish Parliament, unless when otherwise expressed, included, and, so far as appeared from its language, was framed to take effect upon the entire country, it was in practice and reality neither enforced nor regarded outside the districts inhabited by the Anglo-Irish settlers. Under James I. was first introduced the principle, thenceforward recognized, that the laws enacted, unless restricted in operation by their own language, should bind the whole kingdom, and that the people, who were all to be treated as subjects of the Crown, should be compelled to obey them.

Was jurisdiction of Irish Parliament exclusive? From this time there does not appear any open resistance to the authority of enactments made by the Irish Parliaments: some chieftains might continue to disobey them, but even these professed to admit their obligation. Still this did not terminate the questions connected with the authority of such assemblies. Others of grave importance had also to be answered. Was their jurisdiction exclusive? Was the English legislature possessed of paramount or concurrent power within the same sphere and area? And long before the time at which we have now arrived the questions had been raised in both the English and Irish Parliaments, and had received different replies in each. They had also become a subject of examination by judicial tribunals, and of judgments by them not always agreeing in opinion.

Before, however, entering on this controversy, some events which, although not directly connected with it, are not without a certain degree of relation to topics discussed during its continuance, deserve notice. On more than one occasion, representatives of Irish constituencies were summoned to, and attended in, England. The most remarkable of these incidents occurred in the reign of Edward III., A.D. 1376, when a mandate was issued, directing that the Irish clergy from each diocese should send two persons, and the Irish counties, cities, and boroughs also each two persons, to England, to treat, consult, and agree (*ad tractandum, consulendum, et concordandum*) with the King and his Council (*cum domino rege et ejus consilio*), as well concerning the government of Ireland as concerning the war there (*tam super gubernatione ejusdem* (*i.e. Hibernicæ*) *terræ quam super auxilio et sustentatione*

Irish representatives summoned to England.

guerræ regis). The circumstances under which this proceeding took place were that the King, requiring supplies to meet his expenses in Ireland at a time when all his other resources were exhausted by wars in Scotland and France, had failed in obtaining them from the Irish Parliament, although a special agent (Sir Nicholas Dagworth) went over and attended to explain his needs and the causes of them. In answer to the summons of the King, representatives were returned and sent; but in some instances the returns were accompanied with protests and with declarations that the delegates chosen were not to have any right to tax or impose burdens. These protests asserted that the mandate was in contradiction of the laws, liberties, and customs in use from the conquest of Ireland, and that there was no precedent for sending representatives from Ireland to an English Parliament or Council.*

Controversy as to jurisdiction of English Parliament in Ireland.

Whether any question as to the legislative authority of the English Parliament in Ireland was raised at this time is not certain. There is some similarity in the principles upon which the protests against Irish representatives being summoned to England are founded and those put forward subsequently, when the English Parliament expressly claimed for itself and the Irish Parliament expressly denied to it jurisdiction to

---

* See Note O of Appendix.

make laws for Ireland, that makes it not unlikely there may have been some dispute on this point. But this is merely conjecture; and the first manifestation of actual controversy upon the subject was, as far as I can find, an Act stated to have been passed by the Irish Parliament during the reign of Henry IV., of which no record now remains. This, it is said, declared that to give a statute force in Ireland it must have been allowed and published by its Parliament.*

If such a statute was passed by an Irish Parliament, it is improbable that the declaration said to have been contained in it would have been made without some claim on the part of the English Parliament, either by express words or by the effect of its legislation, to provoke it; but of neither is there now remaining any evidence. Until the next reign nothing of the kind appears. Then the English Parliament enacted a statute specially for Ireland (4 Henry V. chap. 6), which prohibited prelates of the Irish nation collating persons of

English Act (4 Henry V. chap. 6).

---

* Some date the statute of an earlier reign. The existence of this statute of Henry IV., and of another to the same effect, afterwards mentioned (29 Henry VI.), seems to me admitted in the discussions between Sir Richard Bolton and Mr. Justice Mayart, which will be afterwards considered. It is said that Sir Richard Bolton, in an edition of the Irish Statutes which he superintended, stated that he saw in the Treasury at Waterford records or transcripts of them. Grattan, in one of his speeches (22nd February, 1782), assumes that these statutes had been enacted under Henry IV. and Henry VI.

Irish birth, or bringing with them Irish rebels to the Parliaments of Ireland to know the secrets and state of Englishmen. This was followed by other statutes naming Ireland, of which it is enough to mention the Staple Act (2 Henry VI., chap. 4), in itself the most important and afterwards the most prominent in connection with subsequent controversy. Under its provisions the export of wools, wool-fells, leather, and other merchandize of the Staple, not only from England and Wales, but from Ireland also, was ordered to be to Calais, where the King's Staple was, and not to any foreign port, on pain of forfeiture of the goods.*

<small>29 Henry VI., and Acts of 1549.</small>
These statutes are said to have been followed by an Act of the Irish Parliament (29 Henry VI.), which, like the Act of Henry IV., is not now forthcoming, and which, like it, declared that a statute to bind Ireland should be allowed and published

---

* Grattan, in his elaborate argument against the claims of the English Parliament, refers to five of its statutes as those in which Ireland was expressly named, viz. 4th of Henry V., above mentioned; 1st of Henry VI., relative to ecclesiastical benefices; 19th of Henry VII., relative to Perkin Warbeck's confederates; 8th of Henry VII., regarding tithes; and the 2nd of Henry VI., or the Staple Act.—*Speech in the Irish House of Commons*, 22nd February, 1782. Besides these some allege the *Statutum Hiberniæ* (14 Henry III.), respecting the inheritance of females, the *Ordinatio pro statu Hiberniæ* of Edward I., and another *Ordinatio* of Edward III., to be also instances of Acts of the English Parliament to bind Ireland; but they seem to me mere ordinances of the King, not Acts of Parliament. See Note P of Appendix.

by its Parliament. But the most certain and distinct assertion of the exclusive jurisdiction of the Irish Parliament seems to have been in 1549, when Richard, Duke of York, who had previously been Lord Lieutenant, and had then returned to England, took refuge in Ireland from the vengeance of the Lancastrian party, and was recognized by the Irish Parliament as still holding his former office. The Irish Parliament then declared that laws for Ireland must be freely admitted and accepted in its Parliament; that the Irish had a right to coins for themselves different from the coins of England; and that, as Ireland had a Great Seal, the Irish subjects were not bound to answer writs not issued under its authority.*

The reign of Henry VI., when the Irish Parliament thus expressed itself, was a period during which the English interest in Ireland had sunk to a low point of depression. The civil war which at that time raged in England withdrew attention from the country, and prevented a sufficient military force being left there; and it is not improbable that it was this weakness which emboldened the Irish Parliament to make the explicit assertion

<small>Condition of Ireland under Henry VI.</small>

---

* The proceedings of the Parliament in Ireland under Richard, Duke of York, will be found in Leland's *History*, vol. ii., p. 42, and in Richey's *History*, p. 251. Mr. Bagwell considers that it was at this time the local independence of Ireland was first seriously attempted. (*Ireland under the Tudors*, vol. i., p. 90.)

it then did of its exclusive jurisdiction. But the sentiment itself can scarcely be supposed to have suddenly originated at that time. It must have been growing long before; since, although sympathies of race, such as bound the Anglo-Irish who comprised the Parliament to England, may restrain, they can never wholly suppress, the tendency towards its own aggrandizement, which seems by a sort of natural process to develop itself in a representative legislature.

Pilkington's Case.

It was also in the reign of Henry VI. that the questions as to the legislative authority in Ireland of the English Parliament found their way into the English courts of law. The first reference to them is in the twentieth year of this king, when, in a case known as *Pilkington's Case,* Judges Fortescue and Portington are reported to have laid down that, if a subsidy be granted in England, this should not bind in Ireland; Portington assigning as a reason that the Irish did not receive commandment by writ to come to the English Parliament; and this, says the reporter, was not denied by Markham, Yelverton, or Ascough, three other judges present.*

Case of Merchants of Waterford.

In the reign of Richard III. the question of the power of the English Parliament over Ireland was again considered by the English judges—upon this occasion not in respect of taxation, to which peculiar considerations apply, but for

---

* *Year Book*, 26 Henry VI., f. 8.

general legislative purposes. The case which then led to a judicial examination of the subject arose upon the Staple Act, the nature of which has been already explained. In breach of its provisions, certain Irish merchants, residing at Waterford, consigned wool, not to Calais, but to Sluys in Flanders; and an indenture was made between them and the master of the ship to transport the goods to Sluys. The ship, however, on the voyage put into Calais; and thereupon Sir Thomas Thwaites, treasurer of Calais, finding the ship was really chartered for Sluys, seized and confiscated the goods. The merchants petitioned the King to have their goods returned to them, and the petition was referred to the English judges for consideration —one question before them being whether the Staple Act had force in Ireland, so that Irish subjects of the Crown came within it. The judges are reported, when the matter was first debated before them, to have pronounced their opinion that the Irish were not bound by the statutes of England, 'because the land of Ireland had a Parliament and all other courts of its own, as in England, and did not send representatives to the English Parliament.' A distinction, however, seems to have been drawn between statutes relating to lands and affairs in Ireland and statutes relating to matters to be done out of it.*

---

* 'Et ibi (in the Exchequer Chamber) quoad primam quæstionem dicebant quod terr. Hibern. inter se habent Parliament.

Second hearing of this case.

Notwithstanding, however, the weight which this reasoning might be expected to have, the judges in 'the Case of the Merchants of Waterford' themselves receded from their first decision, and, when the matter was brought before them a second time, they were induced to come round to the opinion of Hussey, the Chief Justice—who was then for the first time present—that statutes made in England did bind the people of Ireland.* The grounds of this change in the views of the judges have not been recorded.

10 Henry VII., ch. 21.

These conflicting decisions made by the same judges unquestionably rendered doubtful, even in England, what was, or might ultimately be declared to be, the law in respect of the operation of English statutes in Ireland. And the uncertainty thus caused was probably one of the reasons for obtaining from the Irish Parliament an Act to make English law, as it existed at that time, of force also in Ireland. This was the

---

et omnimodo cur. prout in Anglia, et per idem Parliamentum faciunt leges et mutant leges et non obligantur per statuta in Anglia, quia non hic habent milites Parliamenti; sed hoc intelligitur de terris et rebus in terris illis tantum efficiendo; sed Personæ illæ sunt subjecti Regis, et si sint tanquam subjecti erunt obligati ad aliquam rem extra terram illam faciend. contra statut. sicut habitantes in Calesia, Gascoignie, Guienne, etc. dum fuere subjecti; et obedientes erunt sub Admiral. Angl. de re facta super altum mare.'—*Year Book*, Ric. III., fol. 12.

* 'Le chief justice disoit que les statutes faits en Engleterre liera ceux d'Irland.'—*Year Book*, 1 Henry VII., fol. 2.

second of the statutes which Poynings induced the Irish Parliament to enact, and which were known by his name. It provided that all statutes lately made (interpreted by judicial decisions to mean all previous statutes of the English Parliament) concerning the common and public weal of England should be used and executed within Ireland, in all points, according to the tenor and effect of the same.

The Act of Poynings now referred to related only to English statutes then existing: it had no effect upon future legislation. The question of the jurisdiction of the English Parliament thereafter to make laws for Ireland remained in the same position as it was before. The subject did not again come for consideration before the English judges until immediately after James I. succeeded to the throne of England, when, in the celebrated case of the *Post-nati* (reported as 'Calvin's Case'), the status of persons born in Scotland after the union of the crowns of England and Scotland had to be decided by the English judges. There the relations of the king's subjects in Ireland to the crown of England were referred to, because calculated to illustrate the immediate subject under examination; and, according to the judgment in the case as it is reported, it was laid down that 'albeit Ireland was a distinct dominion, yet the title thereof being by conquest, the same by judgment of law

'Calvin's Case.'

might by express words be bound by Act of the Parliament of England.'*

Judgment in 'Calvin's Case.'

The judgment in 'Calvin's Case' (which was the composition of Lord Coke, one of the judges who decided it), after stating that it had been a question who was the first conqueror of Ireland, and after referring to a charter of Edgar, King of England, claiming dominion over all adjacent islands, including by name Ireland, declares that it is to Henry II. the honour of the conquest of Ireland is to be attributed, as it was wholly conquered in his reign, and that his style by reason of this was: Rex Angliæ, Dominus Hiberniæ, Dux Normanniæ, Dux Aquitaniæ, et Comes Andigaviæ; King of England, Lord of Ireland, Duke of Normandy, Duke of Aquitaine, and Earl of Anjou. The reason why conquest has the effect attributed is explained to be, that the conqueror hath power over life, *vitæ et necis potestatem;* and, as a less exercise of dominion, may alter the laws of the kingdom he has subdued. But it is admitted that when he does alter the laws and establish a Parliament, they cannot be again altered without the assent of Parliament.

---

* Coke's *Reports*, 'Calvin's Case.' Part vii., fol. 17.

CHAPTER III.

PARLIAMENT OF IRELAND.

[1613-1688.]

THE judgment in 'Calvin's Case,' as has been already mentioned, was delivered soon after James succeeded to the English Crown. The Parliament of 1613 and all subsequent Parliaments, therefore, were restrained in their action, not only by Poynings' Law, but necessarily also by the consciousness that the Parliament of England asserted a legislative jurisdiction in Ireland, and that its right was upheld by the highest English judicial authority. *Effect of 'Calvin's Case.'*

The rigour of Poynings' Law had before this time been so far relieved by an Act of Philip and Mary, that if events occurred which rendered immediate measures advisable, the license and assent of the Crown to legislation could be obtained during the sitting of Parliament, and not, as was originally provided, merely before its commencement. *3 & 4 P. and M., chap. 4.*

James's Parliament and Convocation sat from May, 1613, to October, 1615. They proceeded without any conflict with either the King or the English Parliament. They were not summoned *Parliament of 1634.*

again during the same reign. The next time at which an Irish Parliament and Convocation assembled was in 1634, when Strafford, who had some time before been sent by Charles I. as Deputy to Ireland, obtained, but not without difficulty, permission from the King to have recourse to these legislatures for supplies. When Parliament met, discontent long prevalent among the people was found to have extended to its members. The Peers, disregarding the received construction of Poynings' Law, voted Bills without previous approval from the Privy Council. Strafford made a formal protest, in which he said that under the Acts of Henry VII. and Philip and Mary, the Houses of Parliament had power only by remonstrance and petition to represent to the Lord Deputy and Council such considerations as they should think fit and good for the Commonwealth, and so to submit them to be drawn into Acts and transmitted into England, or otherwise altered or rejected, according as the Lord Deputy and Council in their wisdom should judge expedient.*

Parliament of 1640-1.

So long as Strafford remained in Ireland there was no further breach of the rules regulating parliamentary proceedings for purposes of legislation; nor, indeed, was there any other open disagreement with the government on the part of the Irish Lords or Commons; but, so soon as,

---

* Leland, *History*, vol. iii., p. 22.

in 1640, he was finally recalled to England, a quite different spirit manifested itself in the House of Commons. The majority of its members sympathised with the English Parliament in its contention with the King, and soon evidenced their sympathy by action. Imitating the course pursued in England, they investigated what grievances required to be redressed, and what rights were proper to be asserted. Among the subjects which attracted their attention was the legislative authority of the Irish Parliament. Having obtained permission from the House of Lords to submit questions upon various subjects to the judges, they inserted among the queries one, in reference to this matter, which was in the following words . . . 'Whether the subjects of this kingdom (Ireland) be a free people, and to be governed only by the common law of England and statutes in force in this kingdom?' The communication to the Lords asking the questions to be submitted to the judges was accompanied by a declaration that the subjects of this kingdom (Ireland) were firm, loyal, and dutiful subjects to his Most Excellent Majesty (Charles I.), their natural liege lord and king, and to be governed only by the common laws of England and statutes in force in Ireland; and also by a statement that it was not by reason of any doubt or ambiguity in the premises, but for manifestation and declaration of a clear truth, that the judges were consulted.

Resolutions of House of Commons.

After some time the judges considered the questions; and in the end they returned answers to them, which were expressed in cautious language. The House of Commons, discontented with the answers, had a conference with the Lords. At this, a Roman Catholic barrister of eminence, a member of parliament, Patrick Darcy, advocated the views of the Commons. Finally, the House resolved to embody its own ideas upon the questions that had been sent to the judges in a series of resolutions. Accordingly, when it proceeded to carry out this intention, it declared, among other matters . . . 'that the subjects of his Majesty's kingdom of Ireland are a free people, and to be governed only according to the common law of England, and statutes made and established by Parliament in Ireland, and according to the lawful customs of the same.' *

The idea of conquest controverted.

The declaration that the people of Ireland were a free people was, very probably, aimed at the idea of conquest, as put forward by the judgment in 'Calvin's Case.' The subject had been referred to during the impeachment of the Earl of Strafford, at which deputies from the Irish Parliament attended. A statement of this Minister, to the effect that Ireland was a conquered country, seems to have provoked resentment; and one of the articles of his impeachment alleged . . . 'that the realm

---

* *Nalson*, vol. ii., pp. 573–584, and see also Leland's *History of Ireland*, vol. iii., ch. ii.

of Ireland, having been time out of mind annexed to the Imperial Crown of England, and governed by the same laws, the Earl (being Deputy in that realm), to bring his Majesty's liege subjects into a dislike of his Majesty's Government, and intending the subversion of the fundamental laws and settled government of that kingdom, and the destruction of his Majesty's liege people there, did declare and publish—that Ireland was a conquered nation; and that the King might do with them what he pleased.' Strafford, in reply, defended his assertion that Ireland was a conquered country upon the ground of its truth.

During the discussions of this period a treatise of great learning and acuteness was composed to defend the rights claimed by the Irish Parliament. It was entitled 'A Declaration setting forth how and by what means the Laws and Statutes of England from time to time came to be in force in Ireland.' It was not at that time printed; but a manuscript copy of it was brought under the notice of the Irish House of Lords, and by that House other copies of it were ordered to be made. Its composition was attributed to Sir Richard Bolton, Lord Chancellor of Ireland (1638–1650); but by some writers reasons have been suggested for thinking that its real author was Patrick Darcy, the eminent Roman Catholic barrister, to whom there has been occasion already to refer. In April, 1644, the treatise was sent from the Lords to the Commons

Bolton's treatise.

for consideration, by whom it was referred to 'those of the long robe in that House,' while the Lords were requested to ask the judges also to examine it; and this was done in order, as it was stated, that the judges and the members of the Commons of the long robe might 'privately take into consideration the book.' Of what afterwards happened there are no accounts extant; and affairs of more urgency soon occupied the attention of both Houses.*

<small>Practice of originating not Bills, but heads of Bills, begins.</small>

It is to the period immediately after Strafford's return to England that the introduction of a practice, afterwards firmly established in the Irish Parliament, is attributed.† Under Poynings' Law, Bills originated with the Irish Privy Council, and they should be then approved by the English

---

* Manuscript copies of the treatise attributed to Bolton are preserved in the Library of Trinity College, Dublin, along with an answer to it by Mayart, described as Sergeant and Second Justice of the Common Pleas in Ireland. Both were first published in 1749 in Harris's *Hibernica*. They will be subsequently considered. Harris is one of those who, as is above mentioned, think Darcy the author of the Declaration, founding his opinion upon the resemblance between its arguments and the topics and observations of Darcy when he appeared before the Lords. One of the manuscript copies in the Library of Trinity College has marked upon it (in a different handwriting from the body) 'by Sir Richard Bolton.' Harris gives in his Preface the proceedings in the Irish Parliament in relation to the treatise. A manuscript copy of the Journals of the House of Lords of that time is also preserved in the same Library.

† Leland's *History of Ireland*, Appendix, vol. ii., p. 516.

Privy Council before they could be considered by the Irish Parliament. But these provisions were held not to apply to 'heads of Bills.' Accordingly, from this time, whenever either House desired to obtain a measure, it framed and voted heads of the Bill sought to be made law. When this occurred 'the heads' were sent to the Deputy and Privy Council, by whom, with such alterations as they thought fit, they were forwarded to the English Privy Council, who, in most instances, referred them to the English Attorney-General. If approved, 'the heads' were then returned in the form of a Bill with such modifications as the English Council thus advised might require. The Bill, when returned, went through the prescribed stages of first and second readings, committee, and third reading in both Houses of Parliament. It might, at any stage, be rejected, but it could not be altered.*

The desire which, after Strafford ceased to rule, appeared on the part of the Irish Parliament to assert its own independence was increased by the conduct of the English Parliament in passing what is known as the Adventurers' Act; for which, however, they obtained the assent of Charles I. This Act professed to dispose of the lands of the disloyal in Ireland to any persons who would advance money to put down the Rebellion of 1641. The confederate Catholics {Adventurers' Act.}

---

* See Note Q of Appendix.

afterwards, when remonstrating against the statute, complained not only because it was framed to affect persons who were unsummoned and unheard, but because it was the enactment of an English Parliament, since, they said, from the time of Henry II., there had been Irish Parliaments whose Acts they claimed to be alone capable of binding the King's Irish subjects.*

<small>Ireland under the Commonwealth.</small>

During the rule of the Commonwealth no Parliament was ever summoned in Ireland. The Parliament of England assumed sole and absolute dominion over the country. By a statute of its own it defined the penal consequences that were to follow from the resistance to its power, which had been very general over the country, since not merely the Roman Catholic portion of the people, but the loyalist Protestants, had joined in it. The measures adopted seem to have been based, not so much upon the general right to legislate for Ireland claimed by previous English Parliaments, as upon rights supposed to be consequent upon the defeat of a rebellion. The Commonwealth was assumed to occupy the position of a king in a monarchy under similar

---

* Charles I., when instructing Ormonde for negotiations with the Catholics, wrote that the Irish had much to say for themselves in point of being commanded by orders of the Parliament of England, or being obliged by a statute, until confirmed by their own Parliament, and that this had been the notion of the English kings and councils.—Carte's *Ormonde*, Ed., 1851, vol. ii., p. 442.

circumstances, and to be therefore entitled to the same power of inflicting punishment, including confiscation of property, as would in that case have accrued to him.

Acting on these principles, the English Parliament punished, or exempted from punishment, whom it thought fit. Without the sanction of any Irish legislative authority it confiscated and disposed of vast territories, conferring them upon persons who had advanced money for, or served on its side in, the war in Ireland.* *Proceedings of the English Parliament, 1652.*

In 1654, subsequently to the distribution of the confiscated property, Irish members were introduced into the English Parliament. This was in pursuance of a provision contained in the 'Instrument of Government,' framed in the previous year, under which Cromwell became Protector, whereby Scotland and Ireland were required to send each thirty representatives to the English Parliament. It was, however, contrived that the members to be selected from Ireland should be chosen by and from the partisans of the English Parliament. They consisted either of Englishmen, who were then officially employed in Ireland, such as Sir Hardress Waller and Colonels Hewson and Venables; or of persons Anglo-Irish by birth, such as Lord Broghill and Sir Charles *Irish Members returned to the English Parliament, 1654.*

---

* For the legislation of the English Parliament at this time, see Note R of Appendix.

Coote. In like manner the Parliament summoned by Richard Cromwell contained thirty members from Ireland, selected from the same class as they were for his father's Parliament.

Parliament of the Restoration.

At the Restoration the separation of the Parliaments of England and Ireland was renewed, each being summoned by itself as an independent body, without representatives from any country except its own. No provision was then made to define the relation of these assemblies to each other, or to make more certain than had formerly been the case how far the Parliament of England was entitled to make laws for Ireland. Controversy, however, did not arise upon the subject, for in neither country were the Acts of the Commonwealth considered binding: and the Irish Parliament could, without interference, review the distribution of landed property, which was effected under the sanction of what was treated as an usurped authority. The persons who advanced money under the Adventurers' Act had, it was thought, helped the English cause, since through their means Ireland was reduced into subordination: to the same result Cromwell's soldiers had contributed; but other claims were also to be acknowledged.* Parliament had treated as rebels not merely enemies of the

P. 39, supra.

---

* Lord Clare accounted for the favour shown to the Adventurers and to the soldiers of Cromwell by the supposition that Monk had made terms for them with Charles II. (*Speech in the Irish House of Lords*, Feb. 10, 1800).

English authority, but loyalists, and even persons who had remained neutral during the civil war, both Protestant and Roman Catholic. In the end, a compromise between all the various interests concerned was approved, and statutes, to carry out the compromise, known as the Acts of Settlement and of Explanation, were passed by the Irish Parliament without any concurrence or assistance from the Parliament of England. These statutes, and deeds of grant or awards and certificates of right given under their provisions by competent tribunals, became the foundation of title for the proprietors then introduced upon, or confirmed in, the lands which were the subject of allocation.* Acts of Settlement and Explanation.

That the English Parliament of Charles II. abstained from interfering with the redistribution of land which, during his reign, was arranged in Ireland did not arise by reason of its having relinquished the legislative claims of former English Parliaments; on the contrary, the claims were persisted in, and among other enactments of this period which related to Ireland, the cultivation of the tobacco plant there was prohibited.† Tobacco Acts.

But the statutes of the Parliament of England, passed under Charles II., which had most effect upon the interests of the people of Ireland, were Navigation Act and other English Acts injurious to Ireland.

---

* The Acts were 14 & 15 Car. II., ch. 2, and 17 & 18 Car. II., ch. 2 (both Irish).

† See 12 Car. II., 34; 15 Car. II., ib. 7; 22 and 23 Car. II., ch. 26 (all English).

concerned with subjects which, according to every view that may be taken of the relations existing between the two kingdoms, were within the jurisdiction of the English, and not of the Irish, Parliament. No merchandize could be carried in Irish ships to the colonies; nay, not more than one-fourth of the mariners of an English ship trading there could be Irish. The importation of cattle, and also of beef, pork, cheese, butter, from Ireland into England was forbidden.* But over its own ports, ships, and colonies, England must be held to have had dominion. Such Acts were harsh, ungenerous, upon sound economical principles indefensible, but they cannot be pronounced *extra vires*.

---

* See as to the Navigation Acts and other Acts relating to Ireland passed by the English Parliament under Charles II., Note S of Appendix.

CHAPTER IV.

PARLIAMENT OF IRELAND.

[1688-1700.]

NONE of the Acts professing to bind Ireland, passed by the Parliament of England before the reign of William and Mary, came in conflict with any statute of the Irish Parliament relating to the subjects with which they dealt. They were, until that time, concerned with matters not the subject of enactment by the latter Parliament. And so long as both England and Ireland acknowledged the same king this was likely to continue to be the case, since Poynings' Law gave the king and council in England control over the legislation of the Irish Parliament, which could not, without licence and assent under the Great Seal of England, either meet or make laws. *Before William and Mary English statutes not in conflict with Irish.*

In 1689, however, the relations between the Parliament of England and a Parliament which then met in Ireland were of a character without previous precedent. These assemblies did not, like other English and Irish Parliaments, move apart in separate lines: they came in direct collision with each other. One of them had *Irish Parliament of 1689.*

accepted William and Mary as king and queen: the other was convened by, and came together to support, James II., in whose place the new king and queen were substituted.

<small>Act 1 W. & M. ch. 9 (English).</small> In 1690, a number of Acts having been previously passed by James's Irish Parliament, the Parliament of England interfered by legislation in reference to Irish affairs, and enacted a statute which, after reciting that the Parliament convened by James in Ireland was an unlawful assembly, since it was not called by the rightful Sovereign, declared that all the Acts and proceedings of the Parliament were null and void.

<small>The English Act was solicited.</small> This Act of the English Parliament was, it is said, passed at the solicitation of the Irish refugees who had fled to England after James came from France to Ireland, and proceeded to act there as king. Of the statutes of James's Parliament which it nullified, two were especially alleged to demand the interposition of the English Parliament. One of these was entitled 'An Act for repealing the Acts of Settlement, Explanation, Resolution of Doubts, and all Grants, Patents, and Certificates, pursuant to them or any of them'; and the other was entitled 'An Act for the Attainder of divers Rebels, and for preserving the Interest of Loyal Subjects.' The operation of the first, if it were to take effect, would have been to render void all the titles to lands acquired since the 22nd of October, 1641 (the day before the rebellion of that year

broke out), whether under the Commonwealth, or under the Acts of Settlement and Explanation of Charles II., and to reinstate the proprietors, or descendants of proprietors, who owned them at that date. The second attainted by name and visited with the penalties of high treason more than two thousand persons, a large number of whom were absent from the country, unless they came within prescribed periods to establish their innocence before the tribunals appointed by the Act.*

If the English Parliament had taken no notice of the Acts of James's Irish Parliament, they must have remained apparently undisputed, for, owing to the war then waged in Ireland between James and William, no Parliament was or could be convened there by the latter to repeal them. This circumstance, combined with applications for protection from Irish subjects to the English Parliament, has induced even zealous opponents of the authority claimed by this legislature over Ireland, to waive such objections in the case of the nullifying Act of 1690; to treat it as exceptional, necessitated by circumstances, and therefore, they would concede, legally binding.† *As an act of legislation it has been defended because necessary.*

But it were an error to suppose that the English Parliament founded its jurisdiction to annul *Other English Acts.*

---

* The legislation of James's Parliament, A.D. 1689, will be more fully referred to in Note T of Appendix.

† See Molyneux's *Case*, afterwards referred to, ed. 1719, pp. 63-65.

the Acts of James's Parliament upon anything peculiar in the nature of the Acts themselves. It exercised a like power of legislation, when no reasons similar to those suggested in their case applied. Thus it suspended an Irish statute (17 & 18 Car. II.), which disabled clergymen from holding benefices at the same time both in England and Ireland. By another Act it abrogated the oath of supremacy then required in Ireland, and substituted new oaths and declarations.*

Irish Parliament, 1692. In 1692 a Parliament, for which writs were issued by Lord Sidney, Lord Lieutenant under William and Mary, met at Dublin. One of the provisions of the statute of the English Parliament, which has been last referred to, imposed on members of the Irish Parliament an obligation to take the new oaths and declarations which the Act prescribed, and as these could not be accepted consistently with the tenets of the Church of Rome, this provision, if held operative, was equivalent to an enactment expressly excluding Roman Catholics. The Irish Parliament acted

---

* See the English Acts, 1 W. & M., sess. i., ch. 29, and 3 W. & M., ch. 2. Archbishop King, in a letter to the Bishop of Worcester, dated 3rd February, 1699 (cited by Mant in his *History of the Church of Ireland*, vol. ii., p. 100), complains of both these Acts, and instances them among the causes which created discontent in Ireland in William's reign. The legislation in the first of these Acts being a repeal of an Irish Act is, he says, 'absolutely new to us, there being no such precedent before.'

upon the English Act, and must be held by so doing to have admitted the right of the English Parliament to make laws for Ireland.* The most important Act of the Parliament of 1692 was an Act to recognise and ratify the title of William and Mary to the Crown.† At this time the House of Commons unsuccessfully claimed a right to initiate money bills.

In 1695 an Irish Parliament again met. It proceeded to repeat, in a statute of its own, the declaration already made by the English Parliament, that the proceedings or acts of James's Parliament were illegal, and absolutely null and void; and it ordered that all records of them should be burned.‡ *Parliament of 1695.*

The acknowledgment that the English Parliament had legislative authority over Ireland, which was implied in the conduct of the Irish Parliament in 1692, was neither revoked nor repudiated by any of the subsequent Irish Parliaments called by William. There is no evidence that even an expression of disapprobation fell from any member at the meetings of either House of Parliament. So also as to the jurisdiction of the Irish and English Privy Councils no objection was made. But submission to the *Irish Parliament acquiesces in English legislation for Ireland.*

---

* Macaulay has collected what is recorded of the Parliament of 1692: *History*, vol. iv., p. 366. See, as to exclusion of Catholics, Note U of Appendix.

† 4 William & Mary, ch. 1, A.D. 1692.

‡ 7 Wm. III. ch. 3.

The people discontented.

Parliament of England was confined to the Parliament of Ireland, and did not extend to such portion of its people as concerned themselves with public affairs. The traders, manufacturers, and middle classes (generally of English or Scotch race, and Protestants) were dissatisfied that any assembly not national should have power to make laws for them. Discontent on this ground continued to increase until, about 1698, proceedings took place in the English Parliament which much inflamed its violence. Enactments to hinder the exportation of wool from Ireland, lest its use might assist the foreign manufacturers in their competition with the English in this branch of trade, were at that time suggested. These measures, if passed, would have been in the highest degree detrimental to Irish interests, for the country produced much wool of a quality adapted for making cloth. Had the English Parliament, it was asked, the right to inflict such injury upon Ireland?

Molyneux's Case of Ireland.

The discontent of the period, its apprehension of what the jealousy of English commerce might ordain, and its reluctance to admit an authority in the English Parliament which had been on previous occasions repudiated in Ireland, soon found an exponent. In 1698 appeared a treatise, entitled *The Case of Ireland's being bound by Acts of Parliament in England Stated*. This work at once attained celebrity; and there is no doubt that at the time, and long afterwards, it largely influenced the opinions of the educated classes in Ireland. It was the composition of William Molyneux,* then one of the members for the University of Dublin in the Irish Parliament, who was highly esteemed, both in England and Ireland, no less for his moral qualities than his scientific attainments.

Molyneux's book, immediately upon its publication, was brought under the notice of the English House of Commons, and by it referred to a Committee for examination. The Committee reported against the treatise, and, in conformity with their report, the House voted that 'the book was of dangerous tendency to the Crown and people of England, by denying the authority of the king and Parliament of England to bind the kingdom and people of Ireland, and the subordination and dependence that Ireland hath and ought to have upon England, as being united and annexed to the Imperial Crown of that realm.' These resolutions were followed by an address from the House to the king, in which were contained the charges against Molyneux's book. At the same time it complained that the Irish Parliament had, when re-enacting a statute of the English Parliament, 'for the security of his Majesty's person and Government,' made alterations in it. To these

Proceedings of English House of Commons.

---

* Locke, in his *Essay on the Human Understanding*, has recorded his esteem for Molyneux (Book ii., ch. 9, s. 8). Some of the reasoning in Molyneux's treatise can be traced to the influence of Locke's writings.

representations William answered that he would take care what was complained of by the Commons should be prevented and redressed.*

<small>Both English and Irish Parliaments prohibit export of wool from Ireland.</small>

Notwithstanding the arbitrary conduct manifested on the part of the English Parliament, and the consequent dissatisfaction prevalent in Ireland, the Irish Parliament not only continued to acquiesce in the demands of the English Parliament, but passed an Act which imposed additional duties upon the export of Irish woollen manufactures. It also submitted, without remonstrance, to a subsequent English statute, which prohibited the export of wool and woollen manufactures from Ireland, except to certain specified places in England, on pain of forfeiture of the goods and ship, and of a penalty of £500 for every such offence.† The Irish Act was temporary, the English Act permanent. Their effect was entirely to extinguish the woollen manufacture in Ireland, and also to depress the agricultural interest by leaving no market outside Ireland, except England, open for Irish wool.

<small>7 & 8 Wm. III. ch. 22 (English).</small>

Before the Woollen Act another statute (7 & 8 Wm. III. ch. 22), which also was in the highest degree injurious to the interest of Ireland, had

---

* Macaulay, *History of England*, ed. 1861, vol. v., p. 59. Molyneux died October, 1698. Macaulay thinks that 'had Molyneux lived a few months longer he would have been impeached.'

† See Act 10 Wm. III., ch. 5 (Irish); Act 10 & 11 Wm. III. ch. 10 (English), and note V of Appendix.

been passed by William's Parliament. This strengthened the provisions of the Navigation Act, and effectually prevented any direct trade between Ireland and the colonies.

Before William's death, the English Parliament again interfered with affairs in Ireland. The lands forfeited by the adherents of James II. were granted by William to his generals and favourites. The English Parliament passed an Act resuming the lands from the grantees. Under the authority of this Act, and of a subsequent Act also of the English Parliament, without any statute or order of the Irish Parliament, all this property was sold and conveyed to the purchasers by Commissioners appointed for the purpose.*

English Parliament resumes Irish forfeitures.

---

* The first Act was 11 & 12 Wm. III. ch. 2 (Engl.); the subsequent Act was 1 Anne, ch. 21 (Engl.).

CHAPTER V.

THE TREATISES OF BOLTON, MOLYNEUX, AND MAYART.

<small>Treatises connected with the controversy.</small>

AN account of the controversy respecting the right assumed by the Parliament of England to legislate for Ireland would be imperfect, if it were confined merely to events, and left unnoticed the views and opinions of the eminent persons who took part in it. Molyneux's treatise, which has been mentioned in the last chapter, and the treatise attributed to Sir Richard Bolton, which was before the Irish Parliament in 1644,* are the most celebrated writings in opposition to the jurisdiction claimed. Bolton was answered by Mayart, one of the Justices of the Common Pleas in Ireland, in a tract characterized by much research. Molyneux was also answered, but less ably. Discussion of the subject, at a later date, became involved with the conflicts of political parties in Parliament; but, so far as reasoning, little was added to what was in these discussions put forward. The period at which we have now arrived seems therefore

---

* See page 37, *supra*.

convenient for an examination of the mode in which the question raised was treated.*

Bolton (for in speaking of the treatise of 1644 I shall treat him as the author, notwithstanding the doubt which, as already mentioned, is entertained whether its composition was not due to Darcy), in his argument against the right claimed by the English Parliament, lays down as the basis of his reasoning that Ireland is a separate kingdom. In order to prove this he refers to the fact that Henry II. in his own lifetime granted to his son John the authority of king in Ireland, which continued under Richard I. John held, he seems to suggest, a regal position in Ireland as one kingdom, while his father and brother held a similar position in England as a totally distinct kingdom.† That, under such circumstances, the Common Law of England should be the Common Law of Ireland, he explains by the Acts or Ordinances which, under John and Henry III., were, as we have seen, enacted to provide that English law should be of force in Ireland.‡ When the Common Law was thus introduced, he holds it followed as a necessary consequence that if a

Bolton's treatise.

Page 1.

Page 3.

Bolton's treatise.

---

* The editions of the treatises of Bolton, Molyneux, and Mayart, referred to by the pages noted on the margin, are those mentioned in the Appendix.

† The proposition that Ireland was a separate kingdom does not depend upon the view taken of John's authority under his father; it is admitted on other grounds in the judgment in 'Calvin's Case.'

‡ See page 6, *supra*, and note D of Appendix.

statute was passed in England declaring the Common Law, defining it in some doubtful or ambiguous point, this statute *proprio vigore*, without any re-affirmation by the Irish Parliament, would be law also in Ireland. Of this sort, he says, were *Magna Charta*; the *Statutum Hiberniæ*, respecting the inheritance of females (14 Henry III.); the statute *De Proditionibus* (25 Edward III.). Only statutes of this character, he asserts, came into use without being confirmed by Irish legislative authority. A statute which was (as he expresses it) 'introductory and positive, making new laws, or anyways altering, adding unto, or diminishing the ancient Common Law,' would not be binding in Ireland until such time as it had been enacted by Act of Parliament in Ireland: that is if it were later in date than the ordinance of John, for the words of that ordinance were wide enough to bring in along with the Common Law any then existing English statutes. Examples are then collected of English laws which were again enacted by the Irish Parliament. Others, he admits, were accepted, for which there were not extant Irish statutes confirming them; but this he accounts for by the loss of records, frequent 'in the troublesome and distempered times which have been in Ireland.' That an English Act might be confirmed by an Irish, and the latter not be forthcoming, he shows by an instance. The statutes of Merton, Marlebridge, Westminster (1st), Westminster (2nd),

and Gloucester, were all re-enacted for Ireland by
an Irish Act (13 Edward II.); but the latter was
for a long time not known to exist, and it was
only a short time before he wrote that an exemplification of it had been found in the Treasury
at Waterford. In support of his views, he refers to
the decisions of the English Courts of law, which
there has been occasion to state in chapter ii.
The plea in 'Pilkington's Case,' he observes, was
a plea founded upon an Irish Act, and it was Page 5.
prefaced by a recital 'that the land of Ireland,
time beyond the memory of man, hath been a
land separated and severed from the realm of
England, and ruled and governed by the customs and laws of the same land of Ireland.'
'Pilkington's Case' and 'The Case of the Merchants of Waterford,' were authorities for the
necessity of an Irish Act to bind Ireland.
With respect to the opinions expressed against
the views he was advocating, he suggests that
Chief Justice Hussey, when he said that Eng- Page 12.
lish statutes bound Ireland, might, while using
general words, have meant statutes like that
relating to the Staple at Calais, which was
then in question; and that if conquest had
(which he does not seem to deny) the effect
attributed in 'Calvin's Case,' the effect ceased
when the laws of England were given, since such
as they were when given they would continue until
altered by Parliament. These arguments from
precedent and authority are supported by enume-

Page 13.

Page 14.

rating inconveniences which must result from a contrary theory. If England could make laws for Ireland, of what use were Irish Parliaments? For four hundred years they had been summoned, and upon this supposition it must be held to have been nugatory and superfluous to call them, Again, what stability of legislation would there be? At any moment England could abrogate all the existing laws, and might pass enactments the most opposite. The Parliaments of England and Ireland were then held (he says) at one and the same time; and if they should happen to pass contradictory statutes, which were the king's subjects to obey? Moreover, natural equity and justice were against the claim of the English Parliament. 'It standeth not (he observes) with the rule of reason and politic government that the liberties, laws, and estates of those of the kingdom of Ireland and of their posterities, should be bound by any laws or statutes made in England, whereunto they are not in anyways made privy or parties.' Wales, when 'incorporated to be a member and party of the realm of England, and to be inheritable to its laws,' had members allowed it in the Parliament; and the same occurred with the county palatine of Chester. The claim also was against the nature of a Parliament, for it made the Irish Parliament a subordinate institution, and yet Parliament was *suprema et altissima curia*, and therefore not subject to the control of any other jurisdiction.

Molyneux, who is later in date than Bolton, goes over much of the same ground. He had evidently seen the treatise of the latter (not in print, for it was not then published, but in some of the copies which the Irish House of Lords had caused to be made of it),* and he derived from it assistance in dealing with the legal topics connected with the subject. He has, however, arguments entirely peculiar to himself. Thus he denies the assertion, made in 'Calvin's Case,' that Ireland was a conquered country. Prelates, he says, kings and chieftains in Ireland, did homage to Henry II., but without having been vanquished by him in any battle. What occurred was 'an entire and voluntary submission of all the civil and ecclesiastical states.' Afterwards rebellions were put down; but to put down rebellion is not conquest. Even if there were conquest, it would not prove the claim of the English Parliament; for it gives, he contends, no power over those who conquer along with the conqueror; and so the native Irish who aided Henry II., and the Norman adventurers who preceded him, were entitled to retain the freedoms and immunities of free-born subjects. Nor are the conquered wholly at the mercy of the victor, for his power is only over their own lives and liberties, not over their estates or posterity. Any other idea, he holds, would apply to war the principles on which we

<small>Molyneux's treatise.</small>

<small>Page 13.</small>

<small>Page 19.</small>

<small>Page 22.</small>

---

* See page 37, *supra*.

may act towards rebels. Besides, in the case of Ireland, the consequences supposed to flow from conquest were, he alleges, waived by treaties and concessions of the English kings. This occurred first at the Council of Lismore, when the laws of England were introduced into Ireland, and as part of them 'the freedom of Parliaments to be held in Ireland as they were held in England.' He regards the proceedings at this Council as equivalent to a compact between Henry II. and the people of Ireland, that they should enjoy the like liberties and immunities, and be governed by the same mild laws, both civil and ecclesiastical, as the people of England. John and Henry III. confirmed the English laws, liberties, and customs to the Irish.* But, exclaims Molyneux, the liberties of Englishmen are founded on the universal law of nature that ought to prevail throughout the whole world, of being governed only by laws to which consent is given by representatives in Parliament.† Laws could not be made for Scotland by England. If it was said this was because Scotland was an

_{Page 28.}
_{Page 37.}
_{Page 48.}

---

* But see as to the Council of Lismore, and the ordinances of John and Henry III., Notes A and B of Appendix.

† So also, after showing that, under an Act of James I., all in England are, through representation, deemed to be personally present in Parliament, Molyneux asks, Are we to be denied this birthright of every English subject, by having laws imposed on us, when we are neither personally nor representatively present?

ancient and separate kingdom, so also was Ireland. In explaining how, if England could not legislate for Ireland, laws of the English Parliament were in force in Ireland, he follows Bolton in holding that these were either declaratory of the Common Law or re-enacted in Ireland; but adds to Bolton's suggestions that some of these laws were made in English Parliaments to which *Page 95.* members were returned from Ireland:* and that such as were so made 'might reasonably be of force there, because they were assented to by its own representatives.' Instances of this kind, he says, manifestly show that the King and Parliament of England would not enact laws to bind Ireland without the concurrence of representatives from that kingdom. Hence he infers, that if the Parliament of England is to bind Ireland, the latter country ought to have its representatives in it. 'And this,' he then observes, 'I believe *Page 97.* we should be willing enough to embrace: but this is an happiness we can hardly hope for.'† . . . Against this reasoning the English legislation for Ireland of William and Mary ought not, he thinks, fairly to be relied upon, for it was *Page 106.*

---

* See as to the English Parliaments for which Irish representatives were returned, page 23, *supra*, and Note O of Appendix.

† This passage is said to have been left out in an edition of Molyneux's treatise, published in 1782, during the agitation for parliamentary independence.—See Ingram's *Legislative Union*, p. 12.

acquiesced in, owing to peculiar circumstances, and in the hope of having it re-enacted when a regular Parliament could be called for Ireland; nor, were it otherwise, will he admit that acquiescence, or even alienation, can give away rights of this character. Disposing thus of the arguments from conquest and precedent, he refers to another topic brought forward in 'Calvin's Case,' viz. that as an appeal lay from the Irish Court of King's Bench to the same Court in England, Ireland must be a subordinate country; and he

Page 131. suggests that this right of appeal may have originated in an Irish Act of Parliament, then lost, and that, even if not, yet subordination of a Parliament does not necessarily follow from subordination of a Court of Law. Observations follow upon other arguments which were brought forward from the opposite side. One of these was, that by expenditure to carry on war and put down rebellion England had purchased Ireland. What right could expenditure give beyond a claim to be

Page 148. repaid? Another was, that Ireland was a colony, and the mother country is always held entitled to make laws for a colony. But Ireland, he reasons, cannot be regarded as a colony. It is a separate kingdom. The king is King of Ireland, just as he is king of England and king of Scotland. 'Is this agreeable to the nature of a colony?' He does not style himself king of Virginia, of New England, or of Maryland.

Mayart's treatise. Mayart (as his treatise was designed to answer that attributed to Bolton) reviews the entire range of legal precedent, authority, and argument travelled by the latter. He controverts the assertion that in the lifetime of Henry II., by any authority conferred on John or otherwise, Ireland was made a distinct government, so that England was but a pattern. Ireland was, and is, he says, a member of England, united to it, and as a part and province of it governed. This, he thinks, is expressly declared in statutes which he cites. Thus the Act of Appeals (28 Henry VIII., ch. 6) calls 'the land of Ireland the king's proper dominion of England, united, knit, and belonging to the imperial Crown of the same realm'; and it then asserts that the Crown of itself, and by itself, is fully, wholly, entirely, and rightfully endowed and garnished with all power, authority, and pre-eminence sufficient to yield and render to all and singular subjects of the same full and plenary remedies in all causes of strife, debate, &c. So also the Act of Absentees (28 Henry VIII., ch. 3) describes Ireland as 'the King's land of Ireland'; the Act of Supremacy (28 Henry VIII., ch. 5) says that the 'land of Ireland is depending and belonging justly and rightfully to the imperial Crown of England'; and the Act of Faculties (28 Henry VIII., ch. 9) states that the 'King's land of Ireland is his proper dominion, and a member appending and rightfully belonging to the imperial Crown of England, and united to the same.' Coming from this topic to the second

Page 34.

assertion on which, he says, Bolton grounds his case, viz. that a new law for Ireland requires to
Page 40. be passed by an Irish Parliament, he asks, Why is this so, when it is admitted that a declaratory English law binds Ireland? It is one and the same power that makes declaratory and new laws. Also in practice statutes not merely declaratory were in force, although not affirmed in Ireland. And this was the case even with the statutes re-enacted; since they were obeyed in the interval between their being passed in England and being enacted in Ireland. And for this he refers to the statutes of Merton, Marlebridge, and Gloucester, which were received and executed in Ireland before the 13 Edward II. (Irish), mentioned by Bolton, confirmed them. Of this he ad-
Page 61. duces evidence from extant records. The same he alleges to be true for a long period subsequent, referring to cases which he holds establish the fact. The right claimed by the English Parliament is in analogy with rights exercised by the English
Page 81. Courts of Law in Ireland, which have had their judgments (of which he gives examples) executed there. The alleged necessity of representation of Ireland in the Parliament of England, he sug-
Page 90. gests, is disproved by the fact that before Wales and the county palatine of Chester had representatives in it statutes were enacted to bind both. So also Calais had been legislated for by the English Parliament, although no member was ever sent from that town. Assuming that the

Irish Parliament did by express statutes repudiate the legislative claim of the English, such denial cannot annul a right if it existed; and whether there was or was not the right must be determined by other considerations than the assertion of the party to be affected by its exercise. In like manner to the other inconveniences suggested by Bolton, he offers answers or considerations to abate their force; and in conclusion points out that, for political reasons, it was indispensable that the English Parliament should have power to make laws for Ireland, since otherwise, however judicious the measures which the king might propose to introduce in that country, it would be possible for the Irish Parliament to hinder them from ever being brought into operation. *Page 98. Page 131.*

Molyneux's treatise and the judgment in 'Calvin's Case' show how much stress was laid in their time upon the question, Was Ireland conquered? As these authorities take the affirmative side upon it, so those who answered Molyneux take the negative. Carey, the most able of them, observes that Henry II. had no right distinct from invasion; he was not called by the people; his business was nothing else but to conquer and subdue. What difference, he asks, is there between yielding without fighting and yielding in battle? The Irish made no terms for their own government or laws. *Answers to Molyneux's treatise.*

CHAPTER VI.

THE CLAIM OF THE ENGLISH PARLIAMENT TO LEGISLATE FOR IRELAND CONSIDERED.

Legal decisions as to legislative authority in Ireland.

THE first legal decision favourable to the jurisdiction assumed by the English Parliament in Ireland was upon the second hearing of 'The Case of the Merchants of Waterford.' What reasons (if any) were assigned by the Judges who pronounced it we do not know, for none have been reported. 'Calvin's Case' did not arise out of circumstances which themselves raised the question, and therefore was not a decision upon it; but the judgment incidentally discussed the subject, and laid down authoritatively that the English Parliament had a right to make laws for Ireland, and that it necessarily had the right, because Ireland was a conquered country.* General words, it was admitted, did not suffice to bind Ireland, and this was afterwards by commentators upon the judgment explained to be, because the paramount legislature, in its ordinary

---

* See for 'Calvin's Case,' p. 31, *supra;* and for 'The Merchants of Waterford's Case,' p. 28, *supra*. The part of the judgment in 'Calvin's Case' which relates to Ireland is at fol. 17 of part vii. of Lord Coke's *Reports.*

proceedings, cannot be supposed to have subordinate dominions in contemplation.

The proposition affirmed in the judgment in 'Calvin's Case,' that conquest gives to the nation which prevails a right to make laws for the people it has subdued, was from that time very generally acknowledged among legal authorities.* Blackstone, however, accompanies his support of it by an explanation. He assumes that what is called 'right of conquest' is but another name for a compact either expressly or tacitly made between the conqueror and the conquered people: that if the latter will acknowledge the victors for their masters, the former will treat them for the future as subjects and not as enemies.† {Law of conquest as laid down in Calvin's Case.}

Accordingly, when objections began to be made to the judgment, they took the direction of impeaching its statement of facts rather than its law. Ireland, it was said, was not a conquered country. Some years, however, seem to have elapsed before this was suggested. The language of the judgment was in accord with the notions of its own time. From a very early period 'conquest' had been used in Irish records and statutes to describe the mode in which {Objections to the judgment in Calvin's Case.}

---

* 'A country conquered by the British arms becomes a dominion of the king in right of his crown, and therefore necessarily subject to the Legislature, the Parliament of Great Britain.'—Lord Mansfield, in Hall *v.* Campbell' (A.D. 1774). Cowper's *Reports*, 208.

† *Commentaries*, Introduction, s. 4, vol. i.

Henry II. acquired dominion in Ireland. Indeed, according to some writers, Henry, from the first, in imitation of William I. in England, took the title of Conqueror, *Conquestor Hiberniæ*.*

<small>Whether Ireland was conquered.</small>

Like many other controversies respecting important questions, subsequent discussion of the subject was more engaged in examining the proprieties of phrases than the realities which they represented. These, if we confine attention to them, are free from doubt. Henry II. did not subdue the Irish in actual conflict: their liberties were not struck down in any disastrous battle, as the liberties of the Anglo-Saxons were at Hastings; but this prince, reputed the most powerful of his time, brought with him to Ireland an army which, although not large, was larger than, owing to disunion among the Irish people, there were the means of resisting: and so he obtained,

---

* Molyneux admits that Henry did call himself Conquestor (*Case*, ed. 1719, p. 8). Davis, whose *Discoverie* was written to show that, until the reign of James I., Ireland was never entirely subdued, says the conquest of Ireland was spoken of by many writers. The celebrated Statute of Kilkenny (3 Edward III.) begins, 'Come a la conquest de la terre Dirland' (whereas, at the conquest of the land of Ireland). In the appendix to Hardiman's edition of this statute, an abridgment of a statute passed at Dublin (2 Henry IV.), A.D. 1410, is printed, which begins, 'That Holy Church enjoy their liberties, &c., used since the conquest of this land.' And an Act, 32 Henry VI., has the expression, 'from the conquest of Ireland by Henry Fitz-Empress.' (Leland, ii. App. n. B.)

from the fear and prudence of the native kings and chieftains, the same admission of supremacy as might have been expected at the conclusion of a successful war. Such events may not, in strictness of speech, amount to conquest; but for the purposes of the judgment in 'Calvin's Case,' and so far as the authority and rights therein attributed to conquest, they cannot fairly be distinguished from it.

Of late years the advocates for the Parliament of England have preferred to found its claim to legislative power upon the fact of colonisation rather than upon conquest. In the case of a colony, the mother country has been generally admitted to have a right to make laws for the subjects who emigrate. This being so, it is then urged that England did plant a colony in Ireland, and that only its interests were the objects of her care. If her Parliament legislated for Ireland, it was solely with a view to serve the Anglo-Irish; the natives were neglected, nor would they, if laws had been made for them, have obeyed them.* Supposed effect of colonisation in Ireland.

But can this be regarded as a complete statement of the case? Does it not omit circumstances material to be considered? In Ireland, natives and colonists were subjects of one and the same Sovereign. The King of England was at first Effect attributed to colonisation examined.

---

* Macaulay, commenting on Molyneux's treatise, adopts this line of reasoning in his *History of England*, vol. v. p. 56.

Lord and afterwards King of Ireland. Theoretically, his authority under either title extended to the whole island; practically, it reached far beyond the districts inhabited by the colonists; for in Irish parts of the country it confiscated territories, and was strong enough to set over them lords of Norman or English race. The laws which were passed by the Parliament of England in relation to Ireland named all, and not part of, the kingdom; they were for some centuries operative only in the English districts, but they professed to include the entire island. Moreover, after the reign of James I., neither theoretically nor practically, for legal purposes, was distinction made between colonists and natives: the same laws bound both, and were enforced among both. Colonisation of so small a part of a country as was colonised in Ireland seems a narrow basis for legislative jurisdiction over the whole to rest upon.

Was there compact? Whatever, however, may have been the rights with which conquest or colonisation were adequate to endow the Crown or Parliament of England, it is obvious that these were capable of being relinquished or modified either by treaty or voluntary concession: nay, that even usage might exercise an important influence over them. Hence controversy respecting the authority of the English Parliament did not confine itself to abstract principles: it was fought out as ardently upon the question whether there were binding arrangements in reference to the subject between the kingdoms of England and Ireland. The occasions when it was suggested that such a compact might have been made were the Council at Lismore under Henry II., where the laws of England are said to have been accepted, and Councils under John, where the laws and customs (*leges et consuetudines*) of England were confirmed or enacted for the people of Ireland.* But the utmost that can, by the widest latitude of inference, be deduced from any recorded proceedings of these assemblies does not extend beyond the introduction into Ireland of the English system of Councils to assist the Sovereign; and this might have been effected either with or without a superior legislative authority being conceded to an English Council or Parliament.

The truth is, that the relations which were originally recognised between England and Ireland and their respective Parliaments did not arise out of any consideration of abstract reasonings, or any contracts or ordinances to create or define them. They grew out of circumstances, and were moulded by the demands of the time and occasion. Henry II. and his immediate successors, both in England and Ireland, entertained high notions of their own prerogative: *[marginal note: Why compact unlikely.]*

---

* See as to the Council of Lismore, p. 2, *supra*, and Note A of Appendix; and as to the Councils of John, p. 6, *supra*, and Note D of Appendix.

they found, and acted with, parliamentary institutions in the former country; they gained assistance from them there. Henry probably—his successors certainly—introduced a similar system in Ireland, seeking to strengthen their own influence by obtaining from the Anglo-Norman Knights and Nobles, who had established themselves in the country, assent to their policy. If a Council were called, these kings named the persons who should be summoned to attend. They had, therefore, no reason for apprehending opposition. Hence it was wholly unnecessary to make provision for assistance in the government of Ireland from another legislative assembly. There was then as little need to confer upon some external authority control over the Irish Councils. It is most unlikely that what there was no need to do was done.

Interests of the English and Anglo-Irish at first the same.

Nothing to alter the original state of affairs occurred for a long period. It was the interest of the Irish Parliament, composed of Anglo-Irish, to uphold the power of the Crown of England in Ireland: it was the interest of England to aggrandise the colonists, on whose sympathy and allegiance she could count. With this community of interests the two kingdoms and the two Parliaments had no reason for interfering with each other upon any matter.

Afterwards their interests conflicting.

When first it began to be perceived that the interests of the English and of the Anglo-Irish were not necessarily identical is uncertain.

Under Henry V. and Henry VI. we clearly see the idea manifesting itself in action. English statutes naming Ireland, and intended of their own sole authority, without affirmation by any local government, to bind Ireland, were then passed. England determined to uphold its own interests, and legislation by its Parliament afforded the only means through which this could be accomplished.

An examination of the most important of the laws made at that time for Ireland by the English Parliament—the Staple Act of Henry VI.—will illustrate the motives which induced it to interfere. The statute made Calais the sole mart for wool and certain other merchandise which was specified, if they were exported abroad. The object of the legislation is plain. Calais then belonged to England, and was inhabited by many English merchants. Trade, when directed there, would be wholly under the control of the English Government; also, it would enrich the colonists dwelling in the town. The measure was, therefore, clearly advantageous to England. It was as obviously against the interest of Ireland, whose merchants desired access to all the Continental ports, and not merely to one in the hands of English rivals. Its confirmation by an Irish Parliament, unless coerced, was not to be expected. But to make the enactment effective, Ireland as well as England should be subject to its provisions. Hence the English Parliament,

<small>Staple Act.</small>

if the policy approved was to be carried out, must expressly include Ireland in whatever statute it passed, and the English Government must enforce the statute when enacted.

<small>Acts of Hen. VI.</small> At the time, however, when the English Parliament thus came forward with an explicit demand to legislate for Ireland, the Irish Parliament had been long enough in existence to recognise its own strength. It would seem to have done so as early as Henry IV.; but whatever confidence in its own power it then possessed was increased after the accession of Henry VI., for in his reign civil war in England weakened the power of the Crown, and diminished its ability to attend to or restrain what went forward in Ireland. Accordingly, under this king the Irish Parliament twice by distinct Acts affirmed that statutes made in England were not in force in the kingdom of Ireland unless they were allowed and published in that kingdom by its Parliament.*

<small>Case of Merchants of Waterford.</small> As might be expected, when such adverse claims to jurisdiction were asserted, the question of right involved in them was soon raised before legal tribunals. Irish merchants transgressing the provisions of the Staple Act pleaded in defence that they were not bound to obey a statute

---

* 29 Henry VI., and the Act of the Duke of York's Parliament (see pp. 26, 27, *supra*). The Staple Act was 2 Henry VI. The litigation by the Merchants of Waterford upon the Staple Act was 2 Richard III.

made by an English Parliament. The matter came for adjudication at a period too late for a satisfactory decision. Lapse of time then surrounded the beginning of Irish legislation with obscurity. Many records of important events and transactions had wholly perished:* such as remained were often imperfect. The early annalists made no allusion to the subject. Inquirers, deprived of guidance from precedent or history, turned to abstract principles; but if abstract principles were applicable, there was no evidence to show that those which were at this time suggested had previously been acted upon or even recognised.

Under these circumstances the controversy between the English and Irish Parliaments, as to the legislative jurisdiction of the former, was not and could not be solved by judicial tribunals. From the time when the disputes excited by Molyneux's treatise died away the subject began to be considered more upon political, and

Controversy not then solved.

---

* The loss of records in Ireland has been unusually great. The Rolls of the Chancery in Ireland from 1172 to 1300 (a period of 128 years) were burned along with Mary's Abbey, where they were kept (see Harris's *Hibernica*, p. 149). The same authority says that another chasm occurs in the records of the first twenty years of Henry VIII. (except for the sixth year). It is also to be noted that even of the statutes of which records are preserved little more than a fourth have been printed—most of those omitted, however, are unimportant. (See Hardiman's edition of the *Statute of Kilkenny*, p. iv. n.)

less upon legal, principles than it had previously been. Until eighty years later the question continued to be discussed. Then a final settlement of the matters in dispute was effected through means of express legislation, induced by a series of events which will come to be narrated.

CHAPTER VII.

PARLIAMENT OF IRELAND.

[1700–1719.]

DURING the discussions in the reign of William III., occasioned by Molyneux's treatise, the example of Scotland was cited by those who denied the authority of the English Parliament over Ireland to illustrate the position claimed by them for the latter country. The King of England, it was said, was king of Scotland, just as he was King of Ireland; yet the Parliament of England made no pretence to a right of making laws for Scotland: this could be done, all admitted, only by the Scottish Parliament. Why was it to be otherwise in Ireland? *Parliament of Scotland.*

But the case of Scotland furnished no aid whatever towards solving the question raised respecting the jurisdiction of the English Parliament in Ireland. The independence of Scotland and the exclusive right of its own Parliament to make laws for its people were the result of circumstances peculiar to that country. Before James the Sixth of Scotland had, on the death of Queen Elizabeth, succeeded to the Crown of England, there was no connexion whatever between the *Scotland affords no analogy.*

kingdom of Scotland and the kingdom of England. The King and Parliament of Scotland were then as distinct from the King and Parliament of England as the King and Parliament of France were. James was the first instance of the same person being king of both countries. Until that event occurred there was no conceivable ground for suggesting that the Parliament of England ought to have or had legislative power in Scotland. The union of the crowns might have afforded a reason for enactments to alter this state of affairs, but it could not, of itself, effect a change. There was no such legislation, and consequently the rights of the Scotch and English Parliaments remained exactly what they previously had been.

Some English laws affected Scotland. From James I. to William III. it was not attempted to dispute the application of these principles to the case of Scotland. Their admission saved that country from any attempt by the English Parliament to repeat for its people legislation similar to that by which it had in Ireland interfered with the exportation of wool and woollen goods; but it afforded no bar to, and did not protect from, the laws England had enacted in respect of colonial trade. The Navigation Act was as injurious to Scotch as to Irish commerce. Goods for the colonies could no more be carried in Scotch ships than in Irish.

Harsh treatment of Scotch colonists. In this state of the relations between England and Scotland as to colonial trade, the Scotch began, during William's reign, to turn their attention to mercantile pursuits. Unable to carry on traffic directly with the English colonies, they determined to found colonies for themselves. They selected for the purpose the Isthmus of Darien, a place which had not then been occupied by the English, and which, therefore, Scotland, being a wholly independent kingdom, had a right to appropriate. The project when put in execution failed, but the failure was attended with circumstances which created among the Scottish people much indignation against the commercial policy of the English Parliament. When the Scotch colonists were in distress, the Governors of the English colonies at Jamaica, Barbadoes, and New York, issued proclamations forbidding assistance to be given to them.*

Out of all these causes, when Anne came to the throne (A.D. 1702), there had arisen in Scotland an universal desire to obtain a removal of all restrictions and hindrances which England had imposed upon its trade. Accordingly the Scottish Parliament, sympathising with these feelings, *Proceedings of Scotch Parliament.*

---

* Sir Walter Scott, after entering at length into the ungenerous treatment which the Scotch emigrants to the Isthmus of Darien received, and the consequent universal indignation of the people of Scotland, remarks that owing to these causes William III. was unable to 'wring from that kingdom one penny for the public service, or, what he would have valued more, one recruit to carry on his continental campaigns.'—*Miscellaneous Works*, vol. xxv., p. 48.

and yielding to the external impulse, proceeded to take advantage of difficulties which were likely to arise concerning the future union of the Crowns of England and Scotland, and of the desire of English statesmen to have them settled, and to use them as a means to compel concession of unrestricted rights of trade.

<small>Succession to the Crown of Scotland.</small>
These difficulties arose from the law regulating the succession to the Crown of Scotland. While the Crown of Ireland was, in the language of the Act of Henry VIII.—which conferred the title of King of Ireland instead of Lord of Ireland upon the King of England—united and knit to the imperial Crown of England, so that whoever was King of England was necessarily King of Ireland: the Crown of Scotland was wholly separate and distinct from the Crown of England, and a different person might be entitled to each. James I., his son, and his grandsons, in succession, had been each King of England and King of Scotland; but this was because they were the rightful inheritors of both crowns. William and Mary also, and William were entitled to both crowns; and the Princess Anne, on William's death, had become entitled to both; but this was because the English Convention Parliament, and the Scotch Convention Parliament, had conferred the English and Scotch crowns upon William and Mary, then on William, and then on Anne. But, after Anne, it was uncertain what would happen. The English Par-

liament had by an Act (12 and 13 William III., ch. 2) entailed the Crown of England, in the event of Queen Anne's death without issue, upon Sophia, Electress of Hanover, granddaughter of James I., and her issue; and if this princess and her issue took under the limitation the Crown of England, each in succession would be, *ipso facto*, entitled to the Crown of Ireland. But no such consequence would follow as to Scotland. It still remained for the Parliament of that kingdom to decide who, in this event—which, as Anne's children had all died, was likely to occur—should succeed to the Scottish Crown.

The mode in which the Parliament of Scotland employed these circumstances to attain its objects was by making the descent of the crown depend upon the concession of commercial freedom. In 1704 it passed an Act, called the Act of Security, which provided that, in the case of Queen Anne's death without issue, the Parliament of Scotland was to choose a successor of the royal line and Protestant religion; but that the same person should be incapable of holding the crowns of England and Scotland, unless the Scotch were admitted to share all privileges of trade and navigation equally with the English people. It also contained a clause which enacted that the men of Scotland, capable of bearing arms, should be trained to the use of them by monthy drills.*

<small>Act of Security.</small>

---

* That the Royal assent was given to this Act may well excite surprise. It seems to have been under a sort of com-

Effect in England of the Security Act.

The Security Act obliged statesmen in England to consider the position of their country in relation to Scotland. It was possible that under its provisions the crowns of England and Scotland might be divided: it was certain that the people would be armed. A separate crown with an armed people was an event which could not be contemplated without apprehension. Only one measure was held capable of affording complete security against the danger—an incorporating union of Scotland with England. Then there would be one kingdom, and one crown. To gain such advantages a complete grant of commercial freedom to Scotland might, it was thought, well be made.

Motives to an Union.

When the question of union was raised, Scottish statesmen could not but reflect upon the benefits to trade and commerce which were offered as its attendants. All, except the partisans of the exiled House of Stuart, desired that the difficulties and uncertainties awaiting the succession upon Anne's death should be terminated, and a final settlement made of the crown of Scotland, which would correspond with the

---

pulsion. When, in 1703, it was first voted, the Royal Commissioner would not allow it to become law. The Scotch Parliament offended, refused supplies, shouting, 'Liberty before subsidy.' When it met again, Anne, on the advice of Godolphin, yielded, and gave her assent. (See Sir Walter Scott's *Miscellaneous Works*, vol. xxv., pp. 56 and 58.) Swift says the Scotch Union became necessary when this Act gave the people leave to arm themselves.—*Public Spirit of the Whigs.*

settlement of the crown of England that had been enacted by the English Parliament.

Ultimately, but not without much opposition, there were passed by both the Scotch and English Parliaments, in 1707, Acts uniting the kingdoms of England and Scotland by the name of Great Britain. The succession to the crown of the United Kingdom was, after Queen Anne's death without issue, to remain to the Princess Sophia and the heirs of her body, being Protestants. All commercial and trading disabilities affecting Scotland were to cease. Thenceforward one Parliament, composed of English and Scotch Peers and Commoners, was to legislate for every part of Great Britain. Scotch Union Acts.

These proceedings of the English and Scotch Parliaments necessarily attracted the attention of a Parliament in such proximity to them as the Irish was. Their example pointed to union with England as a certain means of relief from the legislation of the English Parliament, which in Ireland, as in Scotland, hindered colonial trade; and for this reason it tended to recommend the measure as a remedy for financial depression, much felt at that time by Irish industry. The policy of union was, however, not without influential advocates at an earlier period. Molyneux, in his *Case of Ireland*, had said that for Ireland to have representatives in the Parliament of England was a happiness hardly to be hoped for. Sir William Petty, in his *Political* Example of Scotland affects Irish Parliament.
p. 61, *supra*.

Anatomy of Ireland, expressed similar sentiments and gave his reasons.* . . . 'If,' he wrote, 'both kingdoms were under one legislative power and Parliament, the members whereof should be proportionable in power and wealth of each nation, there would be no danger that such a Parliament would do anything to the prejudice of the English interest in Ireland; nor could the Irish ever complain of partiality, when they would be freely and proportionately represented in all legislatures.'

<small>Irish Parliament suggests union.</small>

The first appearance of any tendency in the Irish Parliament towards the policy of union with England was about the end of the year 1703. At that time such a measure was distinctly suggested in a resolution of the House of Lords (October 25, 1703), to the effect that a representation should be made to Queen Anne to induce her to promote it, so as to qualify the states of Ireland being represented there. The House of Commons also in an address referred to a more strict union with Her Majesty's subjects in England. Afterwards, in 1707, the same House, congratulating the Queen on the completion of the Scottish Union, added an emphatic prayer that God might put into her heart to add greater strength and lustre to her crown by a yet more comprehensive union.†

---

* Edition 1719, p. 31. The *Anatomy* professes to be dated 1672.

† See *Journal of Lords*, ii., p. 29, and of *Commons*, 20 Oct.,

Parliament of Ireland, 1700–1719.

But union was not then to be. The Irish Parliament had not any means of compelling attention to its wishes similar to those which the Scotch possessed. There was no difficulty in respect of the succession to the Crown to be overcome. Anne and her Ministers received the addresses presented to them with cold civility, and during the remainder of her reign treated them with neglect. In taking this course they acted in conformity with the sentiments of the mass of the English people, who regarded with apprehension the admission of members of a different nationality to their Parliament, and were jealous of allowing another people to share in the commercial privileges and advantages that they themselves enjoyed. In the instances both of Scotland and Ireland, Union was likened to an inferior or dependent person being taken into partnership, and being thus raised to an undeserved elevation.*

Suggestions of union rejected by England.

1703, and July 9, 1707; Lecky's *History*, vol. ii., p. 416; and Froude's *English in Ireland*, vol. ii., pp. 302, 303. The last contains the most full account of the proceedings in Ireland connected with union at this time. Froude quotes a remarkable letter of Sir Richard Cox, then Lord Chancellor of Ireland, in which he advocates union as especially desirable in a country inhabited, as Ireland was, by several nations, interests, and religions.

* This is the tone of Swift's observations on the Scotch union in his *Public Spirit of the Whigs;* and he adds to the sarcasm by making Scotland boast of the number of Peers and other persons she had quartered on England: just as if

Union unpopular.

Nor can it be said, if we except members of Parliament and such persons as, although not in Parliament, engaged in a scientific study, of political questions, that union was less unpopular in Ireland than in England. Much the greater number were disinclined to relinquish the character of a separate kingdom for the purpose of becoming part of another, even although that other were greater and more powerful. The advantages expected from extended liberty of trade seemed remote and uncertain; while the evils of increased absenteeism, and the consequent withdrawal of a large part of the revenues of the island to be expended outside it, were certain and immediate.

Jurisdiction in Irish causes of the English House of Lords questioned.

The effect of rejecting the project of union was to confirm the legislative relations of the English and Irish Parliaments in the same condition as they were during the last years of William III., and to give confidence to the former in maintaining the claims which it had in his reign, with such fixed determination, advanced. Then the English Parliament, for the maintenance of the position it had taken, proceeded by

---

(he says) a person of quality having been prevailed on to marry a woman, his inferior, she should argue that she was as good as her husband because she brought him as numerous a family of relations and servants as she found in his house. The Scotch (he adds) had acquired more money out of the union than a native of that country, who had not travelled, could before that measure have formed an idea of.

passing resolutions and by addresses to the King: legislation upon the subject would, of course, be a still more decisive mode of asserting a right. And about five years after the accession of George I. to the throne opportunity was afforded for this course. At that time the English House of Lords was the ultimate appellate tribunal from the English Courts of Chancery and Common Law. It assumed the same jurisdiction over the Irish Courts. In a suit in one of the latter, appeals were taken to the Irish House of Lords and to the English House of Lords. These tribunals pronounced disagreeing judgments. Each claimed to be the ultimate Court of Appeal. Neither would give way. Which was to prevail? The Irish Judges, when consulted, pronounced for the right of the Irish House of Lords. The English Parliament resolved to answer their judgment by a declaratory Act in favour of the English House of Lords. But the judicial superiority of the English House of Lords was only a branch of the general superiority demanded for the English Parliament. If it was expedient then to affirm the former, it was deemed equally expedient to affirm the latter.*

---

* The Irish House of Lords, in a Paper drawn up to support their case at this time, had revived the assertion that the Irish chiefs were not conquered by Henry II., but 'without any war or chivalry' submitted to him, and that he in return ordained, at the instance of the Irish, that such laws

6 Geo. I.

Accordingly, the Act—so well known as the sixth of George the First—was passed by the English Parliament. This not only declared the English House of Lords to be the ultimate appellate tribunal for Irish suits, but enacted in express words that the King's Majesty, by and with the advice and consent of the Lords and Commons of Great Britain in Parliament, had, and of right ought to have, full power and authority to make laws and statutes of sufficient force and validity. to bind the kingdom and people of Ireland. It further added, that Ireland hath been, is, and of right ought to be, subordinate unto, and dependent upon, the Imperial Crown of Great Britain, as being inseparably united and annexed thereto.

Effect of 6 Geo. I.

The statute, except as a challenge to the Irish Parliament, was obviously of no value. If the English Parliament and English House of Lords had the authority it claimed for them, the Act was superfluous: if they had not, the English Parliament alone could not, by passing the Act, confer jurisdiction upon them. As a challenge,

---

as he had in England should be of force and observed in Ireland, whereby the privilege of a distinct Parliament was conferred.—*Journals of Irish House of Lords*, vol. ii., pp. 655–660. In the controversy respecting the ultimate appellate jurisdiction from the Irish courts of law, no question seems to have been raised as to the Irish House of Lords being the tribunal before which an impeachment was to be heard. In 1641, when Bishop Bramhall, Sir Richard Bolton, and others, were impeached by the Irish House of Commons, the proceedings were before the Irish House of Lords.

however, the enactment served the purpose of those who procured it; for the Irish Parliament remained silent, and under such circumstances it was not unfair to allege that it no longer disputed the legislative supremacy of England.

The practice of summoning the Irish Convocation along with Parliament, which had been commenced under James I., was abandoned from the accession of the House of Hanover to the throne of England. Convocation in Ireland met in obedience to writ from the Crown for the last time in 1711, being then convened by Queen Anne. She revived it after a discontinuance of its meetings under William and Mary and also under William. For some time, however, before 1711 the clergy of the Established Church had been included among the subjects of the Crown upon whom taxation was imposed by Parliament, and this continued ever afterwards to be the usage. Convocation discontinued.

CHAPTER VIII.

PARLIAMENT OF IRELAND.

[1719-1760.]

Effect of the law preventing the export of woollen goods.

AT the time when the Parliament of England passed the Act of the Sixth of George I., and thus declared its determination to persist in asserting a power to make laws for Ireland, the injurious effects of its previous exercise of the power were becoming visible. Before the English statute of William III., prohibiting the export of woollen manufactured goods from Ireland, except to England, there was a considerable trade from Irish ports connected with this department of industry. After the prohibition came in force the manufacture of wool ceased, and the persons engaged in it either left the country or sank into poverty.

English policy as to Irish trade.

The Woollen Act had been preceded by the Acts excluding Irish ships from, and prohibiting direct trade with, the colonies, and also by the Acts preventing the importation of cattle, sheep, swine, and various agricultural products, from Ireland into England. With the exception of the linen manufacture, which from the time of Strafford had been encouraged, the policy of successive English governments appeared to be to divert Irish enterprize from trade and manufactures. If, in place of making woollen cloth, Irish industry were to turn to any employment other than that which was thus pointed out for its pursuit, those who engaged in the substituted occupation had no security—so long as the English Parliament exercised the power of legislating for Ireland—that it might not in a moment be extinguished. Capitalists feared to invest their money in Irish manufactures, and there were consequently none, beside the linen, of any importance.

It has been already explained that, with the exception of the Woollen Act, all this restrictive legislation of the English Parliament as to Irish trade was unquestionably within its jurisdiction; and that no declaration or admission of exclusive right in the Irish Parliament to make laws for Ireland would have rendered it inoperative, or prevented similar enactments in the future. It is also to be noted that the policy which was embodied in the English statutes grew out of a doctrine then almost universally accepted, that nations ought, by protective provisions, to foster and encourage their own industries. Ireland, although its crown was indissolubly united to the crown of England, was in relation to these matters regarded as a separate country. *The restrictive Acts generally intra vires.*

It is probable that such considerations may *Irish people discontented.*

> P. 89, supra.

have had weight with the Irish Parliament. It could not fail to perceive that to get rid of the Act of the Sixth of George I. would not get rid of most injurious enactments of the English Parliament. But the people in general did not stop to calculate the exact effect of the statute; they objected to the enactment itself. Its provisions seemed to them calculated to fix upon a firmer basis the authority of a Legislature which, in the exercise partly of a power that could not be doubted, partly of a power denied by very able thinkers and reasoners, and on several occasions repudiated by the Irish Parliament, had inflicted great injury upon the manufacturing and mercantile interests of Ireland.

> Swift.

It was at this time Swift came forward, and first appeared as the champion of Irish interests in contradistinction to British. His strength of character, and the extraordinary force and vigour of his writings, at once enabled him to lead and guide public opinion in Ireland. The Sixth of George I. was passed in 1719, and in the next year Swift issued his celebrated proposals for the use of Irish manufactures in clothes and furniture, and the exclusion of British goods. The spirit in which his tract was written will appear from the following extract:—'The fable in *Ovid* of Arachne and Pallas is to this purpose. The goddess had heard of one Arachne, a young virgin very famous for spinning and weaving. They both met upon a trial of skill; and Pallas, finding herself almost equalled in her own art, stung with rage and envy, knocked her rival down, and turned her into a spindle, enjoining her to spin and weave for ever out of her own bowels, and in a very narrow compass. I confess that, from a boy, I always pitied poor Arachne, and could never heartily love the goddess on account of so cruel and unjust a sentence; which, however, is fully executed upon us by England with further additions of vigour and severity. For the greatest part of our bowels and vitals is extracted without allowing us the liberty of spinning and weaving them.'*

Notwithstanding the interference of Swift, the discontent prevailing in Ireland did not result in any movement or other form of action until about four years later, when the conduct of the English Government in reference, not to trade or manufactures, but to an exercise of the royal prerogative, kindled the resentment of the people

Wood's coinage.

---

* The full title of the pamphlet was *A Proposal for the universal use of Irish Manufacture in Clothes and Furniture of Houses, etc., utterly rejecting and renouncing every thing wearable that cometh from England*. It was in this he related the saying of some one, whose name he does not give, but which was told to him by Dr. Vesey, the Archbishop of Tuam— 'Ireland will never be happy till a law be made for burning everything that came from England except their people and their coals.' 'I must confess,' says Swift, 'that as to the former, I should not be sorry if they should stay at home; and as to the latter, I hope in a little time we shall have no occasion for them.'

into a ferment, and gave rise to an agitation against the supremacy of the English Government in Ireland.

Wood's coinage.

The events now alluded to are those which occurred in connexion with a patent for a copper coinage for Ireland, granted by George the Second to an ironmonger of Wolverhampton, named Wood, and the issue under its authority of coin alleged to be below the stipulated standard. With respect to this measure the Irish Parliament was never consulted; and thus offended national pride united with the supposition of pecuniary loss to create resentment, and to stimulate resistance to the scheme being carried into effect. All classes in Ireland combined to prevent the circulation of Wood's money.

The Drapier's letters.

Of this movement Swift placed himself at the head, just as he had done before in the case of the restrictions on trade. Under the assumed name of M. B., a Drapier, he addressed a series of letters to the people of Ireland, in which his extraordinary power of ridicule and invective was without scruple used against Wood and his project. From these topics he turned aside to deal with the general ascendency claimed for England, and as part of it with its legislation for Ireland. 'Some people,' he said, 'who come hither to us from England, and some weak people among ourselves, when in discourse we make mention of liberty and property, shake their heads and tell us, that Ireland is a depending kingdom, as if they would seem by this phrase to intend that the people of Ireland are in some state of slavery or dependence different from those in England: whereas, a depending kingdom is a modern term of art, unknown to all ancient civilians and writers upon government; and Ireland is, on the contrary, called in some statutes an Imperial Crown, as held only from God, which is as high a style as any kingdom is capable of receiving. Therefore, by this expression, a depending kingdom, there is no more to be understood than that, by a statute made here, in the thirty-third year of Henry VIII., the king and his successors are to be Kings Imperial of the Realm, as united and knit to the Imperial Crown of England.' 'I have,' he continued, 'looked over all the English and Irish statutes, without finding any law that maketh Ireland depend upon England, any more than England doth upon Ireland. We have, indeed, obliged ourselves to have the same king with them, and consequently they are obliged to have the same king with us.' *Fourth Drapier's Letter.*

... 'It is true, indeed,' he proceeded, ' that within the memory of man the Parliaments of England have sometimes assumed the power of binding this kingdom by laws enacted there; wherein they were, at first, openly opposed (as far as truth, wisdom, and justice, are capable of opposing) by the famous Mr. Molyneux, an English gentleman, born here, as well as by several of the greatest patriots and best Whigs in England; but the love and torrent of power prevailed.'

Prosecution of the Drapier's Letters.

Observations of this character reviving the ideas of Molyneux, not without exaggeration, and advocating them with the fervour of political partisanship, met with general applause. The existence of a separate Parliament in Ireland, however controlled it might be in action by Poynings' Law or the authority of the English Parliament, had kept alive sentiments of nationality which, much less than the burning words of Swift, would have sufficed to ignite into a flame. Soon it began to be perceived that more than Wood's coinage was in peril. The Irish ministers alarmed, thought that they were called upon to take active measures against the agitation, fast extending through the entire community. They instituted a prosecution of the printers of the Drapier's Letters, in which the fourth letter, that which contained the language which has been cited, was made the subject of an indictment, the legal charge against it being that it was designed to alienate the affections of the king's subjects in England and Ireland from each other.

Failure of prosecution.

But in periods of excitement the success of repressive proceedings of this kind is never certain. The prosecution failed: the grand jury of the city of Dublin refused to find the bill of indictment, notwithstanding observations in its favour addressed to them by Chief Justice Whitshed.

The English Ministry, foiled in their effort to crush the popular movement, yielded to its demands so far as Wood's coinage was concerned, and accordingly revoked the patent, and gave himself compensation. When the original question was decided, the controversy respecting the English Parliament, which had been taken up as subsidiary to it, was no longer continued, and gradually it died away. Not so the principles upon which Swift had conducted the discussion: these survived the question with which they had been associated, and, being universally cherished, they were certain to reappear the moment any favourable conjunction of affairs might open the way for their application.

In the agitation respecting Wood's coinage, just as in the discontent with the legislation respecting the woollen manufacture in William's reign, the Irish Parliament did not take any part. The House of Commons had, since 1692, consisted of 300 members, the number which it continued to retain while it was a separate legislature.* The great majority of these sat for boroughs, and were the mere nominees of their owners and patrons. The smallest borough returned the same number of members as the largest county —each had two. In the counties every holder of a freehold of the value of forty shillings was

Irish Parliament passive.

---

* James I. created about 40 boroughs; before William III. 36 more were created; and in 1692 11 more.—Lecky, *History*, vol. ii., p. 225.

a voter. If a Roman Catholic had the requisite qualification, he could, until the first year of George the Second, vote. Then a clause was introduced in an Act for regulating elections, which prohibited Roman Catholics voting at the election of any member to serve in Parliament as knight, citizen, or burgess, or at the election of any magistrate for any city or other town corporate. From 1692 a Roman Catholic had not been allowed to sit in either the House of Lords or House of Commons. Parliament at this time was called upon every accession of a new sovereign to the throne, and, unless dissolved by an exercise of his prerogative, endured for his life.

<small>1 Geo. II., ch. 9, s. 7.</small>

<small>P. 48, supra.</small>

<small>Mode in which Parliament was managed.</small>

When the representation was thus constituted, it is easy to understand why the Parliaments of William, Anne, and George the First, feebly reflected public opinion. As a general rule, a Parliament sat only every second year. When it met, Ministers, by means of the jurisdiction of the English and Irish Privy Councils under Poynings' Law, prevented any legislation they did not desire. The same system continued after George the Second came to the throne. During his reign the management of the two Houses of Parliament in Ireland was effected through the agency of the great nobles, who, for the time, predominated in society. To them was entrusted the distribution of patronage in Ireland, and they, in return, undertook to ensure success for the measures brought forward by the Administration.

Taxation afforded a subject upon which, notwithstanding the influence thus brought into use, there was much difficulty in securing the allegiance of the Irish House of Commons. In 1692, under William and Mary, it had, as we have seen, claimed to initiate money Bills. In 1731 it proceeded to assert its independence in connection with a financial question. The revenues for national purposes were partly what were termed the hereditary revenues of the Crown, in which were included those derived from the customs and excise, and partly temporary revenues voted to supplement the hereditary. There had at this time accumulated a surplus, and the House of Commons, against the wishes of the ministry, determined to reduce proportionately the supplemental grant. The resolution was passed by a majority of only one vote.*

House of Commons and Taxation.

P. 49, *supra*.

After this incident Parliament relapsed into its usual course, and for a long time resembled its predecessors.† Before, however, the death of George II. an external agitation arose which ultimately acted upon the opinions and pro-

Lucas.

* The vote which carried the resolution was given by a member, Colonel Tottenham, who, having to ride sixty miles to attend the debate, arrived when it was coming to an end; and, in order to be in time, came to the House, which always met in full dress, in his travelling apparel. Afterwards 'Tottenham in his boots' became a popular toast.

† In 1736 Swift wrote his celebrated satire upon the Irish House of Commons, entitled the *Legion Club*, which, with

ceedings of Parliament. The person who took the lead in stimulating and guiding it was Charles Lucas, a member of the medical profession. He first came forward in relation to the affairs and interests of the Municipal Corporation of Dublin. From such subjects, perceiving that with their limited importance they could not secure him permanent influence, he passed on to questions of national interest, and reproduced the complaints and arguments of Swift and Molyneux. Enlarging upon the poverty of the country, the want of manufactures, its exclusion from opportunities of trade, he asked—Was the English Parliament to continue to legislate for Ireland? If it was, what safety remained for any Irish interest? It had extinguished the woollen manufacture; it might destroy the linen manufacture also.*

---

an allusion to the position of the building where it met being opposite Trinity College, commenced:—

> As I stroll the city, oft I
> Spy a building large and lofty,
> Not a bow-shot from the College;
> Half the globe from sense and knowledge.

In this satire he hints at the means used to influence the members thus:—

> In the porch Briareus stands,
> Shows a bribe in all his hands;
> Briareus the Secretary,
> But we mortals call him Carey.
> When the rogues their country fleece,
> They may hope for pence a-piece.

* In 1749 Lucas was returned to Parliament as Member for the City of Dublin. The principal difference of opinion ex-

Parliament of Ireland, 1719–1760. 101

It will be remembered that when in Queen Anne's reign the pressure of English commercial legislation began to be felt in Ireland, the example of Scotland induced the suggestion of an union with England in order to obtain freedom of trade. Now, the same example appeared to warn against, instead of inviting to, this policy. With the people of Scotland the Union was for many years unpopular. To a natural regret for the loss of an extremely ancient nationality was added resentment for the mode in which its destruction was supposed to have been accomplished. Corrupt means, even personal bribery, to gain votes were almost universally believed to have been used. The compensating advantages which the Union brought with it were undervalued and imperfectly made use of, owing to the prevalent discontent and to a vague expectation that the National Parliament would be restored, which was encouraged and kept alive by the Jacobite party until their total defeat in 1745.† *Example of Scotland at this time warns against union.*

Nor even if the example of Scotland and other motives operative in 1707 had still continued to recommend the policy of union for Ireland, could it in Lucas's time have been revived. Anne and *Union then had no support in Ireland.*

---

hibited between him and Latouche, the opposing candidate, was in reference to the views of the former on the questions connected with the jurisdiction of the English Parliament in Ireland.

† See Note W of Appendix.

her Ministers rejected the advances made by the Irish Parliament to obtain a measure of this nature; and the whole current of public opinion had, by the repulse of the overtures made to them, been thenceforward diverted towards the acquisition of a distinct national independence.*

Lucas's ideas.

Lucas himself, favouring the popular sentiments, and aware that to obtain power and influence he must advocate them, demanded a free Parliament, with exclusive jurisdiction over every Irish interest. Ireland, he said, was a kingdom: its King, Parliament, and Courts of Law could not acknowledge any superior; yet there have been Parliaments in England which assumed a superiority over the King and Constitution of Ireland: this, he added, made (what he termed) a solecism in the government.†

Effect of Lucas's agitation.

Lucas did not possess the intellectual power of Swift or Molyneux; yet he attained considerable

---

* In 1759 the extreme unpopularity of a union with England was, in Dublin, evidenced by a violent riot, which broke out upon a rumour that it was intended. The account of this riot in the *Annual Register* for that year (p. 129) states that a mob of several thousands of persons broke into the House of Lords, and insulted them, and then obliged members coming to the House of Commons to take an oath never to consent to an union, or to give a vote contrary to the interests of Ireland.

† *Dedication to the King* of tract on Dublin Charter, p. xx; and see also *Political Constitutions*, 1751. As to Lucas, see Wills' *Lives of Illustrious Irishmen*, and Gilbert's *Dublin*, vol. iii., p. 98.

influence. He spoke to an audience predisposed to hear him. The community was poor and depressed; and the cause was said to be the legislation of the English Parliament concerning Irish trade and commerce. But the growth of opinions such as he advocated in the Irish Parliament of the time was slow, nor can it be said that within it they ever during the reign of George II. arrived at complete maturity. All that, during this period, appeared was the formation of a political party professing to regard merely the interests of Ireland and to desire only the advancement of those interests. In the House of Commons this party became a regular Opposition, engaged in criticising severely such measures as the Government brought forward, while it demanded for Parliament a right to control all financial arrangements, and jealously objected to the number of places and pensions which were supported out of the Irish revenues.

CHAPTER IX.

PARLIAMENT OF IRELAND.

[1760-1780.]

<small>New Parliament at accession of George III.</small>

THE accession of George III. to the throne caused a new Parliament to be summoned in Ireland. The tendencies towards a policy of nationality, which had appeared in the preceding House of Commons during the last years of its existence, were renewed in that which was now returned, and with much greater strength. Its members, more accurately than their predecessors, represented the opinions in favour at the time, and their own sentiments were more in sympathy with them.

<small>Octennial Act.</small>

The Parliament of George II. had continued for his entire reign—a period of thirty-three years—without being dissolved. Its long duration attracted attention to the evils resulting from the rule which made the continuance of Parliament depend upon the life of the sovereign. The constituencies of the counties and open towns, and the owners of boroughs who could nominate the members, were alike dissatisfied with a system which opened for them such rare opportunities to exercise their power, and both now instructed their representatives to insist upon having a limitation of reasonable length placed upon the duration of Parliament. The question was at once brought forward in the House of Commons; but at first even the pressure of those to whom its members were indebted for their seats failed to induce an abridgment of the term for which they sat; and seven years elapsed before an Act was passed which fixed eight years as the utmost period of existence for an Irish Parliament.

The Octennial Act, as the Statute limiting the duration of Parliament was called, effected great changes in the character of the Irish House of Commons. Previously its members had practically only one immediate source of insecurity in the tenure of their seats to fear—the Crown might dissolve Parliament. Their interest, therefore, led them to support the King's Ministers, since this was the way to avert a dissolution. Now, instead of a possible undisturbed possession for the reign of, it might be, a youthful sovereign, a representative of the Commons had the certainty, in the case of a county or city, of meeting his constituents, or, in the case of a small borough, the patron who nominated him, at the latest eight years after his return. The electors, not the Crown, became the taskmasters to be obeyed. Another important result from the measure was, that increased means were

Effects of Octennial Act.

afforded of introducing new men into the Legislature. The most distinguished abilities might, under the former system, have waited in vain for an opening to admit them.

<small>New Parliament elected A.D. 1768.</small>

Contemporaneously with the passing of the Octennial Act Parliament was dissolved, in consequence of a provision to that effect contained in the Act. A new House of Commons was accordingly elected. The influences which the Statute brought into operation were apparent in the character, and subsequently in the conduct, of the members returned by the electoral constituencies, and sent by the patrons of boroughs. From this period may be traced in the House of Commons an increased manifestation of the sentiments popular among the people generally. At the same time more zeal for the public service, greater political knowledge, and improved capacity in the management and discussion of affairs, became perceptible.

<small>Use of patronage to influence Parliament.

See p. 98, *supra.*</small>

About the time of the Octennial Act the Ministers then in power, instead of adopting the means employed during the reign of George II., to influence the Irish Parliament by allowing the great families to distribute the patronage of the Crown, determined to substitute a more direct system under which they themselves would confer places and pensions upon their supporters.* Such arts, however, could not avail to prevent

---

* See Note X of Appendix.

the existence of an independent minority, who from the time of the Octennial Act increased in number and importance.

To examine the merits of those who in the first Parliament of George III. attained eminence would detain too long. Among them the foremost rank must be conceded to Flood. Possessed of extensive knowledge upon political subjects (the fruit of much study and reflection), speaking with force and clearness, an acute thinker, and an accurate reasoner, he, more than any other leader of his time, contributed to elevate the tone of discussion in the House of Commons. It was by his example that its members were first guided to the excellence in debate which they afterwards attained. Flood.

Improvement of the House of Commons in intellectual power would have had little practical effect, if Parliament had been confined in its action strictly to actual legislation. But its power of discussion was wider than its power of enactment. It could pass no Statute without the previous consent of the English and Irish Privy Councils; but either House might vote 'heads of Bills,' and pass resolutions expressing its opinion upon any question it took in hand. Nor does it seem possible that this could have been otherwise, since every Legislature must, so far as mere discussion, be master of its own proceedings; and the only penalty which an external authority, Power of Parliament to debate wider than its power to enact.

Page 38, *supra*.

however superior in actual power, can inflict for violation of rules to restrain debate must be to decree the futility of the resolutions in which debate may result.

<small>Discontent of the Irish Parliament with its position.</small>
If a legislative body have unlimited power of discussion, and but a limited power to legislate its acquiescence in its position can be relied upon only while it is weak and conscious of its weakness. Assuming the Irish House of Commons to have been under William and George I. such <small>Page 99, n. *supra*.</small> as Swift described it to be under George II., there can be no surprise that it remained silent, notwithstanding the extinction of the woollen manufacture, and the enactment of the Sixth of George the First. But with improvement, with the perception of its own development, came the promptings of ambition: what was accepted in the hour of weakness was repudiated in the hour of strength. It compared the fetters forged for it by Poynings' law and the Sixth of George the First with the freedom and independence of the sister legislative assembly of Great Britain upon whose model it had been framed, and chafed at the restrictions by which it was surrounded.*

---

* Bowes, the Irish Lord Chancellor, wrote to Dodington, an English minister, immediately after the accession of George III., that the English House of Commons was looked to 'as the model, and in general they think themselves injured in the instances in which theirs, upon the legal constitution, must differ.' This letter is printed in full in the appendix to the first volume of Adolphus's *History of*

Parliament of Ireland, 1760–1780.

But it was long before this discontent embodied itself in action. The question as to the claims of England to legislate was, Hardy says, alluded to in similes and metaphors; and it was thought an instance of political courage in Pery, a Member of Parliament of the highest reputation, to say .... 'I see no reason for indistinct or figurative language. I will speak out. The Parliament of Great Britain has no right to make laws for Ireland.' *

Discontent without action.

The subordinate position of the Irish Parliament, the legislation of the English Parliament for Ireland, and the restraints this legislation imposed on trade and commerce, continued without any attempt to procure alteration until about 1778, when events occurred which ultimately effected an entire revolution in the relations between Great Britain and Ireland. At that time the former kingdom had become engaged in a war with France, and, occupied in protecting its own coasts and possessions, could not spare an adequate supply of troops to repel a foreign army, if it were to land in Ireland. The only hope or means of defending that country lay in the voluntary formation of associations for the purpose. And accordingly, in 1778, invasion being at that time apprehended, such associations were every-

Volunteers.

England. Hardy also had remarked the emulation excited by English example.—*Life of Charlemont*, vol. i., pp. 79–82; and see Lecky also, vol. iv., p. 352.

* See Hardy's *Life of Charlemont*, vol. i., p. 161.

where in process of being organized. The Volunteers regulated, without the interference of external authority, their own proceedings; they elected their own officers, and defrayed most of the expense of their own arms and equipments. They were nearly all Protestants, but Catholics were not excluded. Persons of high social distinction were at their head. They were drilled and instructed in military discipline. After the lapse of little more than a year, according to the computation of Hardy,* who had peculiar opportunities of acquiring information on the subject, they numbered about 42,000.

<small>Effect of the Volunteer movement.</small>

The organization of the Volunteers did not withdraw them from their positions, whatever they might be, in social life. They continued to be citizens as well as soldiers, and were necessarily imbued with the ideas and sentiments of those among whom they lived. In common with the rest of the people, they were discontented with the commercial policy of England. This had never varied from what it had been under Charles II. and William III. So far from the statutes of these kings being repealed, the prohibition of the export of glass had been added to the prohibitions upon other exports enacted by them.

<small>19 Geo. II.</small>

---

* Hardy was the biographer of Lord Charlemont. He had been his intimate friend during his life. This nobleman was elected President of the Convention of Volunteers in 1783. (See Hardy's *Life of Charlemont*, vol. i., p. 382.)

The Opposition in the House of Commons associated themselves with the Volunteers upon the popular side, and, emboldened by their support, pressed the Government to abolish all restrictions affecting commerce. Both the Volunteers and the Opposition were urged on by the working classes, who were then suffering much distress, and who attributed it to the want of trade and manufactures. If, they asked, the export of manufactured goods was not allowed, if trade were not made free, whence were employment and relief to come to them? *[Opposition combines with the Volunteers.]*

The course which Swift had fifty years before recommended in order to obtain concessions from England was now adopted. A combination was formed to use only home-made goods. Agreements against importing, or purchasing what was imported, from England were entered into and signed by numbers. The Volunteers, leading the way, insisted that their uniforms should be made of cloth woven in Irish looms. *[Combination against English goods.]*

In October, 1779, when this movement was at its height, Parliament met. Grattan, who had about four years before entered the House of Commons, and had already won for himself a position of the highest eminence, brought forward the question of commercial restrictions by an amendment to the Address which was proposed in answer to the speech of the Lord Lieutenant. The views that Grattan advocated received also the support of Flood and Burgh; the former *[Resolution in favour of free trade.]*

then holding the high office of Vice-Treasurer under the Crown, and retaining no small part of his former almost paramount influence: the latter being the Prime Sergeant, and at the head of the Irish Bar, both in rank and attainments. The result of the discussion which ensued upon the amendment was, that a resolution was unanimously carried which affirmed that 'nothing but a free trade could save the country from ruin.'

Address in favour of free trade. After the resolution in favour of free trade had been voted in the Commons, an Address to the Lord Lieutenant, expressing similar sentiments, was carried to the Castle (the residence of the Lord Lieutenant) by a procession of Peers and Commoners, between lines of Volunteers in arms the entire way. Nor was this the only evidence which this body gave of its determination to support the House of Commons in its policy. In the month of November following, when, upon the anniversary of King William's landing, they assembled around his statue, many significant signs and mottos evidenced their zeal in the cause of commercial liberty, and two pieces of cannon drawn up before them bore the inscription— 'free trade, or this.'

Free trade conceded. In the end the British Government and the British Parliament gave way. The English Acts of William and George II., which prohibited the exportation of woollen goods and of glass were repealed. Trade with the English settlements and plantations in America, the West Indies, and

Africa, was thrown open, with the condition only that Irish trade should be subject to the duties then, or at any time thereafter to be, imposed for like exports or imports in British ports and harbours.*

These concessions became law early in 1780, but the announcement that the Government would submit them for enactment to the British Parliament had been made by Lord North on the preceding 13th of December, in a speech reviewing the commercial relations then subsisting between Great Britain and Ireland, and advocating a liberal policy on the part of the former. It is remarkable that, when proposed, the concessions met no opposition. Speech of Lord North.

---

*See Acts 20 George III., ch. 6 and ch. 10 (English); and for the Acts repealed, see pages 44, 52, 110, *supra*. 'Free trade' in the resolution of the Irish Parliament is not used in its modern sense. It means merely freedom from the prohibitions and restrictions on trade to and from Ireland imposed by English legislation.

CHAPTER X.

PARLIAMENT OF IRELAND.

[1780.]

Effect of concession.

SUCCESS in obtaining concessions connected with trade and commerce taught the Irish parliamentary Opposition their strength. They saw that measures aimed to advance the prosperity and greatness of the nation would command the support of the Volunteers and the sympathy of the people; and now experience had proved that with such aid resistance on the part of the British Parliament might be overcome.

English Parliament continues to be unpopular.

The concession of commercial privileges did not put an end to the unpopularity of the English Parliament. Discontent does not necessarily cease because the grievance in which it originated has been removed. Now it was suggested that the laws repealed could be again imposed; that without a Parliament strong enough to cope with the English legislature they were certain to be renewed; that the only security for freedom of trade and manufacture was the establishment, beyond controversy, of an exclusive right in the Parliament of Ireland to make laws for its people.

There were, however, difficulties in the way of a movement for constitutional rights which did not impede the demand for commercial privileges. Most statesmen in England, and many in Ireland, at this period feared to concede independence to the Irish Parliament, lest it might be used to impair the connection between the two kingdoms, and thereby to endanger their acting in concert. Besides, gratitude seemed to dictate that when so much had been done to liberate colonial trade, (a benefit that must be referred to bounty, not right), some delay ought to be interposed before further claims upon Great Britain were put forward. *[margin: Difficult to assert constitutional rights.]*

Considerations of this nature seem to have operated with the chief leaders of the party which allied itself with national interests, Grattan excepted. He, when discussion as to the commercial privileges which had been granted arose in the Irish House of Commons, and some speakers declared that topics tending to prevent the good understanding of the kingdoms of Great Britain and Ireland ought to be postponed, expressed his opinion that 'the time for constitutional relief was when commercial relief had been obtained.'* Acting upon this view, he soon afterwards assumed to direct the course of the patriotic party, and intimated that he would *[margin: Grattan urges action.]*

---

* So the Marquis of Buckingham, then Lord Lieutenant, states to Lord Hillsborough. (See letter of 17th February, 1780, printed in full in *Grattan's Life*, by his Son.)

move in the House of Commons a resolution declaratory of the rights of Ireland.

<small>Obstacles.</small> When he thus came forward and appropriated to himself what was the supreme political question of the period, Grattan stood almost alone. The influence of the Crown was directly used to oppose him. 'The King,' wrote an English Minister to the Lord Lieutenant, 'commands me to signify that it is expected from you that you do oppose and resist any attacks upon the constitution in every stage of their progress.'* The Irish House of Lords, by a decided majority, pronounced against further agitation, and resolved that it would discourage and defeat every attempt which misguided men might make towards raising groundless jealousies in the minds of the people, and diverting their attention from commercial advantages.†

<small>19 April, 1780.</small> But neither influence nor opposition could divert Grattan from his purpose. On the 19th of April, 1780, he proposed the following resolution in the House of Commons: '... That the King's Most Excellent Majesty and the Lords and Commons of Ireland are the only power competent to make laws to bind Ireland.'

---

* Letter of Lord Hillsborough to Earl of Buckinghamshire, March 28th, 1780, printed in full in *Grattan's Life*, by his Son, vol. ii., p. 31.

† The resolution was carried by forty-six to eight. It was moved by the Duke of Leinster. (See *Grattan's Life*, by his Son, vol. ii., p. 27.)

This resolution was introduced in a speech adapted with singular skill to overcome the difficulties by which its advocate was surrounded. Molyneux and Swift had supported the proposition which it expressed by reasoning, and all educated Irishmen were familar with their writings. It was enough to glance at topics of this character: action was what was now wanted. The sentiment of nationality lay languid, dispirited, and, unless aroused into energetic life, useless for practical purposes. *[margin: Grattan's speech.]*

No division took place upon the resolution. It was evaded by an amendment which led to the question being adjourned indefinitely. But the case against England had been stated, the motives for immediate decision supplied; and it is no exaggeration to say that, when Grattan ceased to speak, he had dictated and moulded the whole Irish policy of the future. A speech pregnant with such consequences rightfully claims to be noticed, at least in a summary, which shall retain an outline of the topics and arguments discussed.* *[margin: Result of motion.]*

I have entreated, Grattan began, an attendance on this day that you might, in the most public manner, deny the claim of the British Parliament to make law for Ireland, and with *[margin: Grattan's speech, 19 April, 1780.]*

---

* See Hardy's *Life of Charlemont* (2nd ed., vol. i., p. 394) for the effect of this speech at the time. 'It fulmined,' he says, ' over Ireland : imperfect as the copy was, those who produced it could not conceive how it could be resisted.'

one voice lift up your hands against it. If I had lived when the Act of William took away the woollen manufacture, or when the Sixth of George the First declared this country to be dependent and subject to law to be enacted by the Parliament of England, I should have made a covenant with my own conscience to seize the first moment of rescuing my country from the ignominy of such acts of power; or if I had a son, I should have administered to him an oath that he would consider himself as a person separate and set apart for the discharge of so important a duty. Upon the same principle am I now come here to move a declaration of right, the first moment occurring since my time in which such a declaration could be made with any chance of success, and without aggravation of oppression.

<small>Grattan's speech continued.</small> Notwithstanding (so the speech proceeded) the import of sugar and the export of woollens (referring to the concessions in relation to trade and commerce), the people are not satisfied. A greater work remains. Your ancestors lost to Ireland trade and liberty; you, by the assistance of the people, have recovered trade; you still owe the kingdom liberty: she calls upon you to restore it. The power which took away the export of woollens and the export of glass may take them away again; the repeal is partial: the ground of repeal is upon a principle of expediency. But expedient is a word of appro-

priated and tyrannical import—an ill-omened word, selected to express the reservation of authority, while the exercise is mitigated. . . . The repeal of the Woollen Act, pointed against the principle of our liberty—present relaxation, but tyranny in reserve—may be a subject for illumination to a populace, or a pretence for apostasy to a courtier, but cannot be the subject of settled satisfaction to a free-born, an intelligent, and an injured community. It is therefore they considered the free trade as a trade *de facto*, not a trade *de jure;* a license to trade under the Parliament of England, not a free trade under the charters of Ireland—to maintain which Ireland must continue in a state of armed preparation, dreading the approach of a general peace, and attributing all she holds dear to the calamitous condition of the British interest in every quarter of the globe.

The opportuneness of the time for an assertion of right was then enlarged upon. England, Grattan urged, smarts under the American war: the doctrine of imperial legislature she feels to be pernicious; the revenues and monopolies annexed to it she has found to be untenable: her enemies are a host pouring upon her from all quarters of the earth; the balance of her fate is in the hands of Ireland. You are not only her last connexion—you are the only nation in Europe that is not her enemy. Besides there does, of late, a certain damp and spurious su-

Grattan's speech continued.

pineness overcast her arms and councils, miraculous as that vigour which has lately inspired yours; for with you everything is the reverse. Never was there a Parliament in Ireland so possessed of the confidence of the people. You are the greatest political assembly in the world; you are at the head of an immense army: nor do we only possess an unconquerable force, but a certain unquenchable public fire, which has touched all ranks of men like a visitation.

<small>Grattan's speech continued.</small> Grattan then alluded to the Volunteers, whom he estimates at 40,000, 'conducted by instinct, as they were raised by inspiration,' and the zeal and promptitude of every young member of the community. Yes, there does exist, he exclaimed, an enlightened sense of right, a young appetite for freedom, a solid strength, and a rapid fire, which not only put a declaration of right within your power, but put it out of your power to decline one. . . . You have done too much not to do more; you have gone too far not to go on. . . . It is very true you may feed your manufacturers, and landed gentlemen may get their rents, and you may export woollens, and may load a vessel with baize, serges, and kerseys, and bring back directly from the plantations sugar, indigo, speckle-wood, beetle-root, and panellas; but liberty, the foundation of trade, the independency of Parliament, the securing, crowning, and consummation of everything, are yet to come. Without these the work is imper-

fect, the foundation is wanting, the capital is wanting, trade is not free, Ireland is a colony without the benefit of a charter, and you are a provincial synod without the privileges of a Parliament.

Referring to the sixth of George the First and to the Mutiny Act and other Acts of the English Parliament being enforced in Ireland without being re-enacted by an Irish Legislature, Grattan asked whether a country so circumstanced is free? Where is the foundation of trade? Where is the security of property? Where is the liberty of the people? I here in this declaratory Act see my country proclaimed a slave! I see every man in this House enrolled a slave! I see the judges of the realm, the oracles of the law, borne down by an unauthorized foreign power! I see the magistrates prostrate, and I see Parliament witness of these infringements and silent. . . . What, are you, the greatest House of Commons that ever sat in Ireland, that want but this one Act to equal that English House of Commons that passed the Petition of Right, or that other that passed the Declaration of Right—are you afraid to tell the British Parliament that you are a free people? *[Grattan's speech continued.]*

The weakness of former periods, the want of courage in their leaders, the servility of previous Parliaments, were then touched upon. Recently, he said, the people had recourse to two measures, viz. a commercial and a military association. *[Grattan's speech continued.]*

The consequence, he asserted, was instant: the enemy that hung on their shores departed; when the Parliament asked for a free trade, the British nation granted it. Still the people of Ireland are not satisfied: they ask for a Constitution. What have these walls for the last century resounded? The usurpation of the British Parliament and the interference of the Privy Council.

Grattan's speech continued. There is no objection, he said, to this resolution, except your fears. I have examined your fears: I pronounce them frivolous. The woollen trade and the Act of Navigation made England tenacious of a comprehensive legislative authority; as she has now ceded that monopoly, there is nothing in the way of your liberty except your own corruption and pusillanimity. . . . Take notice, the very Constitution which I move you to declare Great Britain herself offered to America. . . . What, has England offered this to the resistance of America, and will she refuse it to the loyalty of Ireland?

Grattan's speech continued. I shall hear of ingratitude: I name the argument to despise it. . . . I know of no species of gratitude which should prevent my country from being free, no gratitude which should oblige Ireland to be the slave of England. In cases of robbery and usurpation nothing is an object of gratitude, except the thing stolen, the charter spoliated. A nation's liberty cannot, like her treasure, be meted and parcelled out in gratitude: no man can be grateful or liberal of his conscience, nor woman of her honour, nor nation of her liberty; there are certain unimpartible, inherent, invaluable properties, not to be alienated from the person, whether body politic or body natural. . . . Anything less than liberty is inadequate to Ireland, dangerous to Great Britain. We are too near the British nation, we are too conversant with her history, we are too much fired by her example, to be anything less than her equal. Anything less, we should be her bitterest enemies—an enemy to the power that smote us with her mace, and to that Constitution from whose blessings we were excluded.

CHAPTER XI.

PARLIAMENT OF IRELAND.

[1780-1782.]

Grattan's speech considered.

THE speech, of which a summary is given in the last chapter, deserves attentive consideration, not only on account of the demands it put forward, but of the reasons and arguments by which they were supported. The sole object aimed at was to arouse a spirit of nationality. It claimed, and sought to induce Parliament to claim, that Ireland and its Legislature should rank as the equal of Great Britain and its Legislature; that, except so far as superior wealth and strength might create a difference, there should be no distinction between the powers and authority to which they were respectively entitled. With the exception of the Act which declared the supremacy of the British Parliament for legislative and judicial purposes, and the Mutiny Act, which was objected to as a signal manifestation of that assumed supremacy, Grattan made no complaint of any legislation of the British Parliament then continuing in force. He founded his case not on the misdoings of Great Britain, but on what he asserted to be the rights of Ireland: her national and legislative rights—liberty and independence. Great Britain, he admitted, had annulled former restrictions upon the manufacturing industry of Ireland, had freely opened to the people foreign and colonial trade, but, if the rights he claimed were withheld, neither these benefits, nor any others that might be added to them, could, he urged, afford adequate compensation for their loss.

The objection to the Mutiny Act was not on account of the provisions it contained; they were, of course, as much needed in Ireland as in Great Britain for the government of the army. But it was an Act of the British Parliament; whereas, it was contended, soldiers quartered in Ireland were like the rest of the people properly only amenable to Irish law, and a Mutiny Act should have been obtained from the Irish Parliament. Much discontent prevailed in reference to this matter; and Grattan's speech having given an impulse to its consideration, a Bill to deal with it was soon after introduced in the Irish House of Commons, when several members declared that neither as jurors nor as magistrates, nor in any other capacity, would they suffer a British Mutiny law to be enforced.* Ultimately

<small>Mutiny Act.</small>

---

* See letter of Lord Buckingham, the Lord Lieutenant, to Lord Hillsborough, May 8, 1780, cited by Lecky, *History*, vol. iv., p. 511.

an Irish Mutiny Act was passed by the Irish Parliament, which the Government had sufficient influence to have made not temporary, but perpetual—a provision which afterwards gave rise to as much dissatisfaction as had been before caused by the control of the army in Ireland being founded upon British authority.

Effect of Grattan's speech. The ardent sentiments aroused by Grattan's speech gave rise to discussions in the Irish House of Commons on other subjects of importance beside the Mutiny Act:—Poynings' Law; a Habeas Corpus Bill, which was ultimately enacted; the disabilities then affecting persons professing the Roman Catholic religion. But the chief effect of the speech was among the people outside Parliament. Through all classes, with the exception only of persons holding office under the Crown, or connected intimately by ties of property with Great Britain, the spirit infused by Grattan's eloquence spread (to use his own language) 'an unquenchable public fire.' Differences of race and religion ceased to create division. All combined: lesser aims and interests merged in the almost universal desire for national and legislative independence. This, as in itself the supreme good, became the one object sought.

Same combination in Swift's time. The same combination for a common object of all the various elements whereof in Ireland society was composed occurred when Swift, during his opposition to Wood's patent, came forward to proclaim principles similar to those now advocated by Grattan. Then the popular discontent caused by a supposed debasement of the coin was, by the former, turned against English supremacy: just as now the excitement, which began but did not end with the commercial restrictions, was, by the latter, guided to insist upon independence. *Page 96, supra.*

But while on each occasion the mass of the community moved in the same direction, the motives which impelled the separate portions which formed it were by no means the same. The descendants of the original inhabitants, almost all of whom had adhered to the Roman Catholic religion, inherited the feelings which animated their ancestors, when for four centuries they were excluded by an injudicious policy from the rights and privileges of British subjects; and moved by such influences they welcomed whatever appeared calculated to fortify the independence of their country against an external sovereignty which had reduced themselves to a subordinate condition. On the other hand, the descendants of the colonists, whether of English or Scotch origin, had nothing in their own history to account for the course which, under the lead of Swift and Grattan, they took. They were the ruling class, and that they were was due to the protection of Great Britain. It was to her they were indebted for their ascendency. Moreover, kindred, agreement at all times in religion, general harmony of sentiments, drew them towards alliance with her *Causes of combination.*

Page 19, supra.

people. What overpowered these influences was that the existence of a separate legislature, and of a separate executive, fixed in their minds the notion of a kingdom, not less morally than geographically distinct from England.

Agitation reaches the Volunteers. When the agitation which followed upon Grattan's speech had spread through the people, it necessarily came in contact with the various associations of Volunteers then established through the country, and quickly communicated to them the impulses by which it was itself urged on. The same had happened during the movement for commercial freedom; but since that time the organization of this force had assumed proportions of great magnitude.

Their influence. From their first institution the Volunteers had continually increased in number and importance. Recruited from every class, officered by persons of rank and education, regularly trained, and so attaining a high standard of military efficiency, they exercised an influence in the community equal, if not superior, to that possessed by Parliament.*

Meeting of Volunteer officers. About the close of the year 1781 the Volunteers began to manifest much concern in political affairs, and especially in the questions raised as to the jurisdiction of the English Parliament in Ireland. This was chiefly the case with the regiments recruited in the northern parts of the

---

* See further observations as to the Volunteers in Note Y of the Appendix.

island; and on the 28th of December in that year a meeting of the officers of one of these regiments, led to important results. Before separating, those who attended issued invitations to all the Ulster associations of Volunteers to send delegates on the 15th of February then next (A.D. 1782) to Dungannon (a small town of Ulster, conveniently situated for the purpose), in order that they might deliberate respecting the interests of the country.

Upon the day which had been thus appointed the representatives of one hundred and forty-three corps of Ulster Volunteers assembled. They passed a series of resolutions, among which it is sufficient to mention those which immediately relate to the subject of this treatise: . . . 'That a claim of any body of men, other than the King, Lords, and Commons of Ireland, to make laws to bind this kingdom, is unconstitutional, illegal, and a grievance; that the power exercised by the Privy Council of Great Britain and Ireland under, or under colour or pretence of, the law of Poynings, is unconstitutional and a grievance.' *[margin: Convention at Dungannon.]*

From the time when in 1780 Grattan brought forward in the House of Commons the resolution declaratory of the exclusive legislative jurisdiction of the Parliament of Ireland, he had been the acknowledged leader of the movement to attain that object. Pre-eminence was conceded to him without a dissentient; and it was amply justified by eloquence of unrivalled brilliancy, *[margin: Grattan.]*

an extensive knowledge of political subjects, and an ardent and disinterested patriotism.*

<small>Address moved Feb. 22, 1782.</small>

Grattan is said to have assisted in framing the resolutions of the Convention of Volunteers; but however this may have been, he immediately, when they were announced, perceived the impulse which they would communicate to the cause of national independence, and the probable effect which such an example would have upon Parliament. Accordingly, on the 22nd of February, a week after the date of the meeting at Dungannon, he moved an address from the House of Commons, to assure His Majesty that the people of Ireland were a free people, the Crown of Ireland an imperial Crown, and the kingdom of Ireland a distinct kingdom, with a Parliament of its own, the sole Legislature thereof; that by their fundamental laws and franchises the subjects of this separate kingdom could not be bound, affected, or obliged by any Legislature save only by the King, Lords, and Commons of His Majesty's realm of Ireland, nor was there any other body of men who had power or authority to make laws for them: that in this privilege was contained the very essence of their liberty.

<small>16 April, 1782.</small>

A motion to adjourn the consideration of the question was carried; and without anything further being then done in respect of it, Parliament was, on the 14th of March, prorogued until the

---

* See Note Z of Appendix.

16th of April. In the interval a new Ministry came into power in England. They proceeded at once to review the condition of Ireland; and, arriving at the conclusion that it was expedient to make concessions to the popular demands, they arranged that the Duke of Portland, who was sent over as Lord Lieutenant, should address to the Irish Parliament, when it would meet after the prorogation, a message indicating what was intended in the future. The message, expressed in the following terms, was read on the 16th of April: . . . 'His Majesty, being concerned to find that discontents and jealousies were prevailing among his loyal subjects in Ireland upon matters of great weight and importance, recommends Parliament to take the same into their most serious consideration, in order to effect such a final adjustment as may give mutual satisfaction to his kingdoms of Great Britain and Ireland.'

Hutchinson, the Minister in charge of the measures of Government in the House of Commons, expressed from himself sympathy with the objects aimed at by the popular movement. Grattan, assuming that legislative independence was about to be conceded, at once rose[*] to congratulate the

Grattan's speech.

---

[*] From what Hardy states (*Life of Charlemont*, vol. ii., p. 20), it appears that Grattan acted on this occasion with the concurrence of the Earl of Charlemont—a nobleman whose abilities, social accomplishments, and moral worth, gave him great influence in the Irish House of Lords. With respect to Hutchinson, who represented the Government on this occasion, see Note AA of Appendix.

House of Commons, expressing himself in words which mark how completely predominant in Ireland was at that time the idea of a separate nationality : . . . 'I am,' he said, 'now to address a free people ; ages have passed away, and this is the first moment in which you could be distinguished by that appellation. . . . Spirit of Swift ! spirit of Molyneux ! your genius has prevailed ! Ireland is now a nation ! In that new character I hail her ! and bowing to her august presence, I say, *esto perpetua*.'

<small>Terms insisted upon.</small> The precise nature of the measures about to be submitted to Parliament by the Government did not appear, and Grattan determined to leave no doubt as to the conditions which he demanded. He enumerated them in the following words :—(1) Repeal of the perpetual Mutiny Bill, and dependency of the Irish army upon the Irish Parliament ; (2) the abolition of the legislative power of the Council ; (3) the abrogation of the claim of England to make laws for Ireland ; (4) the exclusion of the English House of Peers, and of the English King's Bench from any judicial authority in Ireland ; (5) the restoration of the Irish Peers to their final judicature ; the independency of the Irish Parliament in its sole and exclusive legislature. 'These,' he said, 'are my terms. I will take nothing from the Crown.'

CHAPTER XII.

PARLIAMENT OF IRELAND.

[1782.]

THE demands of Grattan as they were stated in the speech which at the close of the last chapter has been referred to, were by subsequent legislation substantially granted. The first step taken towards their accomplishment was by an Act of the British Parliament to repeal the English statute (the Sixth of George the First), which had been the chief cause of complaint, and (as it was expressed in the repealing Act), 'all the matters and declarations contained in that statute.' Repeal of 6 Geo. I.

Objections were made to this measure as insufficient to meet the requirements of the case. Merely to repeal, it was said, left matters as they were before the enactment of the measure which was repealed; and could not, therefore, finally decide the controversy which had so long existed between the Parliaments of England and Ireland concerning the jurisdiction of each. Those who thus argued sought leave to introduce into the Irish House of Commons a Bill which was Resolution declaring the effect of the repealing Act.

explicitly to declare the exclusive right of the Irish Parliament to make laws for the kingdom of Ireland. The motion for this purpose was opposed, upon the ground that repeal of an Act which had asserted a claim to a right was equivalent to renunciation of the claim. The House refused leave to bring in the Bill, and afterwards recorded that it had adopted this course because the exclusive right of legislation in the Irish Parliament in all cases, internal and external, had been already asserted by Ireland, and had been fully, irrevocably, and finally acknowledged by England.

Reason for the word 'external' in the resolution. The word 'external' was designedly introduced into this resolution for the purpose of explicitly negativing the supposition, which might otherwise have been entertained, that in respect of the range of its jurisdiction the Irish Parliament admitted the propriety of a distinction drawn by some English statesmen between 'the external' and 'the internal'* affairs of Ireland, and of a claim made by them to retain for the English Parliament the exclusive right to make laws in relation to the former.

---

* The protest against this supposition again appears in an address to the Lord Lieutenant at the end of the session, where, referring to what had occurred, it is said . . . that the sole and exclusive right of legislation, external as well as internal, in the Irish Parliament had been firmly asserted on the part of Ireland, and unequivocally acknowledged on the part of Great Britain.

The truth is, that if the Irish Parliament had been then excluded from legislating for external affairs, the results of the victory it had won must have been small. Matters would have remained very much as they had been in practice, whatever they might have been in theory, from the accession of George II., as, during the intervening time, the laws regulating the internal affairs of Ireland had almost altogether been made by its own Parliament.

If jurisdiction over external affairs not admitted, little had been gained.

When the repeal of the Sixth of George the First was conceded the Marquis of Rockingham was Prime Minister. Upon his death, in July, 1782, he was succeeded by Lord Shelburne, who had been one of his Cabinet. The Chancellor of the Exchequer, under Lord Shelburne, was William Pitt. This administration being defeated upon a motion in the House of Commons on the 21st of February, 1783, Lord Shelburne resigned, but his successor was not appointed, nor did he come into office until the month of April.

Prime Ministers in 1782 and 1783.

Before Lord Shelburne's resignation, a Bill was (on the 21st January) introduced in the British Parliament, which afterwards became law, whereby it was declared that the right claimed by the people of Ireland to be bound only by laws enacted by His Majesty and the Parliament of that kingdom in all cases whatever, and to have all actions and suits at law or in equity, which might be instituted in that

Renunciation Act, 23 Geo. III. c. 28.

kingdom in His Majesty's Courts therein, decided finally and without appeal from thence, was established and ascertained for ever.

<small>Poynings' law repealed and new provisions substituted.</small>

The statutes of Repeal and Renunciation, as the two English statutes relating to the authority of the British Parliament were called, would have effected no more than to prevent its interference: if they were to stand alone, Poynings' law would have still made the legislation of the Irish Parliament subject to the control of the Privy Council of Ireland, and the Privy Council of England. It was therefore necessary, in order to complete the independence intended to be conferred upon the Irish Parliament, that Poynings' law should be repealed or modified. This law having been enacted by the Irish Parliament, recourse was had to the same authority for its repeal, and in lieu of the former legislation upon the subject, an Act was passed by the Irish Parliament (21 & 22 George III. c. 47), which provided that the Lord Lieutenant, or other Chief Governor of Ireland, was to certify to the King all such Bills, and none other, as both Houses of Parliament in Ireland should certify to be enacted under the Great Seal of Ireland, without alteration: that such of the same as should be returned under the Great Seal of Great Britain, without alteration, and none other, should pass in the Parliament of Ireland: that no Bill should be certified as a cause or consideration of holding a Parliament in Ireland, and that Parliament might be holden without any Bill being certified, but not without license for that purpose being first had and obtained from the King, under the Great Seal of Great Britain.

The condition contained in this Act, which required the Bills of the Irish Parliament to be submitted to the King in England, and to be thence returned under the Great Seal of Great Britain, was in addition to, not substitution for, the royal assent being given in Ireland. It was supposed that the condition would prove a protection against legislation injurious to British interests, because the minister who was to be responsible for affixing the British Seal would be a British Minister, and amenable to censure in the British Parliament. *Object of a condition imposed by the Act.*

Thus, the Constitution of the Parliament of Ireland, which became known as the Constitution of 1782, was the result of three statutes (two British, and one Irish). By them this Parliament was rendered free and independent. It could no longer be controlled or interfered with by the Parliament of Great Britain; its Bills were no longer to be sent to either the English or the Irish Privy Council for approval or rejection. There was no limit imposed upon the subject-matter of debate or legislation. Whatever was within the province of a national Parliament might come before it. Its relations to Great Britain and the British Parliament were substantially the same, as before 1707 the relations had *Constitution of 1782.*

been of the Parliament of Scotland to England and the English Parliament, with one exception—that, in order to a Bill becoming law, the royal assent had been given in Scotland by a Commissioner attending to represent the Crown of Scotland, while in Ireland the Bill should not only receive the royal assent in Ireland, but be transmitted to England, and be thence returned under the Great Seal of Great Britain.

Omission to provide for disagreement between the British and Irish Parliaments.

In the Constitution of 1782 there was no provision for the case of disagreement in policy between the Parliaments of Great Britain and Ireland. They were equal and co-ordinate, without any paramount authority being provided to overrule or reconcile them. No matter how injurious to British interests the intended legislation of the Irish Parliament might be, the only restraint upon it which the Constitution provided for the British Government was the power of refusing to return, under the Great Seal of Great Britain, the Bill sent over, and to refuse the royal assent in Ireland. But neither of these checks applied to resolutions or proceedings of Parliament not taking the form of Bills. The Irish Parliament could adopt, and give expression to, whatever views it chose upon questions of trade and commerce, foreign policy, treaties, and other relations with foreign powers. And even in the case of Bills where these checks did apply, little was to be expected from them, since statesmen would be reluctant to use a power which must place the Crown by itself in an attitude of hostility to one of the nations subject to its rule.*

That controversies were likely to arise between the British and Irish Parliaments in reference to the subjects which have been mentioned, and the injurious consequences likely to follow from them, were foreseen by the Duke of Portland in 1782, and he proposed to guard against the danger by retaining for Great Britain a supreme control in respect of the matters which were of most importance. His views were embodied in a letter to Lord Shelburne, in which he expressed a hope that the Irish Parliament might be induced to pass an Act by which 'the superintending power and supremacy of Great Britain in all matters of State and general commerce would be virtually and effectually acknowledged,' and Ireland be bound to contribute ' a share of the expense of carrying on a defensive or offensive war, either in support of the dominions of the Crown of Great Britain, or those of its allies, in proportion to the actual state of her abilities'; and also be bound to adopt 'every such regulation as might be judged necessary by Great Britain for the better ordering and securing her trade and commerce with foreign nations or her own colonies and dependencies, consideration being duly had to the circumstances of Ireland.'†

<small>Suggestions of Duke of Portland.</small>

---

* See on this subject Note BB of Appendix.

† Letter from Portland to Shelburne, 6th June, 1782. This letter is printed in full in the *Life of Grattan*, by his

Portland's suggestions found to be impracticable.

These suggestions then received the approbation of Lord Shelburne, but no steps were ever taken to give them effect. The Duke of Portland found that he had formed too sanguine expectations; and in about a fortnight after he had first communicated his ideas to Lord Shelburne he wrote that 'any attempts to conciliate the minds of this nation to any such measure as I intimated the hope of, would at this moment be delusive and impossible.' *

They were opposed to the views of the patriotic party. Page 122, supra.

Nothing, indeed, could have been less in accordance with the aims of the patriotic party than Portland's propositions. Grattan had for Ireland insisted upon equality: if not the equal, she must, he said, be the enemy of Great Britain. These propositions would have reduced Ireland to a subordinate position. Besides, they retained for Great Britain absolute dominion over commerce, and on no point had the statutes of the

---

Son, vol. ii., p. 291. At the time of the debates in connexion with the Union, Parliament first became aware of the correspondence, of which it is part. This was then produced and printed in the Parliamentary papers on the motion of Pitt. Portland seems from the beginning to have desired that what he calls 'some middle term' should be thought of, and to have entered upon unsuccessful negotiations for that purpose. (See his letter to Fox, 28th April, 1782, printed in *Grattan's Life*, vol. ii., p. 273.)

* See Letters, Shelburne to Portland, June 9th, 1782; Portland to Shelburne, June 22nd, 1782. The whole correspondence, extracted from the Parliamentary Papers, will be found in *Grattan's Life*, by his Son, vol. ii., p. 286-294.

English Parliament been more objected to than upon this. They would, in effect, have accomplished the very restriction of the Irish Parliament to internal affairs, which its House of Commons, as we have seen, by an express resolution repudiated.

These circumstances explain why neither in 1782 nor 1783 was any qualification of the Acts of Repeal and Renunciation proposed. Moreover, any proceeding of the kind was discouraged by the consideration that, even if such a measure were carried, there was no certainty of its permanence. The existing Irish Parliament might enact it; the succeeding might demand its repeal. An intermediate policy necessarily does not of itself and by its own nature claim finality: the point ultimately to be reached seems still beyond it; and this is especially true when the policy relates to the constitution of representative institutions; for such institutions have within them a principle of growth. In Ireland Councils had expanded to Parliaments; Parliaments without representatives of the Commons to Parliaments with representatives of the Commons; Parliaments without the native Irish to Parliaments with representatives from the native Irish; Parliaments restrained by Poynings' law, and overawed by fear of another Legislature claiming pre-eminence, to Parliaments free, independent, subject to no external authority. Why, then, might not Parliaments excluded from dealing

And they were open to other objections.

with commercial questions, foreign policy, the great affairs of State, arise out of their depressed condition, and in time regain the elevated position which had, in a moment of weakness, been surrendered?

<small>Ministers silent as to Portland's suggestions.</small>
When the British Ministers decided that they would not seek to impose restrictions upon the capacity of action conceded to the Irish Parliament, no hint was given that they had ever contemplated or desired them. The British Parliament was thus enabled to present itself to Ireland as the willing and generous donor of a constitution whose freedom and independence equalled its own.

CHAPTER XIII.

THE PARLIAMENT OF IRELAND.

[1782–1786.]

THE changes made in 1782 in the Irish Constitution weakened in important points the authority of the English Government over Ireland. The control of Irish legislation exercised by the English and Irish Privy Councils existed no longer. There was no check upon the proceedings of the local Parliament except such as was afforded by the power of refusing to return under the Great Seal of Great Britain a Bill when passed. Under the former system a measure could not only be vetoed, but if approved, be moulded into its final form and shape by the Councils; under the new, a statute owed its being and provisions to Parliament, and was indebted to the Government only for an assent, difficult to withhold. With respect, also, to the measures which Ministers might desire to pass, Parliament had been rendered more independent, by being freed from any apprehension that, in case of their being rejected in Ireland, resort could be had to the British Parliament.

Constitution of 1782 weakens the authority of the English Government.

Yet leaves important sources of influence untouched.

As, however, these changes only interfered with legislative jurisdiction, they still left for the English Government important sources of power and influence undiminished. It retained within its dominion the direction of the executive department in Ireland, and administered this through the Lord Lieutenant and Chief Secretary, nominated by and removable at its pleasure. Neither the Ministers in England for the time being, nor these their representatives in Ireland, depended on the Irish Parliament for the tenure of their offices: an adverse vote of the British House of Commons would lead to the resignation of both the English and Irish Ministers; but no such consequence was expected to follow as to either if a ministerial measure was to fail in the Irish House of Commons. Moreover, the British Government retained, either directly or indirectly, all the important patronage; for after 1782, just as before that date, peerages and the highest class of offices (such as the Bishoprics and Deaneries in the Church, and the judicial offices in the legal department) were in the appointment of the Crown, acting under the advice of its English ministers; and whatever offices connected with the State were not so circumstanced, were disposed of by the Lord Lieutenant, the nominee and colleague of these Ministers.

Patronage used to influence Parliament.

Before 1782 the patronage exercised in Ireland by the English and Irish Ministers of the Crown was largely used to influence the votes of the members of both Houses of Parliament. With the same object pensions also were often granted to many of these members, or to their relatives and friends upon their application. As no alteration was, in 1782, made in the composition of Parliament, as the number of seats commanded by owners of close boroughs was undiminished, the same practices were certain to continue, and did continue, under the new Constitution. Indeed, the increased freedom of Parliament, the wider range of subjects within its jurisdiction, made it still more requisite that the allegiance of its members should be secured by each Administration that came into office in England.

But, quite independent of such inducements, the Parliament of Ireland contained at this time elements which powerfully promoted harmony with England. In both kingdoms the right to sit in Parliament was confined to Protestants, and those who elected representatives were also Protestant. Nor was religion the only subject on which the electors and elected were imbued with the same tone of thought and sentiment in both countries. There were few questions respecting which there was any difference in their opinions. Besides, Irish Peers and Commoners were almost universally owners of land, very many deriving under titles resting upon grants of forfeited estates, for which the most effectual defence was to be found in the protection of England.

Other motives to concord.

L

Hence, at first agreement.

These various causes enabled the British Government for some time after 1782 to retain its former influence in the Irish Parliament, and to obtain support for its policy from majorities in the two Houses. While they continued, no conflict of opinion or action between the Parliament of England and the Parliament of Ireland, such as was apprehended when freedom was conceded to the latter, arose. Nor, indeed, did the subjects which were submitted to each during this time give an opportunity for disagreement.

A.D. 1785.

In 1785 the relations between the two Parliaments were altered. The same political questions then came for discussion before both, were regarded by them with entirely different sentiments, and ultimately received from them the most opposite decisions. As there is no doubt that what then occurred materially contributed to recommend the policy which afterwards terminated the separate existence of the Irish Parliament, it is requisite to narrate the events of this period at more length than would otherwise be consistent with the plan of this treatise.

Previous proceedings in Ireland.

In 1780 statutes to annul the restrictions which British legislation had imposed upon trade from Ireland to the colonies and on the export of some Irish manufactures were enacted; but neither then nor in 1782 had there been any compact to prevent the British Parliament reimposing the former laws as to the colonies:

and what was done as to the manufactures could not be considered more than a part of the arrangements requisite in order to place the commercial intercourse between Great Britain and Ireland on a satisfactory basis. These circumstances attracted especial attention in Ireland during the winter of 1784-5, when there was much distress, which, it was supposed, might be alleviated if the commercial relations of Ireland with Great Britain were improved. The Irish House of Commons, induced by the condition of the people, appointed a Committee to inquire into the state of Irish trade and manufactures, by whom, after examining witnesses, a Report was made. The Report was followed by an Address from the House of Commons, voted May 13, 1784, in which, after stating that the interval between the present and next Session would afford an opportunity to propose a well-digested plan for a liberal arrangement of commercial intercourse between Great Britain and Ireland, it was declared that such a plan would be the most effectual means of strengthening the empire at large, and cherishing the common interest and brotherly affection of both kingdoms.*

When this Address was voted Pitt was Prime Minister, having been appointed in the previous

Pitt.

---

* *Grattan's Life*, by his Son, vol. iii., pp. 233-236. Lecky's *History of England*, vol. vi., p. 354.

month of December upon the dismissal of the Coalition Government of Lord North and Fox. In 1782, when the Sixth of George the First was repealed, Pitt neither was in office nor took part in the debate upon the subject; but in 1783, when the Renunciation Act was passed, being one of the Ministers, he had supported it. At a much later period (in 1799) he took occasion to refer to the legislation of 1782, and to the sentiments he entertained at that time, and he described himself as having disapproved of the 'system which, before 1782, held (as he expressed it) the two countries together,' because 'unworthy the liberality of Great Britain, and injurious to the interests of Ireland.' What was enacted in 1782 and 1783, he contended, ought to be regarded as mere demolition, and was not, even by those who were its authors, intended to be a final adjustment of the relations between the two kingdoms.*

<small>Pitt favours commercial concessions.</small>

Assuming that Pitt, in 1785, held the opinions which he thus afterwards attributed to himself, they would necessarily predispose him to consider, not unfavourably, the suggestions contained in the Address of the Irish House of Commons. It had been found impossible to introduce into the Constitution of 1782 an acknowledgment of the supremacy of Great

---

* See Pitt's speech of 31st January, 1799.—*Speeches*, vol. iii., p. 363.

Britain in reference to commercial subjects; but if now a treaty between Ireland and Great Britain, regulating their relations in respect to these subjects, which could not be rescinded except by mutual consent, were enacted by the legislatures of both countries, many of the advantages expected from the acknowledgment which had been refused would be attained. At all events, such a treaty must diminish the topics and occasions of controversy, otherwise almost certain to arise between two kingdoms whose interests were not always the same in reference to the matters which the treaty dealt with.

But it would be an error to suppose that Pitt regarded the Address of the Irish House of Commons only from this (an English) point of view. He desired to serve Ireland, and his ideas in reference to commercial policy being more enlightened than those of other statesmen of his time, he saw that he could do this without injury to the interests of Great Britain. Free trade between the two countries might enrich both, and consequently tend to the aggrandisement of the State. Liberty of foreign trade he held to be an act of justice; liberty of colonial trade, an act of bounty, but also of wisdom. *Other motives for free trade.*

Commercial relations, however, were not the only relations which it was expedient to adjust between Great Britain and Ireland. The Duke of Portland, in 1782, had sought to have Ireland bound to contribute to the maintenance of the *Contribution to naval expenses to be claimed.*

naval establishment. Pitt was likewise anxious to effect this object; and now he perceived that, if he dealt with trade and commerce, an opportunity would open to have the question of contribution for this purpose at the same time settled. Ireland, in return for the benefits which his policy of free trade would confer upon her, might reasonably be expected to aid in meeting the expenses requisite for the protection of the whole empire.*

<small>Commercial propositions, 1785.</small>

Pitt therefore determined to answer the Address of the Irish House of Commons by offering a scheme for the final settlement of the commercial relations between Great Britain and Ireland; and, accordingly, the result was that propositions (eleven in number) known at the time as the Commercial Propositions, were prepared by himself and his colleagues, in order that they might be submitted to the British and Irish Parliaments. Ten of them related to matters of trade and commerce, while the eleventh provided that any surplus of the hereditary revenue (which in Ireland was at the time largely derived from the Customs and Excise, sources of income which free trade was expected to increase) should be appropriated to support the naval force of the empire. These Propositions originated in sug-

---

* Pitt's Speeches in 1785, on 22nd February, 12th May, 22nd July, should be compared with his speech 31st January, 1799.—*Speeches*, vol. i., pp. 198, 246, 269, and vol. iii., p. 372.

gestions from Ireland, and were drawn up after consultation with advisers summoned from Ireland.*

There is preserved a full explanation by Pitt of the views and objects with which the Propositions were framed, in a letter to the Duke of Rutland, then Lord Lieutenant in Ireland, dated January 6, 1785.† He describes them as representing 'the unanimous opinion of the Cabinet on the subject of the settlement to be proposed as final and conclusive between Great Britain and Ireland. . . .' 'The general tenor,' he says, ' of our propositions not only gives a full equality to Ireland, but extends the principle to many points where it would be easy to have urged just exceptions, and in many other points possibly turns the scale in her favour, at a risk, perhaps a remote one, of considerable local disadvantages to many great interests of this country. I do not say that in practice I apprehend the effect on our trade and manufactures will be such as it will probably be industriously represented; but I am

Letter of Pitt to Rutland, 6 Jan., 1785.

---

* The Propositions are said to have originated with Joshua Pim, a member of a mercantile family then and now eminent in Dublin. What he suggested was added to by Foster, afterwards Speaker of the House of Commons, who went to England and took the draft to Pitt. (See *Grattan's Life*, by his Son, vol. iii., p. 239.)

† Pitt's letters to the Duke of Rutland were privately printed. The letter of the 6th January, 1785, from its importance, has been printed in full in the *Quarterly Review*, vol. lxx., p. 300. It occupies eight pages of the *Review*.

persuaded (whatever may be the event) that, by the additions now proposed to former concessions, we open to Ireland the chance of a competition with ourselves on terms of more than equality, and we give her advantages which make it impossible she should ever have anything to fear from the jealousy or restrictive policy of this country in future. Such an arrangement is defensible only on the idea of relinquishing local prejudices and partial advantages, in order to consult uniformly and without distinction for the general benefit of the empire. This cannot be done but by making England and Ireland one country in effect, though for local concerns under distinct legislatures—one in the communication of advantages, and of course in the participation of burdens. If their unity is broken, or rendered absolutely precarious in either of these points, the system is defective, and there is an end of the whole.'*

<small>Propositions modified.</small> To meet objections made in Ireland, an alteration was introduced in the clause of the Eleven Propositions that related to the surplus hereditary revenue by defining the surplus to be what accrued above a fixed sum—£656,000 in each year of peace, wherein the annual revenues should equal

---

* Subsequently in the letter, referring to the passage above cited, Pitt says: . . . 'the fundamental principle, and the only one on which the whole plan can be justified, is that I mentioned in the beginning of my letter—that for the future the two countries will be to the most essential purposes united.'

the annual expense, and in each year of war without regard to such equality. And with this alteration these propositions were carried in the Irish Parliament. When, however, they were then brought forward in the British House of Commons they encountered such resistance, not only from the Opposition, but from a violent agitation against them among the English merchants and manufacturers, as obliged them to be withdrawn and remodelled. Other propositions, twenty in number, were substituted in their place. They extended to additional subjects, and varied also in other particulars from the former. The most important of the alterations was a new clause to the effect. . . . That it was highly important to the general interest of the British Empire that the laws for regulating trade and navigation should be the same in Great Britain and Ireland, and that therefore it was essential for carrying into effect the present settlement that all laws which had been made, or should be made in Great Britain for securing exclusive privileges to the ships and mariners of Great Britain, Ireland, and the British colonies and plantations, and for regulating and retaining the trade of the British colonies and plantations, such laws, imposing the same restraints and conferring the same benefits on the subjects of both kingdoms, should be in force in Ireland by laws to be passed by the Parliament of that kingdom for the same time and in the same manner as in Great Britain.

The modified propositions fail to secure support in Ireland.

The Propositions, as they were finally modified, were adopted by the British Parliament, but in the Irish House of Commons they failed to secure adequate support, and were, therefore, after this was seen to be the case, not proceeded with. In the end they were altogether abandoned.

Objections made to them.

The grounds of objection to these propositions assigned by their opponents were, that by obliging the Irish Parliament to accept and ratify the commercial legislation of England its independence was infringed upon; that this amounted to a surrender by Parliament of the right of external legislation which had been conceded to it in 1782, and so, as to that point, it would be brought back to the position from which it had been then emancipated. If the principle, it was said, were adopted of establishing one will in the Parliament of Great Britain and Ireland as to commercial affairs it would soon be extended to other matters (as, for example, the army, the Mutiny Act, the nature of the taxes to be imposed). Thus the result would be a virtual Union, but without the compensation which a real Union must bring, providing, as it would, means through representation of influencing the Legislature, whose greater strength gave it predominance.

CHAPTER XIV.

REVIVAL AND PROGRESS OF THE POLICY OF UNION.

[1785-1798.]

FROM 1707, when an Union of Ireland with Great Britain was distinctly suggested to Queen Anne and her ministers by the Irish House of Commons, and was by the former discouraged, there had been no attempt in either the British or Irish Parliaments to revive the project. During the debates upon the Commercial Propositions of 1785 in the British Parliament Union began again to find favour, and was mentioned with approval by some speakers. It was also then suggested by an Association of English and Scotch Manufacturers formed to resist Pitt's scheme.* As a substitute for what he proposed, and as a means of arriving at a satisfactory settlement of commercial relations between Great Britain and Ireland, they advised 'a real Union under one Legislature;' which, they said, 'would take away every difficulty.'

Policy of Union revived.

---

* The President of this Association was Wedgewood, the celebrated manufacturer of earthenware : Mr. Peel, father of Sir Robert Peel, the Prime Minister, was a member of it. (See *Grattan's Life*, by his Son, vol. iii., p. 249.)

Effect of failure of the Commercial Propositions.

But if reasons for Union were supplied by the obstacles hindering the enactment of the Commercial Propositions they were much increased and strengthened by the failure to carry them in the Irish Parliament. This incident afforded a striking instance of that disagreement of sentiment and action between the British and Irish Legislatures, which Ministers had in 1782 foreseen was likely to occur, but foreseen without making provision to meet the event. It suggested the possibility of other conflicts of a like character, and it manifested that it was useless to attempt to pass through the Irish House of Commons measures that proposed to withdraw from its legislative jurisdiction departments of public affairs in which the interests of Ireland were concerned, or that might tend to subordinate its Parliament to the Parliament of Great Britain; for if any such could have been expected to conciliate acceptance they would be those which had been rejected, accompanied, as they were, with substantial commercial benefits in return.*

Financial effects of Union in Scotland.

Suggestions of Union as the best means of solving the difficulties attending an adjustment of the commercial relations between Great Britain and Ireland derived much support from

---

* During the agitation in Ireland which gave rise to the Commercial Propositions of 1785, the Duke of Rutland had written to Pitt (June 16, 1784):—'Were I to indulge a distant speculation, I should say that without a Union Ireland will not be connected with Great Britain in twenty years longer.' (Cited by Lecky, *History*, vol. vi., p. 404.)

the consequences which had followed from the Scottish Union. Previous to that event the relations between Great Britain and Scotland were much more disadvantageous to the latter country than those at this time existing between Great Britain and Ireland were to Ireland. But Union had removed all restrictions on Scotch trade and commerce, and opened unlimited freedom of intercourse with England and her colonies. From taking complete advantage of these benefits, and from the full industrial progress which they were calculated to stimulate, the people were at first diverted by the discontent with which they regarded the loss of their Parliament and by the hope of regaining it. But these hindrances to advancement had long before 1785 passed away, and at that time increased wealth and improved civilization were everywhere in Scotland acknowledged to be the consequences of having been admitted to share in the superior greatness and prosperity of England.*

---

* Queen Anne, when recommending Union to the Scottish Parliament, said . . . that it would secure the religion, liberty, and property of the Scottish people, remove animosities among them, and jealousies and differences with England; that it would increase their strength, riches, and trade; that as a consequence the whole island, freed from apprehension of different interests, would be able to resist its enemies, and maintain the liberties of Europe. Dundas, citing her words in the debate on the Irish Union, added, that not one syllable of her predictions had failed. (Speech, Feb. 7, 1799.)

Social effects.

Nor were the improved commercial relations of Scotland with Great Britain the only consequences of its Union which recommended the precedent to statesmen as one to be followed for Ireland. Union had in the former country enabled the abolition of the heritable jurisdictions—a cause of invidious distinctions between classes, previously attended by an unjust depression of some and an unjust exaltation of others; and in Ireland there were equally invidious distinctions of a different character, originating in differences of race and religion which an Union, if enacted for that country, might be expected equally to remove.

Literary advocacy of Union.

There has been occasion in a former chapter to mention that before the Scottish Union Molyneux had approved, and Sir William Petty had advocated the Union of the Parliaments of Ireland and England; it deserves also to be noted that after that event the weight of literary and scientific thought in Great Britain decidedly inclined in that direction. It may be sufficient to refer to three eminent writers upon economical science—Adam Smith, Sir Matthew Decker, and Sir Josiah Child—who, the first in his *Inquiry into the Causes of the Wealth of Nations*, the second in his essay *On the Causes of the Decline of Foreign Trade*, and the third in his *New Discourse of Trade*, gave their support to the measure. Nor did it want foreign authority. Montesquieu, whose writings had, during the eighteenth century, great influence upon the opinions of European society, discussing in conversation the state of Ireland, pointed out the advantages of Union to that country. 'Were I,' said he, 'an Irishman, I should certainly wish for an Union between Ireland and England; and as a general lover of liberty, I sincerely desire it—and for this plain reason, that an inferior country, connected with one much her superior in force, can never be certain of constitutional freedom unless she has, by her representatives, a proportional share in the legislature of the superior kingdom.'*

But whatever may have been the tendency about the date of the Commercial Propositions towards the Union of Ireland with Great Britain, it was confined to the latter country. None of the arguments or considerations which in England recommended it had any effect in the former. Speaking in 1785, the Duke of Rutland, who, as Lord Lieutenant, had the best means of

Union unpopular in Ireland.

---

* These words were addressed to Lord Charlemont by Montesquieu. (See Hardy's *Life of Charlemont*, vol. i., p. 70.)

In the debates at the time of the Union Decker and Child were cited by Addington, Speaker of the English House of Commons. Pitt merely in general terms referred to literary opinions. After saying that it could not be disputed that his measure would augment the general force of the Empire, and that there was no statesman in any court in Europe so ill-informed as not to know it would be increased by consolidating the strength of the two kingdoms, he added that 'every writer of any information on the subject had used the same language.'

forming a judgment upon the point, declared that the man who should attempt to carry an Union with England into execution in Ireland would be tarred and feathered;* and a reference to the debates in the Irish House of Commons upon the second set of commercial propositions will show that these strong expressions were not used without foundation. Union ought to be, but never will, said its most influential English advocates.†

Question of regency. The Commercial Propositions, and the ideas to which they gave birth, had ceased to interest statesmen, whether English or Irish, when another disagreement between the Parliaments of the two kingdoms again drew attention to the consequences which followed from their power of separate and independent action. This was in connexion with the question of the Regency. In 1789 the King was affected with mental infirmity. During the continuance of his illness, who was to exercise the regal authority? The

---

* This statement was made by him to Watson, Bishop of Llandaff. (See the speech of this Prelate in the English House of Lords, 19th March, 1799, as reported in the *Annual Register* for that year, p. 232.)

† As to the sentiments of the Irish Parliament in 1785, concerning an Union, compare Froude, *English in Ireland* (first edition, vol. ii., p. 439); and as to the fears of failure, with which the English suggestions of Union made about 1785 were accompanied, see Lecky, *History*, vol. vi., p. 404. He cites both Wilberforce and Lord Lansdowne as friendly to a legislative Union, but as, at the same time, pronouncing it impracticable.

British Parliament held that it was within its province to choose the person, and to define the power which he was to possess. Accordingly the British House of Commons selected the Prince of Wales, and prescribed the rights and duties of his office. For these purposes it passed a Regency Bill. On the other hand, the Irish Parliament treated the Prince of Wales as rightfully entitled to act with the same authority as his father might have done; and, imposing no restrictions upon his rights, invited him to assume the government of Ireland during the continuance of the King's illness, and, under the style and title of Prince Regent, to exercise the powers of the Crown. While in England the Regency Bill was being discussed in the House of Lords, the King recovered his mental health. Thus the conflict between the British and Irish legislatures was put an end to. Had it not, in this or some other mode, been interrupted, the Prince would in Ireland have possessed all the prerogatives of a king; in Great Britain only such of them as Parliament might have endowed him with.

The question of the Regency was of a constitutional character: it arose because there was no express provision by any written law to determine what was to be done in the event that had happened. Upon that point there was a difference of opinion in England, Fox and those who followed his lead dissenting from Pitt and concurring with the Irish legislature. England and Ireland had *Why the course pursued as to Regency important.*

no separate interests connected with the solution of the question. What gave importance to the course pursued by the Irish Parliament was less the decision to which it came than the circumstance of the decision being in opposition to that of the English Parliament. As the same person was to be Regent in both countries, disagreement would in this instance probably lead to no serious consequences; but with what mischief might it not be attended, if repeated in relation to such subjects as alliance with a foreign power, maintenance of the army and navy, war or peace?

Dispute with Portugal, 1782.

With respect, indeed, to the first of these matters an incident had occurred in 1782, which illustrated in what jeopardy the engagements of the Crown with a foreign kingdom might be placed from the separate action of the Irish Parliament. At that time, the old restrictions upon the exportation of wool being abolished, the Irish Parliament claimed that Irish wool should have access into the harbours of Portugal in the same manner as English wool then had; but this being refused by the Portuguese Government, the Irish Parliament addressed the Crown to insist that Irish wool should be admitted by Portugal—a proceeding which, if adopted, must have led to a breach in the friendly relations between Great Britain and that country.*

p. 113, *supra*.

---

* On the disagreement with Portugal, see Lecky, *History*, vol. iv., p. 520. Sir Robert Peel, referring to the Address of

The evil effects of any conflict between the Parliaments of Great Britain and Ireland, and the likelihood of conflict, so long as they were independent of each other, afforded arguments in favour of the policy of Union, which connected themselves with the interests of the Empire. But not long after the decision of the Regency question other motives that had reference almost exclusively to Ireland began also to recommend the measure to statesmen. These arose out of a desire to improve the position of the Irish Roman Catholics. In the reigns of William III. and Anne, statutes—known, from their excessive severity, as emphatically 'The Penal Code'—had been passed, designed to reduce this portion of the people to a condition of extreme weakness and depression. To the enactments of that period had been added some others, under George I. and George II., of like tendency. But before the time at which we have now arrived it had begun to be perceived that the policy which dictated such laws was as unwise as unjust, equally injurious to the financial prosperity and to the moral well-being of the community. Accordingly, many of their provisions had been repealed, and Catholic question.

---

the Irish Parliament, says: . . . 'One of two events might have occurred—either the foreign relations of Great Britain with a friendly power might have been disturbed, contrary to the wish of the British Parliament and of the British minister, or Ireland might have been involved in a war, in which Great Britain refused to be a party.' (*Speeches*, vol. ii., p. 425.)

a movement for the removal of all that yet remained in force was proceeding under the guidance of very able and distinguished leaders. So far as this movement was directed to procure relief from oppressive provisions connected with the ownership of property, it met general support, but to the abolition of the restrictions on political power, which excluded the Irish Catholics from sitting in either House of Parliament and from voting at elections for members of the House of Commons, there was much resistance; those who opposed concession contending that it would lead to a Catholic ascendency, hostile to the existing constitution in Church and State. Objections on this ground, powerful with a local legislature, could not continue to be of force in an Imperial Parliament, where the Irish representatives would be outnumbered by those from England and Scotland.

Pitt begins to favour Union.

It was by considerations of this character that Pitt seems to have been first induced to favour the Union of Ireland with Great Britain. In 1791 and 1792, the question of emancipating the Catholics from their parliamentary disabilities came into especial prominence in Ireland, and was discussed there with great difference of opinion. Much angry feeling was manifested by the contending parties. English statesmen, who had for some time turned their attention away from Irish affairs, were forced to reflect upon the peculiar circumstances of the country, and to examine what policy might best tend to reconcile the conflicting interests and claims which divided the people. On the 18th of November, 1792, after previous correspondence with the Irish Government, Pitt, writing to Lord Westmoreland, then the Lord Lieutenant of Ireland, expressed his own views upon the subject in the following terms: ... 'The idea,' he said, 'of the present fermentation gradually bringing both parties to think of an Union with this country has been long in my mind. I hardly dare flatter myself with the hope of its taking place; but I believe it, though itself not easy to be accomplished, to be the only solution for other and greater difficulties. The admission of Catholics to the suffrage could not then be dangerous. The Protestant interest in point of power, property, and Church Establishment, would be secure, because the decided majority of the supreme legislature would necessarily be Protestant, and the great ground of argument on the part of the Catholics would be done away with, as, compared with the rest of the Empire, they would become a minority.' *

[margin: Pitt's Letter, 18th Nov., 1792.]

For several years, however, after this letter, Pitt seems not to have taken any further step towards carrying out the ideas he approved; and so far as appears they made little way among his

[margin: Policy of Union delayed.]

---

* Letter of Pitt to Lord Westmoreland, then Lord Lieutenant of Ireland, November 18th, 1792: one of the many additions to the materials for Irish History brought to light by Lecky. (See his *History*, vol. vi., p. 573.)

English colleagues in the Government, although Lord Clare—the Irish Chancellor—constantly pressed upon them the expediency of Union:—'I make,' said this strenuous advocate for the measure, speaking in the Irish House of Lords on the 10th of February, 1800, 'no scruple to avow, that in every communication which I have had with the King's ministers on the affairs of Ireland for the last seven years, I have uniformly pressed upon them the necessity of Union, as the last resource to preserve this country to the British Crown. I pressed it without effect, until British Ministers and the British nation were roused to a sense of the common danger by the late sanguinary and unprovoked rebellion.'

Probable reasons for delay. In abstaining from acting upon his own views Pitt was probably influenced by the obstacles which, if he brought them forward, he would have had to encounter. They were then in Ireland just as unpopular as they had been in 1785; while for the English Parliament there were reasons to induce at least a reluctance on its part to adopt them. The British and Irish legislatures could not be made one without admitting into the United Parliament Irish Peers and Commoners. It was uncertain what their number in that event would be, but it could not be trifling; and it was equally uncertain what opinions they would support. Hence no political party desired to introduce an unknown force which, even if weak in itself, yet might be adequate to give preponderance to whatever side it happened to choose.*

Lord Clare, as we have seen, attributed to the Rebellion of 1798 that the doubts and apathy of British Ministers towards the policy of Union were overcome. The events immediately preceding the actual outbreak of the Rebellion ought to be included in this statement, for that was only the final development of designs previously prepared and matured; and in pursuance of them much had occurred which, if we would ascertain from what causes came the immediate impulse to the policy of this period, must be taken into account just as much as the civil war to which they led. Of equal importance, certainly, were the detection of conspiracies in Ireland, formidable from the energy and abilities of those concerned in them, for the purpose of establishing a separate and independent State, and an attempt which, induced by the solicitation of some of the leading conspirators, the French Republic made, in December, 1797, to land an invading army upon the coast of Munster.

Events leading to Union.

---

* In 1792, Burke regarded the Union with Ireland as 'next to impossible.' 'To it,' he says, 'neither nation (*i. e.* neither England nor Ireland), nor any sect or party in either, has shown the least inclination.' (Paper *On the State of Ireland*, written in 1792. *Correspondence*, vol. iv., p. 65.) In the same Paper he seems to doubt that Pitt could desire to see from 50 to 100 members from Ireland in the British House of Commons.

Existing connexion between Great Britain and Ireland.

It was this combination of circumstances—foreign war in concert with domestic treason, and both seeking to sever Ireland from Great Britain—that especially drew the attention of English Statesmen to the nature of the connexion between the two kingdoms. Were the ties which bound the countries together adequate to resist the assaults of such adversaries? If under ordinary circumstances they were, would they stand the additional strain that, if there should arise disagreement between the Parliaments, would be imposed? For at least two years before 1798 these questions pressed for answer and compelled consideration of the subjects to which they related. Distrust of existing constitutional arrangements, doubts as to their stability and permanence, such as were suggested at the time when the legislative system of 1782 was conceded, revived and produced more general effect than they did then. It was seen that, whatever might at home be thought concerning the nature of the connexion between the two countries, their foreign enemies acted upon the supposition of its weakness, and therefore endeavoured to strike against it as a vulnerable point.

War tends to suggest Union.

If peace had at this time come, these considerations would probably have failed to produce any practical result. In a period of war, and especially during the war then waged, statesmen could not with prudence disregard them. England had assumed a position among the European kingdoms in league against France, which drew upon her the especial enmity of this great military power. Against such an antagonist every possible precaution was needed; if there were any defect in the political system of the British Empire, which tended to diminish its means of defence, it was indispensable to amend it. Could, then, the relations between Great Britain and Ireland be allowed to continue as they were? The crisis demanded consolidation of resources, unity of counsel, unity of action; but so long as the two kingdoms remained independent of each other, neither consolidation nor unity could be ensured. If, as was then thought, the same cause rendered their connexion uncertain, would less, it was asked, than its total removal meet the exigency of the case?

Union, it was admitted, was a policy not free from objections, and obstructed by grave difficulties; but to the safety of the Empire all objections and difficulties must give way. Whatever else the measure might fail to accomplish, that object it would certainly tend to promote. The connexion between the two countries was especially assailed, and this connexion would be placed out of reach of the peculiar dangers which menaced it. The weakness caused by the distinct existence of separate kingdoms would be removed. Instead of being, as they then were, isolated and divided, the constituent parts of the Empire would be fused into one mass. Ireland

Decisive reason for Union.

would present no more opportunity or encouragement to foreign enemies than Scotland or any other part of Great Britain. If, nevertheless, invasion should be again attempted, the resources of the whole Empire, directed by one paramount authority, could be concentrated, and made available for its defeat.

CHAPTER XV.

HINDRANCES AND AIDS TO THE POLICY OF UNION IN IRELAND.

WHEN the Union of Scotland with England was under consideration, the difficulties obstructing the measure arose in the former not in the latter country. It was to be expected that the same would also occur in the case of Ireland, since there, just as in Scotland, the Union, if accomplished, would be of a weaker, with a far more powerful, kingdom; and in every such instance the greater, receiving merely an addition to its magnitude, is little affected, while the less, by losing its separate existence, loses also whatever political importance the power of independent action may have conferred. *Hindrances to Union.*

These considerations will explain why, both in Scotland and Ireland, when Union was proposed the sentiment of nationality rose in hostility against it. Among the people of the former kingdom this sentiment had been intensified by peculiar circumstances in their history and social condition. Until little more than a hundred years before the Scottish Union was proposed by Queen Anne's Ministers, the Crown of England *In Scotland.*

and the Crown of Scotland had never been united in the same person. When they were so united there was no permanent or indissoluble connexion established between them; it was possible—nay, as the Security Act had proved, it was not improbable—that they might be disunited again. So long as the inhabitants of the two nations were ruled by different monarchs there was little alliance or intercourse between them, and so late as the reign of Henry VIII. they were engaged in actual warfare. Such an Union of the Crowns as took place under James I.—effected not by permanent arrangement, but by the same person becoming entitled to both—was not of itself adequate to fuse together the subject peoples. Each retained its own distinct legislature and its own distinct code of law. Scotland, too, offered no inducement for colonization: its inhabitants, therefore, remained without any new intermixture, and down to the Union of the kingdoms they tenaciously adhered to the customs, usages, sentiments, and opinions which characterized them when they formed a separate nation with a separate Crown.

Ch. vii., supra.

In Ireland. In Ireland the course of events had been quite different from what occurred in Scotland. More than six hundred years before the period we have now arrived at the Irish princes and chieftains acknowledged the paramount authority of a King of England. His successors, at first under the title of Lord, and afterwards of King, had during the interval exercised regal authority over the island. The Crown of Ireland was held to be indissolubly annexed to the Crown of England.* The country was extensively colonized from England and Scotland; and although much the larger number of its people were descended from the original inhabitants, the ruling class was formed from the colonists, and in habits, opinions, and pursuits, differed little from the parent stock.

Ireland having before the English Invasion existed in a distinct independent political form, it can excite no surprise that the sentiment of nationality was cherished among such of its inhabitants as were of Irish race, the more especially as a mistaken policy on the part of the English Government for four centuries treated them not merely as aliens but as enemies. What is remarkable is, that the idea of a nationality separate from, and, it might be, opposed to that of England, was at an early period as definitely fixed in the minds of the settlers as of the natives. English towards the Irish, the Anglo-Norman knights and nobles, among whom, wherever English supremacy was established, the lands of the subjugated owners were parcelled out, had in no long time become Irish towards the English. The subsequent colonists, according as they successively arrived, naturally acquired

Nationality.

---

* See Note CC of Appendix.

the notions of such of their own countrymen as had preceded them; and these notions were again transmitted by them to those who succeeded to their authority in the country.

Irish Parliament. Exclusion, until the reign of Henry VIII., of the natives from Parliament, and their subsequent niggard admission within it, rendered that assembly down to the reign of James I. representative only of the English portion of the people. It was imbued with their views of political affairs, and it necessarily shared whatever of a national spirit existed among them. Parliament, however, until it had acquired strength and had become conscious that it was too powerful to be repressed, did not speak out.

Ch. ii., supra. When it did, it insisted upon national and legislative independence.

Claims of English Parliament. The claims of the Irish Parliament were met by the English Government and the English Parliament with a counterclaim for the latter of a paramount authority. What they assumed in theory they asserted in practice. Resistance on the part of the Irish Parliament followed, but without avail until 1782. Then a wave of popular enthusiasm swept away all the checks that controlled the legislative capacity of the local Parliament, and with them every restraint upon the independence of the nation.

National spirit in Ireland in 1782. Although, therefore, the circumstances which fostered a national spirit in Scotland did not exist in Ireland, it may be doubted whether, owing to these other causes, the Irish people were not even before 1782 animated by as decided an attachment to their nationality as the Scotch had been previous to 1707. But whatever may have been the case before 1782, it was then that complete independence was won by the Irish Parliament after a struggle which (to use Grattan's words), 'had braced up every faculty of the nation.' Endeared for its own sake, it was rendered still more dear on account of the exertions made, and the difficulties overcome, in order to its attainment.

The interval between 1782 and the time when the policy of Union was adopted by the British Ministers was not sufficiently long to produce much abatement in the ardour thus excited at the former date: besides, the effect of time was counteracted by the events of the intervening period. The reputation of the Irish Parliament for eloquence, high in 1782, had risen still higher; its debates bore comparison with the contemporary debates in the British Parliament. Every Irishman was proud, and justly proud, of the intellectual eminence which the legislature of his country had attained. *Continues to 1798.*

In Scotland, so far as her statesmen and her Parliament were concerned, the sentiment of nationality was in 1707 outweighed by the commercial advantages to be gained by Union. But in Ireland the British Government had already conceded without Union the most important of *Commercial motives to Union less in Ireland than in Scotland.*

the benefits which Scotland had purchased by Union. In 1780 access for Irish ships to colonial ports was opened, and previous restrictions upon the export of Irish manufactured goods were removed. Trade had consequently increased, and the general prosperity of the people been promoted. That without Union the most beneficial of these concessions might be revoked; that their continuance depended upon the arbitrary discretion of the British Parliament, although recognised by statesmen and admitted in debate, was not sufficiently considered by the public, seldom disposed to look beyond what immediately presses.

<small>Why some benefits of Union undervalued.</small>

Another commercial advantage certain to flow from Union was more obvious, and therefore more generally perceived. There still remained some imposts and restrictions on imports from Ireland into Great Britain, and Union would remove these just as it had removed similar burdens upon the intercourse between Scotland and Great Britain. But circumstances tended to induce in Ireland an under-estimate of the benefits to accrue from this result. It was thought that they would be counterbalanced by other consequences that must also follow. If after Union duties and taxes on imports from Ireland into Great Britain could not be maintained, so likewise could not the duties and taxes on imports from Great Britain into Ireland, which, together with bounties upon exports from Ireland, had been enacted by the protective legislation of its Parliament.*

In Ireland, therefore, the Government, when proposing to unite Great Britain and Ireland, could not rely upon much effect being produced by financial considerations, similar to those that had in 1707 moved the Scottish Parliament. One motive, however, in some degree of this character, which was not without influence at that time in Scotland, would, it might be presumed, have like force in Ireland—the aggrandisement of the community to be expected from incorporation with a kingdom of superior wealth and power. If some instinctive impulses urged to retain independence, others no less prompted to become an integral and governing member of an empire whose pre-eminence was acknowledged in every quarter of the globe. *[margin: Local motives to Union.]*

Government could also appeal to reasons for their policy founded on the existing social and political system in Ireland, of which one, the most important, had been mentioned by Pitt in the letter to Lord Westmoreland, which has been cited in the last chapter. The subordinate position of the Roman Catholic part of the nation called for some remedial measure, not indeed with as great force as when that letter was written—for in 1793 Catholics had been admitted to vote at parliamentary elections—but still urgently, *[margin: The condition of the Catholics recommends Union.]*

---

* See note DD of Appendix.

since their exclusion from seats in Parliament, and from the superior offices of trust and confidence under the Crown (including the judicial), remained as yet in force; and when efforts to improve their condition had been made in the Irish Parliament, the result was neither successful, nor calculated to inspire a hope of better fortune in the future. Even as late as 1797 Grattan had brought forward in the House of Commons a resolution expressed in such moderate terms as ought to have disarmed opposition. Yet the motion was defeated by a majority of no less than 143 against 19 votes.

<small>Need of Reform.</small>

Nor was the position of the Catholics the only question pressing for solution, of which it was difficult, if not impossible, to procure a settlement from the local Parliament. Parliamentary reform was urgently needed. The state of the representation in the House of Commons was indefensible. Out of 300 seats there were sixty-four in the counties, twenty-two in towns, and two in the University of Dublin—eighty-eight in all—that might be considered free. The rest were filled either by the direct nomination of owners of boroughs, or at the dictation of a few persons who exercised in boroughs such influence as was equivalent to nomination.*
Reform meant for these proprietors the loss of

---

* In this estimate I have followed Plowden (vol. ii., App. cxv.). See note EE of Appendix.

an unfailing source of honours and emoluments. How, then, was Reform to be carried, for without their concurrence it could not?

Fully, however, to estimate the difficulties which in the Irish Parliament obstructed Catholic Emancipation and Reform of the House of Commons, they must be considered together. Emancipation without Reform would affect only the free seats, that is, not a third of the House of Commons. Reform without Emancipation would still leave Protestant ascendency. But what would be the result if there were both Emancipation and Reform? The Catholic voters preponderated in the counties; the same would happen in the boroughs if they were opened; and under such circumstances, supposing Catholics to be eligible as members, the result anticipated was a Catholic House of Commons. Such a House, it was alleged—and so far as an opinion can be formed from divisions in Parliament, it was by a majority of those who possessed political power thought—would not contentedly acquiesce in the existing establishment of a Protestant Church, or in the existing settlement of landed property. But of the Church the Peers and Commoners were members, and in the settlement of property they had a deep personal interest. They, therefore, regarded any alteration in the policy of the past as equivalent to a revolution, and any variation in the constitution of Parliament as a measure leading to this consequence, and for that reason to be resisted.

Hindrances to reform and emancipation.

Union expected to remove them. By these obstacles social and political improvement in Ireland was impeded. Without Union there appeared no prospect of their removal. Only an imperial Legislature seemed able to cope with them. Superior to local fears and prejudices, it might be expected to do justice to all sections and classes of the people of Ireland; while the magnitude of the United Kingdom would enable this to take place without danger to the stability of the State from the increased greatness of any portion of the people.

CHAPTER XVI.

TERMS OF UNION PROPOSED BY PITT TO THE BRITISH PARLIAMENT.

[1799.]

IN the month of June, 1798, the Marquis Cornwallis, deservedly of high reputation both as a soldier and statesman, was appointed Lord Lieutenant and Commander of the Forces in Ireland. The selection of this nobleman, and the union in him of these offices, were due to Pitt's estimate of his capacity to overcome the difficulties surrounding the government of Ireland during the continuance of the Rebellion, and afterwards to deal with the troubled state of society that was certain to follow its suppression. When he left England, he seems to have been aware that Ministers approved the policy of uniting Ireland with Great Britain, and he was himself a decided advocate of the measure.

_{Lord Cornwallis}

But for some time before his arrival in Ireland it had begun to be there suspected, and indeed generally rumoured, that at least the tendency of opinion among the English Ministers of the Crown was in this direction. A pamphlet had

_{Cooke's pamphlet.}

been published in Dublin, which, although anonymous, was reported to be, and in fact was, the composition of Edward Cooke, a member of the Irish House of Commons, and Under-Secretary to the Lord Lieutenant, that (not, however, without some disguise) sought to recommend the Union. It was entitled, '*Arguments for and against an Union between Great Britain and Ireland considered.*' In this pamphlet Cooke was supposed to represent the sentiments of his immediate superiors in office, who again were thought to derive their notions from the English ministers.

<small>Union not then decided on.</small> There is, however, no reason to think that the Cabinet had at this time collectively resolved to bring forward Union as a measure of the Government. The most influential ministers favoured it; but in the proceedings of official persons a long interval often separates opinion from action. It was useless to move without support from Ireland, and so little was this to be anticipated that Lord Cornwallis, about a month after his arrival in that country, wrote : . . . ' How or when to bring forward, or even broach, the great point of ultimate settlement (*i. e.* Union) is a matter in which I cannot see the most distant encouragement.'*

<small>When Bill in preparation.</small> But whatever may have been the exact

---

* Letter of Cornwallis to Pitt, 20th July, 1798. *Correspondence*, vol. ii., p. 365.

date when Pitt and his colleagues determined to submit to the Parliaments of Great Britain and Ireland a scheme for Union, there is no doubt that at the end of September and the beginning of October, 1798, the actual provisions of a measure of this character were under their consideration.* The question of most difficulty which presented itself in connexion with them was—whether relief of the disabilities still affecting the Irish Catholics should be included among them. Upon this point there was a division of opinion between the Lord Lieutenant and the Irish Lord Chancellor, the former (Lord Cornwallis) desiring that it should; the latter (Lord Clare) being opposed to any reference in the Act of Union to the claims of the Catholics.

At this period, and for some years previously, no person had more influence with the English Ministers in reference to Irish affairs than Lord Clare. This followed from his official position, his abilities and force of character. Clear and determined in his opinions, he adhered to them firmly. Popular applause he regarded little; popular censure less. On every occasion of diffi-

_{Lord Clare}

---

* On September 26, 1798, Mr. Marshall (Private Secretary to Lord Castlereagh, then acting for Pelham, the Secretary to the Lord Lieutenant) wrote from London to Lord Castlereagh, ... 'the Union is to be brought forward, and the leading points of it are now under consideration.' *Castlereagh Correspondence*, vol. i., p. 378.

culty his courage, self-reliance, and sagacious discernment, were conspicuous. Inheriting affluence, yet of the middle class, educated a Protestant, yet of a Catholic family, he had early come in contact with the interests which contended for supremacy in his native country. So far, therefore, as regards intellectual power and knowledge of the social system, he was well fitted to act the part of a political adviser; but unfortunately with these great qualities were allied others which in no small degree hindered a sound judgment. He was haughty, overbearing in temper and manner, disdaining to conciliate, and impatient of contradiction or dissent. There are no traces in his speeches of philosophic study or reflection; and, as not seldom happens when strength of mind is neither enlarged nor softened by such influences, his opinions were deficient in breadth and generosity.

Lord Clare's views. Lord Clare had never been favourable to conceding political power to persons professing the Roman Catholic religion. He had in 1793 assented to the Bill admitting them to the franchise, but he explained that he did so only because, after what had previously passed on the subject both in Great Britain and Ireland, he would not be responsible for the immediate consequences of rejecting it. His objections, however, in 1798, to including relief for the Irish Catholics in the Act of Union were urged, principally upon the ground that such an addition to the measure would endanger its acceptance by the Irish Parliament.

Early in the month of October Lord Clare, at the request of the English Ministers, proceeded to London in order that they might confer with him respecting their intended legislation. The result was, that his opinions in relation to the course proper to be pursued towards the Roman Catholic portion of the Irish people had much weight with the Cabinet; and that at a later date they resolved to propose measures which should make no reference to the future position of either English or Irish Catholics in the State.* Act of Union not to contain relief for the Catholics.

When the Government had decided what were the terms of Union to be recommended, it was judged proper that the subject should be introduced simultaneously in the Parliaments of Great Britain and Ireland—in the former by a message from the King, and in the latter by the speech of the Lord Lieutenant, but with a reference to the royal authority having sanctioned the communication. Union to be proposed.

Accordingly when, in January 1799, the British Parliament met, a message was delivered from the King and read in both Houses. The message did not expressly mention the intended project of Union, but it so referred to recent events, especially the efforts of the enemies of Great Britain to separate Ireland, and contained Message from the King, Jan. 1799.

---

* See Note FF of Appendix.

such recommendations, that it was understood to suggest some measure of the kind. It was expressed in the following terms: ... 'His Majesty is persuaded that the unremitting industry with which our enemies persevere in their avowed design of effecting the separation of Ireland from this kingdom cannot fail to engage the attention of Parliament; and his Majesty recommends to consider the most effectual means of counteracting and finally defeating this design; and he trusts that a review of all the circumstances which have recently occurred (joined to the sentiment of mutual affection and common interest) will dispose the Parliaments of both kingdoms to provide, in the manner which they shall judge most expedient, for settling such a complete and final adjustment as may best tend to improve and perpetuate a connection essential for their common security, and to augment and consolidate the strength, power, and resources of the British Empire.'

Sheridan. In the House of Commons a formal Address of thanks for the message having been proposed, Sheridan, interpreting the message to favour Union between Great Britain and Ireland, at once announced his hostility to any policy of that character, and insisted upon the finality of the settlement of 1782. Fox had, at this time, ceased to attend Parliament, and Sheridan, in his absence, came forward on behalf of the political party then in opposition. It was the leaders of this party who had made to the Irish Parliament the concession of legislative independence, which formed the basis of the Constitution of 1782; and those who had been the authors of the consequent enactments were naturally indisposed to admit their failure or imperfection. Sheridan, himself an Irishman, and accustomed to act in political association with the party of nationality in Ireland, was impelled in the course he took by the additional motive of sympathy with whatever appeared to elevate and give importance to the country. To place on record his views, he moved an amendment to the Address, which, after declaring that it was with regret the House then, for the first time, learned that the final adjustment of 1782 had not produced the effects expected, implored his Majesty not to listen to the counsel of those who should advise or promote an Union of the Legislatures of the two kingdoms at that crisis.

When supporting the finality claimed by the Amendment for the arrangements made in 1782, Sheridan contended that Great Britain had then admitted what was at that time asserted by the Irish Parliament, namely, that there was no power whatever competent to make laws for Ireland except the Parliament of Ireland. He did not deny that the King's Ministers were actuated by the motive of desiring to avert separation; their policy, he said, originated in fear of the ambitious designs of France. But he could

Sheridan's observations.

not agree with them in regarding those designs as a reason for desiring Union; they seemed to him to furnish an argument against it, since any measure of the kind would revive in Ireland recollections of jealousy and distrust, and, by exhibiting internal disagreement, would be sure rather to encourage external enemies than to drive them from (what he allowed to be) their settled purpose.

Pitt's reply.

Pitt, when he came to speak, replied to Sheridan. He observed that the amendment called upon the House to declare that it would not deliberate upon the matter. To justify such a resolution, the mover was bound to show that the then state of Ireland required no remedy, or that if it did a better might be proposed than that which had Union for its basis. But Ireland clearly required some remedial measure, for it was subject to great and deplorable evils which had a deep root, for they lay in the situation of the country itself, in the unavoidable separation between certain classes, in the state of property, in religious distinctions. If, then, a remedy was needed, must not the most effective be an impartial Legislature, standing aloof from local party connection, sufficiently removed from the influence of contending factions to be advocate or champion of neither? The settlement of 1782, he contended, was not, as alleged by Sheridan, designed to be final. The proceedings at that time (which he then proceeded to refer to) demonstrated, he argued, that some further measure was contemplated.

On a later day (January 31, 1799) the discussion upon the King's message was renewed; and Pitt moved that the Speaker should leave the chair in order that there might be submitted in committee Resolutions which he then laid before the House, affirming the expediency of uniting Ireland with Great Britain, and defining the arrangements to be connected with the Union. In the interval which had elapsed since Pitt's former speech the Irish House of Commons had declared against the policy of Union. He therefore began by explaining, that while he admitted the right of the Parliament of Ireland to express its opinion, he felt that, as a member of the Parliament of Great Britain, he also had a duty to perform, and that was to state distinctly the principles of the propositions which he intended to submit for approval, and the grounds upon which they appeared to him to be entitled to approbation. When they were understood, the Irish Parliament could judge whether finally to accept or reject what would be offered for its consideration. This course was the more necessary because the question involved many subjects likely to be decided upon by passion, not judgment, and was one in which an honest but mistaken sense of national pride was likely to operate,

Pitt's second speech, Jan. 31.

and where, therefore, much misconstruction and misconception must inevitably happen. The measure rested, however, upon such clear grounds of utility, that even under the discouragement of the opinion expressed by the Irish House of Commons, he entertained a confidence that all that could be necessary for its ultimate adoption was, that it should be stated distinctly, temperately, and fully, and then be left to the unprejudiced, and dispassionate judgment of the Parliament of Ireland. In the general principle on which it was founded, he was happy to observe, from what passed in the former debate, all were agreed. This was, that a perpetual connection between Great Britain and Ireland was essential to the interests of both. If so, what was the situation of affairs which called them to the discussion of the existing connection? It was, that the connection had been, and still was, the great object for the hostility of all who were enemies of the country. It was necessary to guard against threatened danger. The settlement of 1782 left the connection exposed to all the attacks of party and all the effects of accident. It left the two countries with separate and independent Legislatures, connected only by these ties, that the third estate in both countries was the same,*

---

* It is remarkable that in the debates at the time of the Union the Crown is always spoken of as the third estate, whereas (as is pointed out by Hallam) the three estates of the that the Irish Acts of Parliament required the assent of the British Crown, and that this was given under the Great Seal of Great Britain, and upon the advice of British Ministers. Such ties, he asserted, were not sufficient in time of peace to unite the countries; in time of war to consolidate their strength against the common enemy; or to guard against local jealousies arising. In connection with this topic he referred to the disagreements between the two Legislatures which had occurred. And, with respect to the disagreement in relation to commercial questions in 1785, he observed, that the only means of obviating differences between two kingdoms concerning such subjects must be either by some permanent compact entered into between their Legislatures, or by blending their Legislatures together. In the case of Great Britain and Ireland the former mode of dealing with the matter had been offered by the British Parliament, but it had been refused by the Irish, and it therefore only remained to resort to the latter. Then with respect to the disagreement upon the question of Regency, he said, it was accident alone (namely, the same person

---

realm are the nobility, clergy, and commons, or, less correctly, their representatives, viz. the Lords Temporal, the Lords Spiritual, and the Lower House of Parliament, over whom (as Lord Chancellor Stillington, in the reign of Edward IV., expressed it) is the State Royal, our sovereign Lord the King. *Middle Ages*, 9th edition, vol. ii., p. 237, n.

being chosen by both the British and Irish Parliaments) that preserved the unity of the executive power, in which consisted the bond and security of the connection of the kingdoms. But its preservation in this manner was attended with the disadvantage that it depended in Ireland on one tenure, and in Great Britain upon another. Moreover, disagreement upon commercial questions and the Regency were only part of the disagreements between the two legislatures that might occur. They had distinct powers in reference to war and peace, alliances and confederacies. Was there any certainty that on these supremely important questions their decisions would always be the same? The present war, he said, which the Parliament of Great Britain considered to be just and necessary, might have been voted by the Irish Parliament to be unjust, unnecessary, perhaps even to be extravagant, and hostile to the principles of humanity and freedom. If this could happen, what security was there, he asked, that, at a moment the most important to the common interest and common salvation, the two kingdoms would have but one friend and one foe?

<small>Pitt's speech continued.</small> These observations drew arguments from the general interests of the whole Empire in favour of such an Union of the Legislatures of the kingdoms which composed it as would ensure harmony of counsel, and consolidation of their distinct

capacities of defence. But it was necessary also to consider what would be the effect of the measures to be proposed upon the special circumstances of Ireland. What inducements were to be held out to her Parliament to adopt them? And, in reference to this department of the subjects necessary then to be considered, Pitt proceeded to examine what wants had to be provided for, and to point out in connection with them the beneficial consequences to flow from Union. It would, he said, communicate to Ireland all the commercial advantages which Great Britain possessed; would open free communication between the markets of the two countries; would lead to a common use of their capital, and to its diffusion through the people of both, thus extending civilization and improvement; would ensure for the weaker kingdom the protection of the stronger against danger from enemies without or treason within, conferring upon it a full participation in the wealth, the power, and the stability of the whole Empire.

Referring to the internal dissensions which divided the Irish people, he contended that an imperial legislature was the only means of terminating them and of restoring tranquillity. When the conduct of the Catholics should be such as to make it safe to admit them to participation of the privileges granted to those of the established religion, and when the temper of the times should be favourable to such a policy, the question

Pitt's speech continued.

o

might be agitated in an united, imperial parliament with much greater safety than it could be in a separate legislature. How far it might be right and practicable to accompany such a measure by some mode of relieving the lower orders from the pressure of tithes, or to make, under proper provisions and without breaking in on the security of the Protestant establishment, an effectual and adequate provision for the Catholic clergy, it was not, he said, necessary then to discuss. It was sufficient to say that these and other points were more likely to be permanently and satisfactorily settled by an united legislature than by any local arrangements.

Pitt's speech continued. To ask the rejection of a measure, calculated to produce such results as he had laid before them, because it put an end to independence, would, he observed, be an appeal to an erroneous and mistaken sense of national pride. Did those who made it mean that in any humiliating sense, when the Governments of two separate countries unite in forming one more extensive empire, the individuals who composed either of the two former societies are afterwards less members of an independent country, or to any valuable or useful purpose less possessed of political freedom or civil happiness, than they were before? If, he said, the principles suggested had been acted upon by their forefathers, not one of the countries the most proud of their present existing independence would exist in the state in which it then stood. In the different unions which have formed the principal states of Europe had their inhabitants become less free, had they less of which to be proud, less scope for their own exertions, than in their former situation? If a nation has not adequate means of protecting itself without the aid of another, and that other should be neighbouring and kindred, speaking the same language, with laws, customs, and habits the same in principle, but carried to more perfection, with a more extensive commerce, and more abundant means of acquiring and diffusing national wealth, does an Union under such circumstances deserve to be branded as a proposal for subjecting to a foreign yoke? Is it not rather the free and voluntary association of two countries which join, for their common benefit, in one Empire, where each will retain its proportional weight and importance, under the security of equal laws, reciprocal affection, and inseparable interests, and which want nothing but that indissoluble connection to render both invincible?

> 'Non ego nec Teucris Italos parere jubebo
> Nec nova regna peto : paribus se legibus ambæ,
> Invictæ gentes eterna in fœdera mittant.'*

---

* This speech being a statement of the case made by the Government for their measures, I have thought it better to attempt a summary of it, necessarily most imperfect. I shall afterwards adopt the same course with a speech delivered by Foster, the Speaker of the Irish Parliament, which I regard as the most effective of the replies to Pitt's speech.

Pitt's resolutions voted.

A division was taken upon the question that the Speaker do leave the Chair, in order that the Resolutions then laid before the House might, at a future day, be considered in Committee. The numbers were: ayes, 140; noes, 15. Ultimately the Resolutions, when proposed, were adopted by the British House of Commons, and subsequently by the British House of Lords. But in consequence of proceedings in the Irish House of Commons, which will be narrated in the next chapter, no Bill to carry them into effect was in this Session introduced in the British Parliament.

CHAPTER XVII.

PROCEEDINGS IN THE IRISH PARLIAMENT.

[1799.]

THE Speech of the Lord Lieutenant at the meeting of the Irish Parliament, in Jan. 1799, was to the same effect as the King's message to the English Parliament. After referring to the industry with which the enemies of the Empire persevered in their design of separating Ireland from Great Britain, it stated the King's anxious hope that this consideration, joined to the sentiment of mutual affection and common interest, might dispose the Parliaments in both kingdoms to provide the most effectual means of maintaining and improving a connection essential to their security. *Speech of Lord Lieutenant, 1799.*

In the House of Commons an answer to the Lord Lieutenant's speech was moved, which promised the fullest consideration to its recommendations. An amendment was at once brought forward intended by its language to pledge the House against the Union. It sought to insert the words: '... but maintaining the undoubted birthright of the people of Ireland to have a *Address in Commons.*

free and independent Legislature resident within that kingdom, as it was asserted by its Parliament in 1782, and acknowledged and ratified by his Majesty and the Parliament of Great Britain upon the final adjustment of the discontents and jealousies then prevailing.'

<small>Amendments to Address.</small>

The amendment became the subject of a lengthened debate, and was in the end rejected, but only by a majority of one, 105 voting for and 106 against it. When, however, the Address itself was under examination, the promise to consider the recommendations of the speech, being supposed to express in an indirect manner approval of Union, led to a renewal of the former discussion. Then by another amendment it was proposed to expunge the paragraph which contained the promise; and this motion was attended with a different result from the former proceeding, 106 (including tellers) now voting with and 111 (including tellers) against the Government.

<small>Analysis of division on second amendment.</small>

When this division is analysed it will be found that in the minority of 106 for Government there were 16 members returned by counties, 6 returned for open seats in boroughs, and 84 returned by close boroughs; that in the majority of 111 against Government, there were 36 members returned by counties, 9 for open seats in boroughs, and 66 returned for close boroughs; that there were absent 11 members for counties, 9 sitting for open seats in boroughs, and 65 returned for close boroughs. The Speaker, who is not reckoned in these calculations, sat for a county.*

In the Lords an Address, which was moved in answer to the Lord Lieutenant's speech, and which engaged to consider the best means of improving the connection between the two kingdoms (describing it as essential to their common security), and of consolidating into one firm and lasting fabric the power and resources of the British Empire, was carried by a majority of 35; the votes for being 52, and the votes against 17. Amendments adverse to the policy of Union which were proposed were defeated. *Address in House of Lords.*

The debates and divisions in the Commons disclosed that against any scheme of Union there was enlisted a remarkable combination of parliamentary ability. Grattan at the general election, when the existing House was returned, did not seek a seat. Flood, his great rival, had died. But while their support was thus withdrawn from the cause of national independence, Plunket, then recently returned to Parliament, brought to its defence eloquence and legal attainments of the highest order. The most important aid, however, to the Opposition came from the co-operation, for the first time, of the Speaker of the House of Commons *The Opposition in Commons.*

---

* The names are given by Plowden; for the places for which they sat, see *Collectanea Politica*, p. 202. As to the towns in which I assume there were free seats, see Note EE of Appendix.

—Foster—who, although he had been one of Pitt's parliamentary supporters, now came forward to resist his measures, and cast in the scale against them the weight of a character without reproach, of a most accurate knowledge of every constitutional and financial question, and of an advocacy which his power of argument and of well-arranged and lucid statement rendered eminently persuasive.

Lord Castlereagh.

The conduct of proceedings in the House of Commons on the part of the Government devolved upon Lord Castlereagh, who had not long before been appointed Secretary to the Lord Lieutenant. Almost alone this young nobleman (he was only in his thirtieth year) confronted the adversaries who, thus formidable as well by their intellectual pre-eminence as by superiority in number, had arrayed themselves against the proposals he was instructed to offer. Inferior in debate to the trained and practised orators whom he had to encounter, he was sustained through the unequal conflict by a union of qualities well fitted to influence a popular assembly. In counsel cautious and dispassionate, he was in action self-relying, firm, and constant of purpose. No provocation could disturb his equanimity: no danger depress his courage. The effect of this strength of character was heightened, because softened and rendered more attractive, by habitual courtesy, by manners the most dignified and graceful, to which a noble form and countenance lent an additional charm.*

When the state of parties in the House of Commons, as well in respect of numbers as of the capacity of their leaders, was such as has been described, Ministers, defeated upon the Address, had to consider what course they were to pursue. Obviously, if they then brought forward a direct proposal of Union, they would have to contend against greater strength. It was therefore decided not to proceed further during the Session of 1799. On the other hand, the Opposition, whom success encouraged, sought to strengthen their position by removing a cause of objection to the existing legislative system, viz. the probability of renewed disagreement between the British and Irish Legislatures upon the question of Regency. With this object they brought forward a Bill (afterwards defeated), which would have provided that, in case of a Regency, the royal authority in Ireland should be administered by the person appointed in England, and with the same powers. In committee upon this Bill, Foster—who, being in the chair of the House of Commons during the debates

A Regency Bill proposed.

---

* Compare the estimates of Lord Castlereagh's capacity for affairs formed by Sir Robert Peel and Thiers, cited in Note G G of Appendix. The character of the general administration of Irish affairs by Lord Castlereagh and Lord Cornwallis (for they cannot be separated) lies outside the limits proposed for this treatise.

upon the Address, could not then intervene—availed himself of the opportunity, and spoke in answer to the statement with which Pitt accompanied the introduction of his Resolutions in favour of Union in the British House of Commons.

Foster's speech.

Foster commenced, as Sheridan had done, by asserting that the settlement of 1782 was then intended to be a final arrangement, and by entering at considerable length into an examination of the proceedings in that year in both Parliaments. He then defended himself from the charge of having in 1785, when, as Chancellor of the Exchequer in Ireland, he advocated Pitt's Propositions, admitted that the Constitution of 1782 required to be supplemented. These propositions were, he said, commercial, not constitutional; and he had at that time stated that he should think himself unworthy of a seat in Parliament, or of the name of an Irishman, if he would consent to barter an atom of the constitution of his country for all the commerce in the world; indeed, so satisfied was he that the Commercial Propositions did not violate it in the smallest degree, that he could not repress his surprise at their being by anyone supposed to do so. The measure of 1782 was all constitutional; the measure of 1785 all commercial. Now even the Commercial Propositions were not, he urged, needed, since subsequent legislation had accomplished what was formerly sought. There had been a Navigation Act, an East India Act, and other Acts affecting the relations of the countries, so that there was, he said, no one question of general or imperial concern, or even of colonial trade, unattended to. The arrangement of duties on the interchange of native productions or manufactures he did not consider an object of imperial concern; and even if it were, the two Parliaments were competent to deal with it, and if they did were more likely to attain that stability for their arrangements which only mutual consent and satisfaction could secure. He admitted that he had formerly said that two independent Legislatures and unsettled commerce could not exist together with safety. But the effect of what had since taken place was that commerce had been settled, and therefore the two independent Legislatures might exist. In reply, therefore, to the argument that there were but two ways of remedying the commercial jealousies of independent Legislatures in the same Empire, viz. by compact between them, or by blending them together, he answered that there was a third, namely, that which the conduct of Great Britain and Ireland had shown, by leaving to the good sense and mutual interest of each country to pass all laws necessary, in order to prevent the operation and inconveniences of commercial jealousies. *Page 191.*

From these topics Foster passed to the supposed danger from disagreement between the *Foster's Speech continued.*

Parliaments upon the question of war or peace, and pointed out that the sole and absolute right of making either war or peace rested in the Executive power: it was the King's prerogative. In case of war, the Executive had to consult Parliament only for the means of carrying it on; so that if the two Legislatures differed as to the propriety of war, the only difficulty which the Legislature dissenting from the policy of the Executive could create was by withholding supplies; and this would only be until the good sense, which was sure in the end to prevail, should induce it to acquiesce. The dissentient power could not, by any refusal to give supplies, stand clear of the miseries, hazards, and losses of war, because the King's declaration would involve it equally with the rest of the Empire in them.

[Foster's Speech continued.] Nor would there be more difficulty as to treaties which did not concern peace or war—such, for instance, as adjusted the course of trade. Concerning these there was no more reason that England and Ireland should permanently disagree than that the two Houses of Parliament should do so. In both cases there would be motives strong enough to induce reconciliation.

[Foster's Speech continued.] It was said that Union must augment the general force of the Empire. Were it really calculated to produce this effect, much, Foster admitted, ought to be sacrificed for such an object; but was it proved that it would? No, he said, the Unionists used general terms, made unsupported assertions, and spoke as if there were no Union—as if Great Britain and Ireland were actually separate—and then they attributed to their own project every merit, every advantage already enjoyed, as if it only could confer them, and as if the advantages did not already exist; whereas the case, he said, really was, that the kingdoms were so united as to confer on the Empire the whole of their strength. The consolidation, he asserted, of their resources was as firm as human policy and individual interest could make it. Would removing the Parliament to London raise one guinea, or give one soldier more for the defence of the nation?

In the course of his observations Foster alluded to the arguments for an Imperial Parliament, which were based upon the religious differences, and upon the supposed inferior civilization, of the people in Ireland; and pointed out, with respect to the former, that an Irish legislative assembly, deliberating at home, and acquainted with the circumstances to be considered, could just as wisely as the British Parliament judge of the course proper to be pursued; and with respect to the latter, that a local Parliament, and the residence of the gentry, which would be a consequence of its continuance, must of themselves promote social improvement.

Foster's Speech continued.

CHAPTER XVIII.

PROCEEDINGS AFTER THE PROROGATION OF THE IRISH PARLIAMENT IN 1799.

Parliamentary difficulties in the way of Union.

THE success of the Opposition upon the amendment to the Address in the House of Commons, which has been narrated in the last chapter, seems not to have been anticipated by the Irish Ministers. They appear to have expected then to receive the same support as they did on other occasions; and had their proposals been of an ordinary character—relating to the administration of affairs, or the general policy of the Empire—this would probably have been the case. But the distinction between any such measure and an Act of Union was broad and plain. The former dealt with the incidents of the national existence, the latter with the existence itself. One was consistent, the other inconsistent, with the continuance of the institution. Union would put an end to a separate Legislature, and therefore in Parliament the proposal to enact it came in contact with the instinct of self-preservation, potent in corporate bodies, equally as in the individuals of whom they are composed.

Nor were the difficulties that impeded the Ministerial policy confined to objections which may be described as of a national character. Union would necessarily affect injuriously powerful private interests. The number of representatives which it was intended to give to Ireland in the House of Commons of the Imperial Parliament was not disclosed in the Resolutions which Pitt moved; but that the ultimate result would be a very large reduction in the number of seats, to which a few individuals then nominated, was well known; and as yet no suggestion had been made of compensation to the owners of those seats which would cease to be filled. Many members, too, of the existing Parliament had purchased their seats, and had done so upon the expectation that they would hold them for the ordinary duration of a Parliament; and such persons would be naturally disinclined to vote for what must terminate their parliamentary existence. It was also seen that the tradesmen and owners of houses in Dublin must suffer considerable loss by the Union, since it would withdraw the benefits conferred by the residence of the Peers and Commoners attending Parliament, and of many others brought thither by the social attractions thus created. For the Bar, who could not consistently with the practice of their profession leave Ireland, Union meant the abolition of an avenue to the noblest distinction.

Power of owners of close boroughs.

Of these interests, thus naturally pre-disposed against Union, the most formidable was that of the owners of the boroughs. Their members so completely outnumbered the rest of the House of Commons, that if they combined to oppose a measure, it could make no progress. Now among the other members Government was in a minority, and therefore required, in order to counterbalance this deficiency, more than a majority of those returned for the close seats. This could not be without the concurrence of their proprietors; for although when a seat was sold the purchaser was not expected to consult its owner as to his vote, it was otherwise when the member owed his possession of it to mere favour.

Pecuniary value of boroughs.

The great difficulty in the way of reconciling the owners of boroughs to the Union was the practice which had grown up, just as much in Great Britain as in Ireland, of regarding the power of nominating members of the House of Commons as a species of property. Seats were sold, hired for a temporary period, entailed in settlements, and otherwise disposed of, just like lands or manorial rights. For permanent sale or temporary letting there was a market price. A seat in the Irish Parliament of 1775 brought from two thousand guineas to two thousand five hundred pounds; in 1793 the price had risen to three thousand pounds. At the general election for the Parliament in which the question of the Union was brought forward—returned in

1797—the price had fallen, and seats were cheaper, a considerable number being in the market. That neither in Great Britain nor Ireland were the majority of these seats sold, that many of them were filled from the purest motives and to advance the public good, did not conflict with the notion that they were property —a potential, if not an actual, source of emolument, of which, if the present owners did not avail themselves, yet their successors might.

The difficulty of overcoming the resistance of the owners of boroughs to change in the parliamentary system had been experienced in both countries, as often as reform of the House of Commons was suggested. In England, Pitt, when in 1785 he brought forward proposals for reform, had met the difficulty by suggesting the creation of a fund to purchase these boroughs from their owners. A reform of the representation such as he contemplated could, he said, only be brought about by either of two means—by an act of power, or by a consideration which might induce bodies or individuals to part with rights which they considered as a species of valuable inheritance, or of personal property. Having, he said, an insurmountable objection to the former course, he adopted the latter.* No Reform Bill proposed for Ireland

marginal note: In 1785, in England, Pitt proposed to compensate for loss of boroughs.

---

* See as to the close boroughs in Great Britain and Ireland, Note HH of Appendix.

had contained a proposition of this kind, and because none had, Reform made, as we have seen, little progress. Union, if it were also offered without compensation for the disfranchised boroughs, was not likely to fare better.

<small>Compensation suggested.</small>

The first suggestion of applying the principle of compensation for boroughs to be disfranchised by the Union appears to have come from Lord Castlereagh. After the division in the House of Commons adverse to the Government, he drew up and sent to the Duke of Portland, who was then the Secretary of State charged with the care of Irish affairs, a memorandum pointing out the difficulties created by private interests in which, he says, 'the borough objection may be removed at once by pecuniary compensation.' The suggestion meeting the approval of the Cabinet, it became after some time known that, whenever the question of Union was renewed, pecuniary compensation for the disfranchised boroughs would be proposed.

<small>Effect of compensation for disfranchised boroughs being proposed.</small>

There is no doubt that the determination to compensate the owners of disfranchised boroughs removed an almost insuperable obstacle to the policy of Ministers. It may also have afforded, in some instances, a motive to adopt it; but its effect in this way has been overestimated. The compensation to the proprietor of a borough was quite irrespective of his vote; he was equally to receive it, whether he voted for or against the

Bill. It was not proposed to make it higher than the market price; and while an owner, poor or in embarrassed circumstances, might desire the money, the owners whom it was of most consequence to secure were more likely to prefer the retention of a power, whose exercise gave them supreme importance in political and social life.

Of much more effectual operation in gaining the support of such owners of close boroughs, and of such other persons possessing political authority as were to be moved by considerations of personal advantage, was the power which the English Government commanded, and had long been accustomed to employ, of using the patronage of the Crown to reward those upon whose votes they could count in both Houses of Parliament by conferring upon them peerages and other honours, and by granting to them offices, places, and pensions.* In what instances these inducements were at the time of the Union actually had recourse to has been a subject of controversy which I have excluded from the scope of this treatise, because requiring, as has been mentioned in the Preface, a more lengthened examination of evidence than is consistent with its intended limits, and also because the object I proposed to myself was, not to ascertain the motives personal to themselves which may have influenced individuals

---

* See Note II of Appendix.

in the course they pursued, but to present the reasons for and against each of the successive legislative systems of Ireland assigned by those who advocated or opposed their adoption.

<small>Exertions to gain external support.</small>

Neither, however, compensation for disfranchised boroughs nor the exercise of patronage would have produced any effect outside Parliament; and as this assembly was most inadequately representative, the necessity of securing some further support for the measures of Government was recognised. After the parliamentary discussions in 1799, public opinion was, according to Lord Castlereagh, circumstanced as follows:— The Protestants were divided upon the question of Union — Dublin (he says) and the Orange Societies being against it: while the Catholics (he adds) held back, under a doubt whether Union would impede or facilitate their object. It being supposed that if some assurances were given to the latter they might be gained over, Lord Castlereagh went to London to consult the Cabinet Ministers, and obtained from them permission to communicate to Lord Cornwallis, that so far as their sentiments were concerned he need not hesitate to seek Catholic support.*

<small>Inducements offered to Catholics.</small>

When this permission had been received from the Cabinet, the Irish department of Govern-

---

* See letter of Lord Castlereagh to Pitt, written after the Union, dated 1st January, 1801. (*Castlereagh Correspondence*, vol. iv., p. 8.)

ment proceeded to act in conformity with their own judgment, and (as Lord Castlereagh states) 'they omitted no exertions to call forth the Catholics in favour of the Union.' They gave no direct assurance that Emancipation would necessarily follow as a consequence; but it appears to me they held out that if there were any hindrance to its enactment it would not come either from themselves or from the English Government in its collective capacity. It seems also to have been at this time clearly understood that Ministers were favourable to making a provision for the Roman Catholic bishops and clergy.

Lord Castlereagh, in the letter to which I have referred, says that the efforts of the Irish Government to conciliate the Catholics were very generally successful; and that the advantage derived from them was highly useful, particularly in depriving the Opposition of the means they otherwise would have possessed in the southern and western counties of making an impression on the county members. There seems to me no reason to dissent from this statement, made by one who certainly had the means of accurate knowledge. No doubt the Irish Catholics, if they could have obtained relief from their disabilities without Union, would have preferred the existing legislative system; but of this they despaired, and consequently many of the most influential among them, both lay and

Effect of the inducements.

clerical, reconciled themselves to Union with Emancipation.*

Reasons inducing the clergy of the Established Church to favour Union.

The policy of Ministers seems to me to have also at this time gained ground among the clergy of the Established Church. Without Union their position was anomalous. Exclusively possessing the national endowments for the maintenance of religious worship, they ministered to a portion of the people which, when it is compared with the number of the entire nation, must be considered small. So long as Ireland continued to be a separate kingdom, the Church was the Church of a minority, surrounded by a not merely dissenting, but hostile majority, who regarded the privileges which Establishment conferred upon it with extreme discontent. By the Union it was proposed to incorporate not merely the kingdoms of Great Britain and Ireland, but also the Established Church of England and the Established Church of Ireland. Then the people of England and the people of Ireland being regarded as one aggregate, the United Church would command the allegiance of a majority; it would be an imperial, not a local institution, and each of its component parts might be expected to share in whatever security was thereby conferred.

---

* See Note KK of Appendix.

CHAPTER XIX.

UNION.

[1800.]

THE Session of the Irish Parliament for 1799 was brought to a close in June. Upon the 15th of January, 1800, the next Session began.   *Lord Lieutenant's speech.*

When Parliament at that time assembled, the speech of the Lord Lieutenant contained no allusion to the question of Union, as it was thought better to reserve the subject for a separate message. The leaders of the Opposition, perceiving what was designed, determined to anticipate the action of the Government, and, accordingly, moved in the House of Commons an amendment to the Address which was proposed in answer to the King's Speech. By the amendment it was sought to pledge the House to maintain the independence of the Irish Parliament. It was expressed in the following terms:—' To assure his Majesty that his kingdom of Ireland is inseparably united with Great Britain, and that the sentiments, wishes, and real interests of all his subjects are that it should continue so united, in the enjoyment of a free Constitution, in the support of the honour and dignity of his Majesty's crown, and in the advancement of the welfare of the whole Empire: which blessings (it added) we owe to the spirited exertions of a resident Parliament, the paternal kindness of his Majesty, and the liberality of the British Parliament in 1782, and which we feel ourselves at all times, and particularly at the present moment, bound in duty to maintain.' The amendment was defeated by a majority of 42, the votes (including tellers) being, for 98; against 140.

Resolutions of 1799 passed both Houses.

As the House of Lords had been, in the previous year, favourable to Union, this division put an end to any doubt that the measures of Government to effect it would be carried through the Irish Parliament. The Lord Lieutenant, therefore, on the 5th of February, sent to both Houses of Parliament the Resolutions upon the subject which had been passed by the British Parliament in the previous year, and accompanied them with a message, in which he stated that he was commanded by his Majesty to lay the Resolutions before the Houses of Parliament, and solemnly to recommend to their attention the great objects they embraced. Upon a motion in the House of Commons that it should resolve itself into a committee to consider the message, there was on the 6th of February a division in which Government obtained a majority increased by one above that which had supported it on the Address, the numbers (including tellers) being—for the

Page 196.

motion 160, and against it 117. In the House of Lords Government had a majority of 75 votes against 26.

When the House of Commons met upon the 15th of January writs were issued for new elections in twenty-eight seats, of which five had been vacated by death, one by succession to a peerage, and the rest by acceptance of offices under the Crown, or of the escheatorships of Ulster and Munster, the acceptance of these escheatorships having the same effect in vacating a seat in Ireland as the acceptance of the stewardship of the Chiltern Hundreds had in England. Five more writs were issued on the 17th, three more on the 18th, and eight more on the 20th of January. The vacancies in respect of which the writs were issued were caused by acceptance of the escheatorships or other offices. {.sidenote}Writs issued by House of Commons.

Thus there were, between the day on which Parliament met and the day of the division on the motion to consider the King's message, elections for forty-four seats in the House of Commons. In a few instances, where the vacancies were caused by the acceptance of offices of value, the same persons were re-elected, but in all the others new members were returned, almost all supporters of the Government. {.sidenote}43 writs before 6th February.

If the division in the House of Commons on the 6th of February be analysed, the following, or nearly the following, results will appear. The majority on that occasion (160) was composed {.sidenote}Division, 6th Feb.

of 22 members for counties, 8 members for open seats in towns, 129 members for close boroughs, and 1 for the University of Dublin. The minority against Government consisted of 38 members for counties, 9 for open seats in towns, 69 for close boroughs, and 1 for the University of Dublin. These calculations exclude the Speaker. Those absent (22) consisted of 3 members for counties, 5 for open seats in towns, and 14 for close boroughs.*

Saurin, Bushe, Grattan, are returned to Parliament.

The debating power of the House of Commons arranged upon the side of the Opposition was, in 1800, augmented by the addition of Saurin, Bushe, and Grattan. The great legal attainments of the first placed him at the head of the Irish Bar; the second was also a distinguished member of the Bar, one of its most accomplished orators, unrivalled in grace of diction and manner. Grattan took his seat during the debate on the Address, in which he at once took part; and, in a speech characterised by the most brilliant eloquence, commented upon the arguments urged by Pitt in the previous year.†

---

* For names see Plowden, vol. ii. 363; the classification of seats may slightly err, being made from a list in *Collectanea Politica*, p. 202, some changes having occurred after its date.

† Grattan, during the progress of the Bill for Union through the Irish House of Commons in the Session of 1800, delivered four speeches against it—January 15–16, February 5, March 19, May 26. I had in the previous edition given a summary of the first; but I have now withdrawn it, since it

In the House of Commons Ministers had again, just as in 1799, to rely chiefly upon Lord Castlereagh to advocate their measures. In the House of Lords, when the King's message was considered, Lord Clare took the opportunity to deliver an elaborate speech in favour of the proposed Union, announcing his conviction that nothing else could save the kingdom, and eventually uphold the stability of the British Empire. The speech was in effect a review of the whole course of Irish history, the facts and incidents of which he used as the foundation for an argument of great power directed to establish the conclusion that it was to the protection of Great Britain, and therefore to Union, as the most effective means of rendering this protection certain, that the descendants of the English settlers must look for the security of themselves and of their titles to the landed estates, which by the grants of the Crown had been transferred to them from the original native proprietors.*

Lord Clare's speech:

---

could not be adequately represented by any summary, consistent with the limits of this treatise. Besides, it ought to be considered not by itself, but in conjunction with the three other speeches which followed and supplemented it.

* Lord Clare's speech was of great length, having occupied four hours in the delivery. A summary of it, given in the former edition of this treatise, I have in the present omitted; as that was—what any other that could be substituted for it of suitable length must also be—necessarily imperfect.

Motion for Address asking for dissolution

The Opposition, perceiving that the Government commanded a majority in each House of Parliament upon the main question, endeavoured to compel a Dissolution, and with this view they proposed in the House of Commons an Address to the Crown, praying that a new Parliament should be called before any final arrangement was concluded in relation to an Union. The motion was defeated by a majority of 150 votes against 104.

Propriety of dissolution considered

The question whether, when a great political measure is about to be submitted to Parliament, there ought to be a Dissolution, so as to enable the constituencies returning members to the House of Commons to express their opinions in reference to it, cannot be answered upon principles of abstract right. In every instance the reply must depend upon considerations of expediency, upon the circumstances of each particular occasion, and the conclusions proper to be drawn from them. To lay down that in no instance is it proper for the House of Commons to adopt a measure new in its nature and of importance without an appeal to the electoral body, would reduce its position to that of a congress of agents for special interests, who have continually to ask the direction of their principals. The question, however, then before the Irish Parliament must be held to have been one of those respecting which, unless the peculiar social condition of the country forbade a

Dissolution,* the constituencies might justly claim to be consulted, for it involved no less than the extinction of national independence. At the same time there is no reason to think that, if there had been a Dissolution, the balance of parties in the House of Commons would have been altered, so decided was, and would in that event have been, the influence of Ministers among those who dictated the representation of the close seats.

When the motion for a Dissolution was defeated, the Resolutions framed to define the terms of Union were proceeded with, and in the end they were, with some unimportant alterations, voted by both Houses of the Irish Parliament. Immediately after they had been thus passed in Ireland they were referred to the British Parliament by a message from the King, in reply to which an Address was voted in the Commons, and afterwards adopted by the Lords, which was to the effect that after a few alterations and additions, which they had found it necessary to suggest, they considered the Resolutions which had been passed by the Lords and Commons of Ireland fit to form the

Resolutions passed.

---

* Considerations of this character were the reasons assigned by the Duke of Wellington for not advising a Dissolution of Parliament before introducing the Bill for Catholic Emancipation in 1829. (*Speech*, April 4 of that year; see also Sir Robert Peel's observations on the same matter in the House of Commons, March 6, 1829.)

Articles of Union between Great Britain and Ireland.

Motion for suspension of proceedings for Union.   While the Resolutions transmitted from Ireland were under consideration in the British House of Commons a motion was made in that House for an Address to the King, praying that he would be graciously pleased to direct his Ministers to suspend all proceedings on the Irish Union till the sentiments of the Irish people respecting the measure could be ascertained. The motion, it will be observed, is worded in a different manner from that which, with somewhat the same aim, had been proposed in the Irish House of Commons. The latter asked a Dissolution of Parliament, which would have ascertained the opinions of the electoral body; the former sought to test the sentiments of the people generally. The mode contemplated for doing this would seem to have been by having public meetings convened in the counties. In reference to the suggestion, Pitt, speaking against the motion, said, . . . 'I adhere to the opinion of the Parliament of Ireland, and I will, therefore, not consent to a convocation of primary assemblies and of bodies of men to vote addresses founded on French principles, arrayed as they would be against legislative authority and constitutional freedom. Even if we did resort to the people, who would take the expression of their opinion, given amidst tumult, in the fury of passion?' The motion was rejected by a majority of 236 votes to 30.

The arguments against the Resolutions in the British Parliament, so far as they were presented from an English point of view, had very much less force than those which were in Ireland urged from an Irish point of view. The addition of one hundred Irish Members would, it was said, increase the influence of the Crown, which was already too great, and might even injuriously affect the nature of the assembly into which they were introduced.* The strength of the case made by the English Opposition lay altogether in the assertion that the Resolutions transmitted from Ireland represented the will merely of Parliament, and not at all of the people. Had the Irish Parliament been so constituted as to have been fairly representative of the nation, and had it, being so constituted, voted the Resolutions by the same majorities as the existing Parliament had done, there seems no reason to doubt (so far as I can perceive) that all English political parties would

marginal note: Arguments against Union from English point of view weaker than from Irish.

---

* That Union would increase the power of the Crown was objected by Lord Holland in the House of Lords, and by Dr. Lawrence in the House of Commons. The offices and places which were then used to influence 300 Members of the Irish House of Commons would, the latter said, be available for the 100 to be sent to the Imperial Parliament. (*Ann. Reg.* for 1800, pp. 117–121.) Dr. Lawrence added that disturbance was to be apprehended from the quickness of disposition and propensity to duelling of these new Members. He had, on a former occasion, remarked that the Irish tendency to long speeches must embarrass the progress of business. (*Ann. Reg.* for 1799, p. 214.)

have been ready to give effect to them, and probably have also expressed their approval of them as tending to increase the strength of the Empire.*

Acts of Union passed.

After the Irish and British Parliaments had thus conclusively pronounced their decisions in favour of the measures of Government, nothing occurred in either assembly that need detain us. Bills for the purpose of effectuating Union and of defining its terms were brought forward in both Parliaments, went through all the requisite stages, and ultimately received the royal assent.

Act to compensate for disfranchised boroughs.

In Ireland the Act of Union was accompanied by another Act, which provided a pecuniary compensation whenever a borough was entirely disfranchised. Under its provisions £7500 (about the market price) was paid for each seat in 84 boroughs. As there were two Members for every borough, the total amount expended for this purpose amounted to £1,260,000. The compensation was paid to the persons by whom the members for the boroughs had been nominated, and who were therefore regarded as their owners, except in the instances of Swords (where it was laid out to found schools), and of three boroughs under the influence of the bishops of the dioceses in which they were situate (the compensation for these being paid to the Board of First Fruits, as an addition to funds they already held for the benefit of the Established Church).

---

* See Note LL of Appendix.

CHAPTER XX.

THE ACT OF UNION.

BY the Acts of the Parliaments of Great Britain and Ireland, which have been referred to in the last chapter, these kingdoms were from the 1st of January, 1801, united into one kingdom, under the name of the United Kingdom of Great Britain and Ireland. For this 'United Kingdom' a single Parliament was provided, and the succession to its Crown was declared to be the same as the succession which then stood limited for the Crown of Great Britain and Ireland, according to the existing law and to the terms of the Union between England and Scotland.

<small>Union.</small>

These Acts contained also a variety of provisions in reference to matters with which this treatise is not concerned. Thus they declared that the Churches of England and Ireland, as then by law established, should be united into one Protestant Episcopal Church, to be called the United Church of England and Ireland, and that the doctrine, worship, discipline, and government of the said United Church should be and

<small>Provisions of Acts.</small>

remain in full force for ever, as the same were then by law established for the Church of England.

United Parliament.

The constitution of the Parliament of the United Kingdom was to be as follows:—It was, like the separate Parliaments which were about to be fused together, to consist of two Houses— a House of Lords and a House of Commons. The former was to be composed of all the Peers of Great Britain, with the addition of thirty-two Peers from Ireland, of whom four were to be Lords Spiritual, taken by a prescribed rotation each year from the Bench of Bishops, and of twenty-eight Lords Temporal, elected for life by the Peers of Ireland. The latter House was to be composed of members from the same counties, cities, and boroughs of Great Britain, as were before entitled to representation, with the addition of one hundred Members from Ireland. Of the hundred Irish Members sixty-four were to be returned by the thirty-two counties (two for each), four by the cities of Dublin and Cork (two for each), one for the University of Trinity College,* and one for each of thirty-one cities and boroughs, selected as being the most important. Of the latter, twenty-three were, and after the Union

---

* It is singular that the University should be described as the University of Trinity College, instead of, as it had previously been more properly, 'the University of Dublin.' The College was, however, in its statutes termed *Mater Universitatis*.

continued to be, close boroughs. The power to create new Irish peerages was reserved for the Crown, subject to the condition that so long as the number of Irish Peers, who were not also British Peers, was more than one hundred, the power should not be exercised except upon the extinction of three peerages, nor when the number of such Peers was reduced below one hundred, except upon the extinction of one peerage.

As a measure to deal with the constitution of a new Legislature the Act of Union was complete, and carried out all that was designed by the statesmen who proposed it. As a measure of policy it was incomplete, and did not carry out all that was by them intended should be done. There seems to me no doubt that they contemplated to supplement the Act of Union by enactments of the Imperial Parliament which, both in Great Britain and Ireland, should remove all remaining disabilities that affected persons who professed the Roman Catholic religion, and in Ireland should also make a provision for their clergy, and, probably, at the same time do away with the abuses attending the collection of tithes in kind by substituting a pecuniary composition.*

Union intended to be supplemented by other measures.

---

* Measures of this character were, after the Union, actually in preparation, when the opposition of the King led to their abandonment. (See Note MM of Appendix.)

Proportion of representation. If we consider the Act of Union merely in connection with the first of these objects, namely, constituting an Imperial Legislature, the proportion of representation allotted to Ireland in the House of Commons cannot, it seems to me, be considered unfair. The entire number of Members was to be 658, and of these Ireland would retain 100. No proposition to increase the number to be allotted to Ireland was brought forward in the Irish Parliament.

Lord Lieutenancy continued. The Act of Union did not lead to any alteration in the executive department of government in Ireland. A chief governor, under the name of Justiciary, or Deputy, or Lord Lieutenant, had, from the time of Henry II. (with the exception of some intervals when Lords Justices acted in the same capacity), been appointed; and, at least from the reign of Edward I., the Governor had been assisted by a Privy Council. In Scotland, even when the Crowns were united, there had never been a Lord Lieutenant; but there was, before the Union of that kingdom with Great Britain, a Privy Council. After the Union, however, this body was discontinued, and the country was governed from London, without either a Lord Lieutenant or a local Privy Council. In Ireland the example thus set at the Scottish Union was not followed; nor, with the imperfect means of communication then existing between Ireland and London, could it well have been. Accordingly, both the office of Lord Lieutenant and the Privy Council were continued in the same relations to each other as they were before.*

In narrating the proceedings connected with the enactment of the Union I have endeavoured to present the arguments for and against it, founded upon its supposed expediency or inexpediency, such as they were at the time urged. An objection, however, of a different character, going to the very foundation of the whole legislation, and equally applicable, whether it were dictated by a wise or by an unwise policy, remains to be noticed. *An objection to Union not yet noticed.*

According to this objection the Irish Parliament was not competent to enact its own Union with the Parliament of Great Britain. The reason assigned for the proposition may be summed up in a few words. The Union, it was said, of one Legislature with another was equivalent to a merger of the weaker of the united Legislatures; merger differed in nothing from destruction; *Alleged incapacity of Irish Parliament.*

---

* A letter of George III. to Addington, when the latter was Prime Minister, has been cited by Lord John Russell, May 17, 1850 (*Hansard*, cxi, p. 172), in which, speaking of filling the office of Lord Lieutenant, the King says that his opinion is clearly that, although, perhaps, the cessation of the office may thereafter be proper, at that time it was necessary to fill it, but with a person who shall clearly understand 'that the Union has closed the reign of Irish jobs; that he is a kind of President of the Council there; and that the civil patronage may be open to his recommendation, but must entirely be decided in England.' (See, as to the means of intercourse with England at that time, Note NN of Appendix.)

and self-destruction was inconsistent with the object of its original institution. Parliament, elected to make laws, not legislators, occupied towards the people, or at least towards its constituents, a fiduciary position; legislative power was a sacred deposit entrusted to its care; and a deposit committed to a trustee he was bound to preserve in the same condition as it was when he received it.

Reply to objection. To this reasoning it was replied that the principles assumed in it had been overruled by a decision of conclusive authority. The objection, it was obvious, equally applied to the Union of Scotland with Great Britain. The Scottish Parliament had no legislative capacity in 1707 which the Irish did not possess in 1800. And not only was the objection applicable to the Scottish Union, but it had at the time actually been made by those who opposed the Union. A protest was then drawn and signed on behalf of the dissenting minority, which was expressed in the following terms—'... the members of a Legislature are mere administrators of their trust, and not the owners or masters of a people. They are not entitled to bargain away the nation they represent, and make it cease to exist.'* Nevertheless, the English and Scotch Parliaments, under the guidance of their ablest

---

* See Lord Stanhope's *History of the Reign of Queen Anne to the Peace of Utrecht*, 3rd edition, p. 260.

statesmen, had enacted the Union without the slightest misgiving as to its validity. Nor had the precedent thus established been since then impugned by either statesman or jurist, upon any suggestion that what was enacted exceeded the jurisdiction of the Parliaments: on the contrary, every subsequent expression of legal opinion had been in favour of their power to do what had been done, and of the indisputable effect of their acts. Nor, it was said, could the principles on which their opinion rested—although the language of some eminent writers upon political science seemed in conflict with them—be justly contradicted. Nations, all would admit, could unite: if they could, there must be in each some authority to contract for Union, and to negotiate and determine the conditions of Union: among these to fix where, in future, was to reside the right to legislate for the composite realm to be created. What that authority should be might, of course, be expressly defined in the original framing of the constitution of the country; but, if this were silent, where could the jurisdiction so well be placed as where the power to make laws for the community was vested— in the case of an absolute monarchy, in the Sovereign; in the case of a limited monarchy, in the Sovereign and Parliament? Union was but a treaty between two independent kingdoms.

Moreover, according to the constitutional principles accepted by the highest English legal *Further reply to objection.*

authorities, the legislative jurisdiction of Parliament was of a high and transcendent nature. It had in England been exercised, as if no limits to its extent were recognised, whenever any emergency called for it. Thus it had there changed the ruling dynasty and remodelled the succession to the Crown; it had superseded the establishment of one form of religion, and declared that another, widely different, was to be professed by the nation. Even its own constitution had been altered by the English Parliament, which had at one time abridged, at another prolonged, the period for which, when elected, it was to endure; and had both annulled old and created new conditions in respect of the right to vote for the representatives of the people.

Further reasons for holding Parliament competent. In addition to these reasons, offered in answer to the allegation of incapacity on the part of the Irish Parliament, it was also pointed out that, while no one ventured to allege that to unite Ireland with Great Britain was impossible, those who denied the jurisdiction of the Irish Parliament made it so—for to what other authority could recourse be had for the purpose? Would it be said, to the electoral body? But (to say nothing of excluding the Peers) how were they more competent than the representatives whom they returned? They were a portion only, and but a small portion, of the people; and if Parliament could not give away the rights of the whole, how could they? They were no whit more constituted for such an object than Parliament. Then were the whole mass of the people to exercise a sort of dormant sovereignty? But how was this to be done, when the Constitution had made no provision to define the persons by whom, or the mode in which, the requisite proceedings were to be carried out?

The question of the jurisdiction of the Irish Parliament to enact its Union with the English Parliament is sometimes confounded with another question, which has been already discussed, namely, whether it was right to take this course without reference being made to the constituencies returning Members to the House of Commons. It is unnecessary to observe that the questions are entirely distinct. Parliament might have power, yet not be morally justified in using it without consulting those of whom so important a component part as the House of Commons was representative. And, on the other hand, the proceeding might deserve censure without, in the slightest degree, impairing the validity of the act done.*

Question of jurisdiction distinct from propriety of a proceeding.

Page 220.

To the objection urged against the jurisdiction of the Irish Parliament, now noted, and the objections to the policy of the measure itself, which have been already stated, the opposition

No compromise proposed.

---

* See further, as to the competency of the Irish Parliament to enact the Union of Ireland with Great Britain, Note O O of Appendix.

which it experienced in the British and Irish Parliaments was confined. No third course, no intermediate scheme between the existing legislative system and complete Union, no compromise of any kind, was proposed. The Parliaments voted simply upon the alternatives of Union and the existing legislative system. And this is the more remarkable, because, before they met, a very able pamphlet against the proposed Union—written by Richard Jebb, afterwards a judge of the Irish Court of Queen's Bench—which attracted much attention at the time, had admitted that if an Irish Parliament were allowed to remain, its continuance might well be accompanied by a definitive treaty regulating trade and commerce, and by an obligation, in case of war, to ratify the policy of Great Britain, and, in case of legislation upon the subject of religion, to have the concurrence of the British Parliament.*

Any scheme for a limited Parliament unpopular. It is, however, not difficult to understand why this should be. From the time when the Duke of Portland and Lord Shelburne desired a restricted parliamentary jurisdiction for Ireland, and were deterred from bringing forward any plan of the kind by the resistance it would have encountered

---

* Cooke wrote to Lord Castlereagh that he thought Jebb's pamphlet favourable to the cause; that it was cried up in Dublin and talked of; that he admitted all that was wanted; was against an Irish Parliament with imperial powers, and for a Parliament with local and municipal, cut down to the powers of a grand jury. (*Castlereagh Correspondence*, vol. ii., p. 50.)

in the Irish Parliament, hindrances in the way of such a proposal, instead of abating, had increased. A scheme of this character would, in 1782, have been merely the alteration of one form of subordination into another: now it would supersede and take the place of a Legislature of supreme authority, entitled to deal with every subject, whether external or internal, that could concern the interests of Ireland. To submit to restrictions was regarded as an explicit confession of inferiority. 'Are we,' exclaimed Sheridan, speaking under an apprehension that some intermediate scheme might be proposed by Pitt, and giving utterance to sentiments prevalent in Ireland—' are we to be told that Union will not wholly dissolve the Legislature of Ireland; that independence will survive Union, though in a modified state; that Parliament will be left to judge of the local affairs of Ireland? Really, sir, this seems almost too much for men's feelings—a Parliament! a sort of national Vestry for the parish of Ireland, sitting in a kind of mock legislative capacity, after being ignobly degraded from the rank of representatives of an independent people, and deprived of the functions of an inquisitorial power, exercising and enjoying the greatest authority that any Parliament can possess.'*

---

*Speech in the English House of Commons, January 23, 1799, already referred to. (*Collected Speeches*, vol. iii., p. 279.)

Examples of limited legislatures.

A constitution which confined a local Parliament to making laws for its own people—such laws to be operative only within the boundaries of the soil which the people occupied and in respect of their internal rights and interests, while all their external relations were regulated by a different Legislature—was not without examples at this time. Such systems existed in the Isle of Man, Guernsey, and Jersey. But that they did so exist was not calculated to recommend them to the Irish Parliament. There were few notions more certain to provoke resentment than to class Ireland as an additional Channel island, and offer it only such privileges as were suitable to a community whose proximity and relative unimportance entitled it to no higher position than an appendage to England.*

Observations of Canning.

So far as I have observed, there was in the Irish Parliament not merely no proposal of any scheme intermediate between the existing legislative system and Union, but no allusion to such either in the debates of 1799 or in those of 1800. In the British Parliament some suggestion seems to have been made that whatever settlement or security was proposed to be attained by

---

* Grattan, on one occasion, speaking of the Parliament of the Isle of Man, described it as 'free from the influence of opinion, free from the influence of duty, directed by prejudices, and unincumbered by knowledge.' (*Speech*, Jan. 15, 1800.)

The Act of Union.

Union could be equally well provided by arrangement between the British and Irish Parliaments; and Canning thus expressed himself in reference to it :—. . . 'With this argument I am so far from agreeing, that I would almost be satisfied to rest the whole question on this point singly, and to give up the plea of Union altogether, if it does not appear plain that there can be no mode of arrangement devised for the several possible differences and disagreements between the two kingdoms short of Union, which will not take away from the Parliament of Ireland even the shadow of independence, and deprive it of all freedom and dignity in the points the most essential to its very being as a Parliament.' He illustrated this assertion by the position in which the Irish Parliament would be placed under a limited system, in respect of one of its most important functions—voting supplies—to which it would have to contribute proportionally, without any power to give or withhold: a position, he said, consistent with the Irish House of Commons being 'a grave and respectable council,' but not 'a House of Commons according to the genuine spirit of the British Constitution.' *

In the speeches of Sheridan and Canning, which have been cited, they referred to their connection with Ireland. The former said 'that his dear *Views of Sheridan and Canning compared.*

---

* Speech of Canning, April 22, 1799; and see, for further extracts from it, Note P P of Appendix.

country had claims upon him which he was not more proud to acknowledge than ready, to the full measure of his ability, to liquidate;' the latter described himself as 'connected with Ireland by many ties of blood and of affection.' * Agreeing in attachment to the country, both desired to maintain its dignity and importance, but they disagreed as to the means by which this was to be accomplished. Sheridan would attain the object by preserving the Irish Parliament in all the freedom and independence which it had won in 1782; Canning, by incorporating it into a greater assembly with the consequent acquisition of more important functions. Each, from his own point of view, condemned those schemes which, either by provisions introduced into the Constitution or by a permanent contract, would limit the powers and impair the authority of the local Legislature.

<small>Objections to limited Parliament from an English point of view.</small>

But the objections to a limited Parliament for Ireland were not confined to such as had their origin in Irish national sentiment, or a considera-

---

* Sheridan was by birth Irish. The Sheridan family had been settled in the country for at least two generations. The Canning family was possessed of landed property in Ulster from the reign of James I. One ancestor of George Canning was killed in the rebellion of 1641, and another attainted by the Irish Parliament of James II. His mother was Irish, and her father's family was one of several of Irish race which, until the time of Cromwell, had retained lands in Connaught. Canning himself was born and educated in England.

tion of Irish interests. From an English point of view others disclosed themselves. These reached to the very existence of a Parliament in Ireland. They saw in it a rival, almost certain to be successful, raised up to contest supremacy with Great Britain. The local Legislature would be visibly present to the Irish people, its members constantly coming in contact with them, and its measures consulting only for their welfare, while England and the British Parliament would appear to them occupied wholly with affairs which but feebly and circuitously could affect their interests. Attention, respect, attachment, would be concentrated on what was near and of immediate influence, not on what was remote. Proximity would enable the satellite to obscure the luminary, however superior in dimensions, upon which it was attendant.

CHAPTER XXI.

RETROSPECT.

[1172–1800.]

Retrospect THE period proposed for the limit of this treatise has been now reached, and it only remains to sum up the results which have been ascertained.*

Pages 3, 7. Legislative assemblies, modelled upon contemporary English institutions of a similar character, were convened in Ireland by the kings of England, certainly from, and probably before, the reign of King John. At first they were termed Councils, afterwards Parliaments. Originally all who attended them were personally summoned. In the reign of Edward the First counties were for the first time empowered to send representatives. In the next reign a similar privilege was extended to cities and towns. The number of counties, cities, and towns thus privileged increased along with, and in proportion Page 11. to, the extension of English rule. For more

---

* In the subsequent part of this chapter references are made on the margin to the previous pages where the occurrences, of which a summary is given, have been already narrated.

than a century all members of these assemblies, whether summoned or elected, met and deliberated together. At a later date they are found divided into two Houses, one of which assumed the form of a House of Peers, composed of Lords Spiritual and Temporal, and the other of a House of Commons, composed of the representatives of the counties, cities, and towns to which writs for the holding of elections were from time to time directed.

While the principle of representative government was thus early acknowledged, its development was nevertheless, in some respects, slow and imperfect. Until the reign of Henry VIII. the natives were practically excluded from the Councils and Parliaments; and until the reign of Elizabeth two great provinces—Ulster and Connaught—which had remained in the possession of the natives, not having been reduced into shires, had never enjoyed more than occasional representation, and then only to a trifling extent. Under this queen seventeen counties were either created or reduced into their present form, of which a part before her death, and all after her death, were brought into the Parliamentary system. *Page 13.* *Page 15.*

The Parliament of James I. (summoned in 1613) differed from its predecessors. One hundred more members were returned to its House of Commons than had been to the last House of Commons of Queen Elizabeth. No *Appendix N, and page 17.*

qualification of race or religion was required from either the electors or elected; and persons of English, Scotch, and Irish descent, and of such denominations of religion as were then recognised among the people, were substantially represented.

Page 19. Superior to former Parliaments, in the number and constitution of its representative character, this Parliament was also superior to them in the spirit which animated its enactments. Its predecessors, acting as if they were the legislatures, not of the entire people, but of a colony planted in a hostile country, endeavoured by the most stringent laws to separate the native Irish and their descendants from the English settlers and their descendants. Now every distinction of race was abolished, and the announcement was made that thenceforward all the inhabitants of the island were taken into the protection of the Crown, that so they might grow into one nation.

Page 21. The constitution of the Irish Parliament at this time was apparently an exact counterpart of that of the English Parliament. It had a House of Lords and a House of Commons; and the forms and procedure of these Houses were modelled upon the forms and procedure of similar institutions previously established in England. In both instances nothing that could affect the well-being of the people, for whose interests the Parliaments consulted, was expressly excluded from the jurisdiction. But in reality the resemblance between the two Parliaments was confined to external appearance. Their capacity of action was very different. The English was wholly free, without superior, and not liable to interference from any other Legislature. The Irish was admittedly subject to the restraints imposed by Poynings' law, and was by the provisions of that law obliged, before it could pass any valid enactment, to obtain the approval of the Privy Council of Ireland and of the Privy Council of England. It was also checked in its action by the knowledge that the highest legal authority in England had affirmed the right of the English Parliament to make laws for Ireland, and that it was thus exposed to the danger of having its policy interfered with by another authority, which claimed concurrent, or, it might be, paramount jurisdiction. *Page 14.* *Page 31.*

Restrictions of this character would probably have been acquiesced in if the Irish Parliament had continued as weak and incapable of resistance as it had been before the time of James. But it gradually grew in strength and importance; and with improvement in its condition came dissatisfaction with a system which subjected it to external control. Some time, however, elapsed before discontent openly manifested itself. From 1615, when James's Parliament was prorogued, to 1634, no meeting of Parliament took place; and from 1634 to 1640 Parliament was awed into silence by Strafford. With his *Pp. 35, 36.*

removal from the Viceroyalty freedom of debate and procedure came, and sentiments and demands previously restrained from utterance found expression. The House of Commons at once proceeded to assert the rights which, it alleged, either rightfully belonged, or ought to be conceded, to the Irish Parliament. It resolved that all statutable law to bind the people of Ireland should proceed from the authority of their own Legislature.

Page 40.   This resolution was not, however, followed by any practical consequences. The Rebellion of 1641, and the subsequent civil war, wholly absorbed the attention of all interested in political affairs. Under the Commonwealth no legislative assembly met in Ireland; and the English Parliament arbitrarily reconstructed the entire social system, summoning, however, in 1645, members from Ireland to the English Parliament.

Page 41.   After events of such magnitude, the comparatively unimportant efforts of a local Legislature to elevate its position ceased to attract observation, and gradually faded from men's minds. There is no appearance of their having been even remembered at the Restoration.

Page 43.   Under Charles the Second the English Parliament assumed the authority which the Irish Parliament in the time of his father had refused to acknowledge, and proceeded in express terms

Page 52.   to legislate for Ireland. Under William III. and under Anne the same course was persisted in;

and under the First George the Parliament of Great Britain, which had then taken the place of the Parliament of England, in order to place beyond doubt the extent of jurisdiction which it claimed, declared in distinct language that the King's Majesty, by and with the advice and consent of the Lords and Commons of Great Britain in Parliament, had, and of right ought to have, full power and authority to make laws of sufficient force to bind the kingdom and people of Ireland.

_{Page 88.}

Hence from the Restoration (A.D. 1660), the legislative system operative in Ireland was a divided empire. Both the Parliament of Ireland and the Parliament of England, or (when that ceased to exist) the Parliament of Great Britain, asserted and exercised a right to make laws for the island and its people. In theory there was no boundary-line to define their respective spheres of jurisdiction: in practice there was. Poynings' law enabled the English Government, through the agency of the Privy Councils in England and Ireland, to prevent the Parliament of Ireland from legislating upon any subject which it desired to reserve, until 1707 for the Parliament of England, and afterwards for the Parliament of Great Britain. As a general rule, whatever was of such a nature that the decision in reference to it must be a matter of indifference to the English people was left with the Irish Parliament; whatever might be so dealt with as to injure English interests was withdrawn from it. Under the former class came most of the internal affairs of Ireland: under the latter its trade with foreign nations.

These arrangements, which were in force from 1660 to the accession of George III. averted conflict between the two Parliaments; in other respects they worked ill. Ireland sent no members to the English Parliament; its interests were there unrepresented. The result was that English and Scotch interests were alone considered; and that, whenever these appeared to be adverse to Irish interests, the latter were no more regarded than those of one of the continental kingdoms.

Page 44. To serve English agriculture, the importation into England of Irish cattle was prohibited; to serve English commerce, no Irish ship could enter a colonial port; no colonial ship enter an Irish port: to serve English manufactures, no
Page 52. wool or woollen goods could be exported from Ireland except to England. Few, indeed, are the English statutes relating to Ireland of a date before 1780 for which the motive of promoting Irish, as distinguished from English, interests can be suggested.

Until the end of George the Second's reign, the Irish Parliament was concerned with little beside internal affairs. All its statutes then in force related to subjects of this nature. Restriction upon the range will injuriously affect the character of legislation. In a great empire, and, therefore, in its Parliament, if it be so constituted as to be representative, the grandeur and multiplicity of interests expand and liberalise policy; it is the consequence not of one single impulse, but of a number of impulses reciprocally acting upon each other; and their diversity ensures that the result shall be marked by moderation. Society, in such cases, becomes subdivided into a number of differing sections of opinion, and, without a combination, difficult to effect among them, measures of injustice and oppression cannot be enacted. But of such variety of influences a narrow area and confined scope of action deprived the Irish Parliament. Its views were contracted to the measure of its condition. Never coming in contact with anything higher or nobler, it reflected only the passions and prejudices with which it was encircled. At their bidding it framed its legislation, and consigned the weaker, although much the larger, portion of the people to a state of hopeless inferiority.*

When George III. succeeded to the throne, the consequences of the legislative system which was then operative in Ireland were distinctly apparent. The English Parliament had so regulated external affairs as to extinguish the

Page 90.

---

* In one of his speeches Grattan describes Ireland, before 1782, as 'a squabbling, fretful sectary, perplexing her little wits, and firing her furious statutes, with bigotry, sophistry, disabilities, and death.' (*Speech*, 16th April, 1782.)

trade and commerce of Ireland; the Irish Parliament had so ordered its internal affairs that the majority of the people were subject to intolerable oppression. The country was, as might be expected, everywhere poor and depressed.

<small>Page 163.</small>

<small>Page 111.</small> Out of these circumstances originated a movement which, having obtained success in some demands of inferior importance, directed its energies at first against the commercial legislation of the British Parliament, and then against the jurisdiction over Irish affairs which that Parliament assumed. Members of the Irish House of Commons who would in any legislative assembly, however illustrious, have attained eminence, became its leaders. Under their guidance it made rapid progress, and won almost unanimous favour and sympathy from the people.

A struggle of this character appeals to, and seldom fails to call forth, whatever capacity may be possessed by those engaged in it. The debates and discussions of the time rival in eloquence and thought those of the same period in the British Legislature. Parliament rose to an intellectual greatness, with which its position of imperfect power and inferior dignity was in-
<small>Page 108.</small> consistent. Expanding beyond the limits at that time prescribed for its action, it could no longer endure the restrictions that confined it.

At this crisis the Volunteers came forward for the defence of the country. During their training they still pursued their ordinary avocations, and, living among their fellow-subjects, were imbued with similar opinions. Self-constituted, and at their own expense armed, organised, and maintained, they were beyond the control of the British Government. Subject to no external restraint, acting only under the impulse of their own sentiments, they became the champions of the prevalent discontent. Page 110.

In 1780 the Irish Parliament allied itself with the Volunteers. Acting in concert, both demanded from the British Parliament commercial freedom. The demand was conceded. Limitations which then fettered trade from Ireland with the Colonies, with the continent of Europe, and with Great Britain, were annulled. In 1782 the same confederates demanded legislative independence. They were again successful. The exclusive right of the King, Lords, and Commons of Ireland to bind by their laws that kingdom and its people, as well in respect of external as internal affairs, was unequivocally acknowledged. Page 112. Page 133.

This admission placed the Parliament of Ireland in the same relation to its people as the Parliament of Great Britain was to the people of England and Scotland. The two Parliaments became thenceforward co-ordinate institutions. Another measure of equal importance followed, which provided that the control exercised over Irish legislation by the Privy Council of Ireland and the Privy Council of Great Britain should Page 136.

cease. In every particular, except one, the Legislatures of the two kingdoms were to have similar powers and similar procedure. The one exception was, that whereas a Bill passed by the Houses of Lords and Commons required in Great Britain only the Royal Assent to become an Act of Parliament, there was needed in Ireland that it should also be transmitted to England, and be thence returned under the Great Seal of Britain.

Page 137.

The increased power and jurisdiction conceded to the Irish Parliament in 1782 augmented its dignity and importance. It became in these respects, as it had before been in intellectual power, not unworthy to be the Legislature of an independent kingdom. Its internal constitution was, however, and continued to be, in one important respect, imperfect. Its representative character remained unduly narrow. None but Protestants could sit in either the House of Lords or the House of Commons, and only Protestants could vote for members of the latter. Even as to Protestants, the representation in the House of Commons, owing to the excessive number of boroughs subject to the nomination of a few persons, was quite inadequate.

Page 163.

In 1793 one of these defects was remedied by repealing the law which rendered persons professing the religion of the Church of Rome unable to vote at elections for members of the House of Commons. But the others remained, and, so

Page 177.

long as a local Legislature was continued, were likely to remain, since those on whom they conferred exclusive privileges possessed paramount political power in the House of Commons, and were consequently reluctant to do anything that would impair their own influence in that assembly. _{Page 178.}

The imperfections in the constitution of the Irish Parliament, and the improbability that their removal, if this were to depend upon its own motion, would be accomplished, recommended the substitution of a new legislative system for that which had been called into operation from 1782. At the same time other considerations of even more weight, and with even more force, were gradually conducting public opinion to the same conclusion. These considerations were suggested by events which had occurred in connection with, and were caused by the relations of, the Irish Parliament to the Empire.

Whenever, as was at this time the case in the instance of Great Britain and Ireland, two Parliaments of equal and co-ordinate authority, each framing the laws of an independent kingdom, co-exist within the same realm, it follows as a necessary consequence that a large range of subjects must be submitted to them concurrently. Whatever concerns the protection of the whole Commonwealth, relates to its resources, or may affect its interest, comes within this category: so also do all arrangements connected with trade or other dealings between the nations thus separately represented. The character of many of these subjects is such that the Legislatures to decide upon them may disagree without any evil consequences; but in the case of others their concurrence in action is essential, not merely to the well-being, but even to the safety, of the State.

Under such circumstances, it is obvious that unless upon the latter class of subjects—those where conflicting proceedings may endanger the welfare of the Empire—an agreement can be ensured between the co-ordinate Parliaments, the working of the legislative system will not be successful: and this result, it may as a general rule be laid down, can be reckoned certain only when there exists a general harmony of interests and notions between the kingdoms which return the Parliaments, or such consciousness of comparative weakness on the part of one as may suppress any manifestation of its dissent when it disagrees with the other.

In the case of Ireland and Great Britain, neither of the conditions which have been suggested as alone calculated to produce unanimity in legislation was fulfilled. There were in their position relatively to each other, in their history and circumstances, causes for difference of sentiment and opinion; and Ireland was, both physically and intellectually, too great to submit passively. The consequences which might be expected ensued. Questions arose in respect to matters of the utmost importance, on which it was necessary that the British and Irish Parliaments should, each separately, pronounce its judgment. Disagreement, total and distinct, was manifested in the decisions to which they came respecting them. Other questions, even more momentous, whose solution must affect the highest imperial interests, either actually impended, or were expected to arise, on which similar disagreement was feared; while foreign war and internal rebellion lay in wait to take advantage of whatever weakness might thus be caused. Pages 154, 160.

If, then, as we have seen, the inefficiency of the Irish Parliament, as at that time constituted, to deal with the social wants of Ireland tended to procure its condemnation in that country, these events, and the dangers whose existence they revealed, tended to the same result in England. Two separate and distinct classes of objection assailed the existing legislative system. Ultimately their combined influence induced the British Government to determine that alteration was indispensable.

If there was to be change, what was it to be? The dangers which formed in England the chief motive to desire it arose from the independence of the Irish Parliament and the extent of its jurisdiction. If these were abridged, it would seem that the dangers could be averted. But to procure from the Irish Parliament the acceptance of restrictions upon its legislative authority was thought to be impossible. The obstacles in the way of any

measure of the kind were perceived to be insuperable. It would have been the revival of a policy
Page 134. which had been tried, which had upon trial been found impossible to uphold, and which accordingly been unequivocally renounced in 1782, alike by the Parliament of Great Britain and the Parliament of Ireland, apparently with the concurrence of every statesman of eminence in either country.

When restriction was rejected Union presented itself, and was accepted as the only alternative.
Page 225. The Parliament of Great Britain and the Parliament of Ireland concurred in the enactment which now defines the relations of the two countries. Whatever were the objèctions to the measure on other grounds, it met the needs which then the most urgently required to have provision made for them. Incorporating together the kingdoms, before separate, it rendered, as far as human precaution could, their connection indissoluble: fusing in one their distinct Legislatures, it secured that local jealousies and prejudices should be displaced by the more enlightened dictates of an imperial policy; while for divided counsels and discordant action would be substituted the unity of design, resulting from a single authority representing the will and advising for the welfare of the whole Empire.

Thus the legislative systems operative in Ireland since the accession of James I., when more enlarged ideas as to what should be their nature began to prevail, have successively—if we omit from consideration the interruption caused by their suspension under the Commonwealth, and the illegal assembly held in 1689 under James II.—assumed the forms of a local Parliament subject to restrictions, of a local Parliament free from limitation, and of an Imperial Parliament in which Ireland is represented. The constitution of the first was framed upon the supposition that Ireland was inferior to, and dependent on, at first England, and afterwards Great Britain, and that its subordination ought to be represented in the position of its Legislature: the constitution of the second admitted the equality in dignity of the two kingdoms, and sought to represent it by establishing the independence of their respective Legislatures: the constitution of the third also recognised the equality of the two kingdoms, and, regarding any relations between them except independence or Union as inconsistent with its recognition, created one United Kingdom with one supreme Legislature. The working and results of two of these constitutions, and the reasons which led to the adoption of the third, appear in the foregoing pages: the working and results of the third lie outside the scope of this treatise.

APPENDIX.

NOTES AND ILLUSTRATIONS.

I HAVE placed in the Appendix references to records and authorities which, from their length, would have been unsuitable as foot-notes. I have also reserved for the Appendix observations in relation to some important subjects intended to assist in forming a correct estimate of the events narrated, which yet might not be considered to lie strictly within the scope of this treatise.

The notes from A to P are concerned with the early history of Irish Legislative Assemblies, from the Invasion of Henry II. to their full development under James I. Historical investigation during this period is impeded by the loss of important records, the imperfect nature of many of those that remain, and the brief and unsatisfactory character of the contemporary notices of events which have been preserved. Hence, as might be expected, there has been disagreement on various points among the historical writers who have treated of the early Irish Councils and Parliaments. Controversy as to their nature and proceedings began when doubt was raised as to the jurisdiction of the English Parliament to legislate for Ireland; the tendency of those who advocated this claim being to depreciate, and of those who denied it to magnify, the dignity and importance of the assemblies called for legislative purposes in Ireland during the three centuries succeeding the Invasion. It is inconsistent with the plan of this treatise to enter into a critical examination of the evidence bearing on the questions raised during the progress of the controversy: references are, however, given to the works in which they have been discussed. At the head of these their learning will always place the tracts of Bolton and Mayart (referred to in Chapter V., *supra*). They will be found in the *Hibernica* of Harris, published at Dublin in 1750. Next in importance are Molyneux's *Case of Ireland*, published at Dublin in 1698, and the answers to it. The later authors who have thrown most light upon the subject are Lord Mountmorres in his *History of the Principal Transactions of the Irish Parliament from the year 1634 to 1666*, published in London, 1792; Monck Mason, in his *Essay on the Antiquity and Constitution of Parliaments in Ireland*, published in Dublin, 1820; Lynch, in his *View of the Legal Institutions, Honorary Hereditary Offices, and Feudal Baronies Established in Ireland during the Reign of Henry II.*, published in London in 1830; and Hardiman, in the Introduction and Notes to his Edition of *The Statute of Kilkenny*, published by the Irish Archæological Society in 1863.

Note A, Page 3.

No better illustration of the difficulties obstructing historical research, which are referred to in the preceding remarks, can be found than the subject of this Note. Was there a Council, which accepted the laws of England as obligatory in Ireland, held under Henry II.? Mathew Paris distinctly says there was at Lismore. His words are:— . . Rex, antequam ab Hiberniâ rediret, apud Lismore Concilium congregavit, ubi leges Angliæ sunt gratanter receptæ, et juratoriâ cautione prestitâ confirmatæ. But against this statement is to be set the fact that Giraldus Cambrensis, who treats minutely of the very period, only makes mention of the Synod of Cashel, and that he describes that Synod as if it were concerned with merely ecclesiastical affairs (see p. 2, *supra*). Modern historians disagree in their conclusions upon the subject. Archbishop Ussher (*Parliaments of Ire-*

land) and Sir John Davis (*Discoverie*, &c.) follow Mathew Paris. Sir Richard Cox (*Anglicana Hibernia*) thinks that the only Council under Henry II. was at Cashel; and that, as the Bishop of Lismore, the Pope's Legate, presided at this Council, by some mistake the place of meeting has been confused with his title. Leland, in his *History*, avoids deciding between these opposing opinions. (See p. 76 of vol. i. of the 3rd ed., which is that adopted for reference in this treatise.)

NOTE B, PAGE 3.

The statute which (as stated at p. 3, *supra*) was referred to by Acts of Parliament of a much later date as having been enacted under Henry II., was one to enable a Chief Governor, in certain events on vacancy, to be appointed by certain great officers; and the Acts which so refer to it were of the reigns of Richard III. and Edward IV. (see Mason's *Essay*, p. 3, 18). In a petition to Richard II. it is stated that Parliaments met in Ireland from the time of Henry Fitz-Empress (Mason, p. 5); and the same assertion was made in the proceedings of a Parliament of Henry VI. (Leland, vol. ii. p. 509). Lord Coke attributes to Henry II. that he sent to Ireland a *modus tenendi parliamentum* (4th Inst. f. 12); but Selden and Prynne think that the *modus* was later in date than the reign of Henry II.

NOTE C, PAGE 5.

The writs and mandates for the early Irish Councils and Parliaments have been extracted from the original records, and printed by Lynch in his Treatise on *Feudal Dignities*.

It is curious that in a record cited by the same author (p. 43), of as early a date as the reign of Henry III., there is mention of the Commons of Ireland joining with the Magnates in legislating. This was subsequent to his son

Appendix. (afterwards Edward I.) being granted by him authority in Ireland, and while the Irish Government was administered, in the name of Prince Edward as 'Lord,' by de Ufford, as Justiciary, . . . provisum et statutum est de consilio Domini R. de Ufford capitalis Justiciarii Hiberniæ et aliorum fidelium Domini Edwardi qui sunt periti de ejus consilio et *totius communitatis* Hiberniæ.

NOTE D, PAGE 6.

Note D.   It is not clear whether the introduction, or, if already introduced by Henry II., the confirmation of English law in Ireland by John and Henry III., was, with the sanction of Councils in Ireland, or merely by ordinances founded upon the regal authority. Lord Coke thought that under John it was by a Parliament or Council, and cites in proof a recital in a patent of Henry III., which thus refers to John and his enactment of English law for Ireland: 'Leges regni nostri Angliæ, quas dominus Johannes rex, de communi omnium de Hibernia consensu teneri statuit in terra illa.' He treats 'de communi consensu,' &c., as meaning 'by Act of Parliament.' (Inst. iv. 349.) (See also as to John another record cited in *Calvin's Case*, 7 Rep., f. 22.)

Of Henry III. it is recorded that in his twelfth year, 'mandavit justiciario suo Hiberniæ, ut convocatis archiepiscopis, episcopis, baronibus et militibus ibidem coram eis legi faciat cartam regis Johannis, quam legi fecit, et jurari a magnatibus Hiberniæ de legibus et consuetudinibus Angliæ observandis, et quod leges illas teneant et observent.' (Cited by Lord Coke, Inst. iv. f. 350.)

Henry III. had previously, on his accession, granted Magna Charta to his Irish subjects (Leland, vol. i. pp. 200, 355); and had also in the first year of his reign confirmed to them the liberties granted by John. (See Molyneux, *Case*, p. 47.) By this king it was also ordered that the same Common Law *Writs* should run in Ireland as in England, . . . 'Volumus quod omnia brevia de communi jure quæ currunt in Angliâ similiter currant in Hibernia sub novo sigillo regis. (Cited by Molyneux, p. 53.)

Note E, Page 7.

In England the origin of a Council to advise the King has been traced earlier than Edward I.—according to Stubbs, to the minority of Henry III. The Council comprised, he says, the judicial staff, a number of bishops and barons, and other members, who, in default of any other official qualification, were simply counsellors (*History*, 4th ed., vol. ii., p. 265). Similar counsellors were in Ireland before the end of the same reign (see the record cited in Note C). Under Edward I. and Edward II. these counsellors obtained in England the title of the King's Ordinary or Privy Council (Hallam, *Mid. Ages*, 9th ed., vol. ii., pp. 269, 273). There also occurs in an Irish record of 17 & 18 Edw. II. the expression 'counseil nostre s. le roy en Irelande' (Mason, p. 12). The Irish Privy Council seems to have decided on private rights (see a Roll of 16 Ric. II., published in England in 1879, under the authority of the Master of the Rolls).

Note F, Page 8.

The account of Wogan's Parliament in the Liber Niger, preserved in Christ Church Cathedral, Dublin, is as follows: 'Justiciarius hic de communi consilio domini regis in hac terra, ad pacem firmius stabiliendam ordinavit et statuit generale parliamentum hic ad hunc diem. Et mandatum fuit archiepiscopis, episcopis, abbatibus, et prioribus, quorum præsentia videtur ad hoc esse necessaria, necnon et comitibus, baronibus et aliis optimatibus terræ hujus, videlicet unicuique eorum pro se, quod essent hic ad hunc diem. Et nihilominus, præceptum fuit vice-comitibus Dubliniæ, Louethiæ, Kildariæ, Waterfordiæ, Katherlagh, Kilkenniæ, et Ultoniæ, quod unusquisque eorum pro se, videlicet vice-comes in pleno comitatu suo, et senescallus in plena curia sua libertatis suæ, per assensum comitatus sui seu libertatis, eligi faceret duos de probioribus et discretioribus militibus de

Note F. singulis comitatibus et libertatibus, qui hic nunc interessent, plenam potestatem habentes, de tota communitate comitatus et libertatis ad faciendum,' &c. (Cited by Leland, vol. ii., p. 508.)

This assembly ordained that each county should have its sheriff; that the boundaries of the English territories should be defended from the natives by the lords who had charge of them; that absentee proprietors, as well as their tenants, should contribute to a military force; and that the settlers should assist each other in case of any invasion from the Irish. (See Leland, *History*, vol. i., p. 253.)

Before the Tudor kings the Parliament of Ireland, whose legislation was of most importance, was probably that which met at Kilkenny in 1367, summoned by Lionel, Duke of Clarence, son of Edward III., then Lord Lieutenant. This Parliament enacted the famous Statute of Kilkenny, designed to keep the English and Irish races separate, under which marriage, fosterage, gossipred, with the native Irish amounted to high treason. There is no record óf the persons who attended this Parliament. The last section, however, of the Statute mentions eight bishops by name as present in the Parliament. (See Hardiman's edition of the Statute, p. viii. n. and p. 119.)

Note G, Page 9.

Note G. Sir John Davis is one of those who depreciated the importance of the early Irish Councils and Parliaments. In his address to Sir Arthur Chichester (referred to at p. 18, *supra*) he says: . . . 'This extraordinary court' (*i.e.* Parliament) was not established in Ireland by authority out of England for many years after, in the form it now is, till towards the declining of King Edward the Second's reign. For before that time the meetings and consultations of the great Lords, with some of the Commons, for appeasing of dissensions among themselves, although they be called Parliaments in the ancient annals, yet being without orderly summons or formal proceedings, are rather to be called Parlies than Parliaments.' (Leland, vol. ii., p. 492.)

But it is only necessary to refer to Wogan's Parliament of 1295 (see p. 8, *supra*, and Note F) to see that this, if intended to apply to all the early Councils and Parliaments, cannot be considered accurate. Ussher, speaking of parliamentary assemblies, both before and after Wogan's Parliament, says: '. . . All Parliaments that we read of in the chronicles are not to be accounted to have been of the same nature; but a distinction may be observed therein of *petite* and *grande* Parliaments; for the name is sometimes given to such meetings as were Parlies rather than Parliaments.' (See Ussher's tract on *Parliaments*.)

It will be observed that in Wogan's and subsequent Parliaments counties outside the districts known as the Pale sent representatives. These were parts of the counties Dublin, Kildare, Meath, and Louth. The term Pale does not seem to have been used before the fifteenth century. In a State Paper of 1515 the boundary of the Pale is decribed as passing from Dundalk by Kells, Kilcock, Kilcullen Bridge, Naas, Ballymore Eustace, Rathcoole, Tallaght, Dalkey, round to Dublin.

NOTE H, PAGE 10.

Lynch (pp. 62, 63) gives instances of fines for non-attendance in the reign of Edward III. At that time, and afterwards, attendance on Parliament was regarded as a burden, not only because it was expensive, but also because it withdrew the paramount Lords from superintendence of their numerous followers and retainers. In their absence, too, the neighbouring natives were better able to conspire against their authority. In the reign of Edward IV. Desmond claimed the right to be absent as if it were a valued privilege. (Mason, *Essay*, p. 64.)

Note I, Page 11.

Note I. The *Ordinatio de Statu Hiberniæ* of Edward III. is included in the collection of the English Statutes published by authority in 1810. It deals with several other subjects besides Parliaments. To the clause relating to them Lord Coke attributes the conformity of Irish Parliaments to the English Parliaments (4th Inst.). It is expressed as follows: '. . . Volumus, &c., quod nostra et ipsius terræ negocia *in consiliis* per peritos consiliarios nostros ac prelatos et magnates et quosdam de discretioribus et probioribus hominibus de partibus vicinis, ubi ipsa consilia teneri contigerit, propter hoc evocandos; *in parliamento,* vero, per ipsos conciliarios nostros ac prelatos ac proceres, alios que de terra predicta, prout mos exigit.' The *Ordinatio* appears to recognise the distinction between the *Magnum Concilium* and the *Parliamentum,* which was then observed in England. (See Stubbs, *History,* vol. ii., p. 271.)

Note K, Page 13.

Note K. A record of the Parliament of 1560 is preserved in the Record Office, at Dublin. It is printed in full in the Appendix to Hardiman's Edition of *The Statute of Kilkenny*. The Domini Spirituales enumerated are twenty; of thirteen both names and titles are stated; of seven only names, probably because they did not attend. The names of members from ten counties (two for each) are also given; ten more counties are stated, but there is no mention of any members from them. The names of members from twenty-eight cities and boroughs (two for each) are also given, and, besides, there is mention of one other borough, but not of the names of any members returned for it.

Note L, Page 13.

Official letters respecting the Parliament of 1541, and a list of those who attended, are preserved in the State Papers. This list describes the chieftains as follows:—Procuratores Domini O'Brene; Willelmus de Burgo, seu nacionis capitaneus; Donat O'Brene; Carolus filius Arturi Kavanagh; Dominus O'Rayley; Kedagh O'More; Phelym Roo. Opposite these names are written the words, Isti nondum sunt de parliamento. St. Leger, the Deputy, however, wrote to Henry VIII. that 'the great O'Rayley, with many other Irish Capytaines, attended.' He says the Upper House had three Earls, three Viscounts, sixteen Barons, two Archbishops, twelve Bishops; 'the Commons' House had divers knights and gentlemen of fair possessions.' The only Peer of Irish race seems to have been Lord Upper Ossory (Macgillapatrick), anglicised Fitzpatrick). (*State Papers*, Henry VIII., vol. iii., pp. 304–307.)

The Parliament met in June. In August other Irish chiefs —O'Connor, O'Dwyn, or Dun, and O'Donnell—are said to have acknowledged Henry's authority, and to have been followed by O'Carroll, O'Mulloy, Mac Mahon, Mageniss, O'Rourke, O'Flaherty, O'Melaghlin, Mac Carty, O'Sullivan, and others whose names are not recorded. (Ware's *Annals*, chap. XXXIII.)

Note M, Page 16.

A record of Perrot's Parliament, A.D. 1585, is preserved in the Record Office, Dublin. It is printed in the Appendix to Hardiman's Edition of *The Statute of Kilkenny* (p. 139). It professes to give a list of the lordes spiritual and temporal, counties, cyties, and borough-townes, answerable to the Parlyament in this realme of Ireland: and souche as were summoned. The spiritual lords enumerated are four Archbishops, wenty-two Bishops; the temporal lords twenty-six, of whom

Appendix. Note M. were of Irish race Earl of Thomond (O'Brien), Earl of Clancare (M'Carthy), Lord Upper Ossory (Fitz Patrick), and Lord Dungannon, who was also Earl of Tyrone (O'Neill). Seventeen of the peerages mentioned still exist. The counties required to return members were twenty-seven (two for each); the cities and boroughs thirty-six (two for each). The names of members returned are written opposite the counties and towns; but some are obliterated. About eighteen of the names given indicate the persons whom they designate to have been of Irish race.

In the enumeration of counties there is the county of Tipperary and county crossie of Tipperary. Wexford is also treated as forming two counties, viz. the county of Wexford and the county of Ffernes. The counties of Armagh, Tyrone, Monaghan, Derry, Leitrim, Fermanagh, and Donegal, are not mentioned; Ulster not being then reduced into obedience.

The attendance of a large number of Irish Chieftains, besides such Peers or Commoners as were of Irish race, appears from the *Annals of the Four Masters* (O'Donovan's Edition, vol. ii., pp. 1827-41). According to this authority, 'a proclamation was issued to the men of Ireland commanding their chiefs to assemble in Dublin precisely on Mayday,' for, it adds, 'the people of Ireland were, at this time, obedient to their Sovereign. And, accordingly, they all (the names of about fifty-four are given) at that summons did meet in Dublin face to face.'

NOTE N, PAGE 19.

Note N. James himself defended the creation of the forty boroughs simply on the ground that it was an exercise of his prerogative. 'Did any good subjects,' he said to a deputation from the Irish House of Commons, 'ever dispute their King's power in this point? What is it to you whether I make many or few boroughs? My Council may consider the fitness, if I require it. But what if I had created forty noblemen, and 400 boroughs? The more the merrier, the fewer the better cheer.' (*Desiderata Curiosa*, ed. 1732, vol. i., p. 308).

The increased number of members in this Parliament was caused, not merely by the members from these boroughs, but by members from counties which had returned none to Perrot's Parliament. Davis, in his address (p. 18, *supra*), observed that Ulster and Connaught, as well as Leinster and Munster, had then voices in Parliament, and that the English of birth, English of blood, the new British Colony, and the old Irish natives, did all meet together to make laws.

Note O, Page 24.

The proceedings connected with the summons of Irish representatives to England by Edward III. arè stated in a record, which is printed in the Appendix to the first volume of Leland's *History of Ireland*. Of the protests with which some of the returns (as mentioned at p. 24, *supra*) were accompanied, it will be sufficient to cite that from the county of Louth (convocatis magnatibus et communibus comitatus Loueth). . . . 'Iidem magnates et communes de eorum communi assensu, una voce dixerunt quôd ipsi, juxta jura, privilegia, libertates, leges et consuetudines terræ Hiberniæ a tempore conquestus ejusdem et ante usitatas, non tenentur eligere nec mittere aliquos de terrâ prædictâ ad parliamenta nec concilia in Angliâ tenenda ad tractandum consulendum et concordandum prout hoc breve requirit.'

Under Edward I. and Edward II. there seems also to have been attendance of representatives from Ireland in England. A writ of the former speaks of statutes made at Lincoln and York: ' Per nos de assensu prelatorum comitum baronum et communitatis regni nostri Hiberniæ. (See Mason, 40, 41; Molyneux, pp. 80, 82; Coke's *Institutes*, iv., f. 750.)

Appendix. Note O. The mandate of Edward III. summons those who should be sent, ad tractandum cum rege et consilio (also spelled concilio) ejus; but Sir Maurice Eustace, Speaker of the Irish House of Commons, A.D. 1689, speaks of these attendances of Irish representatives in England as having been upon the English Parliament. (See his address in *Journals of the Irish House of Commons*, vol. i., p. 91.)

NOTE P, PAGE 26.

Note P. The *Statutum Hiberniæ* (14 H. 3), mentioned in the Note to p. 26, *supra*, is printed among the English statutes, but its close (teste meipso, &c.) is that of an ordinance. It declared the law of succession of co-heiresses. The Irish Chief Justice, Fitz Maurice, despatched four knights to the King in England, to ascertain the law and custom of England—whether the younger sisters were to hold of and do homage to the eldest sister—and they brought back the ordinance that all the sisters ought to hold of the chief lord, and not the younger of the eldest sister. The *ordinationes*, mentioned in the same Note, are also printed in editions of the English statutes; but their form, too, is more consistent with their being ordinances than Acts of Parliament. The first of them is sometimes cited as 17 Edw. I., and sometimes as 17 Edw. II. The latter is the date preferred in the authorised edition of the English statutes published in 1810.

NOTE Q, PAGE 39.

Note Q. In the Birmingham Tower there is a MS. book of 'minutes for Bills' considered by the Irish Privy Council, from January 2, 1747, to March 30, 1766. The proceedings seem to have been so regulated, that when 'Heads of Bills' came from the Irish Parliament they were several times brought under the consideration of the Council before they finally transmitted them to England. Thus the entries as to 'the Heads of a Bill for the recovery of small debts in a summary way in the city of Dublin' (February 20, 1758) are:—' Heads of Bill read in Council ; ordered to be put in form ; accordingly done ; read the first and second time, and committed.' When a Bill was approved, it was sent on to the Privy Council in England, with an expression of approbation, *e.g.*, 'Thinking this Act will be good and expedient for this realm, we recommend it to your Lordships, and desire that you will please to have it returned in the usual form.'

NOTE R, PAGE 41.

The confiscations of landed property under the Commonwealth had been preceded by similar confiscations under Philip and Mary, Elizabeth, and James I. In the two first instances colonies from England were introduced (planted as it was termed) upon the lands taken possession of; in the third the same process took place, but the larger number of the colonists were from Scotland. From these examples the Commonwealth derived the idea of a plantation, and applied it to the estates of all who opposed its authority, whether native or settler, Catholic or Protestant, whether they fought for Charles I. or for Irish independence. But both confiscation and plantation were carried out with much more severity than on the occasions of the previous confiscations. By a statute passed in 1752 persons who stood neutral were regarded as delinquents, and when persons professing the Roman Catholic religion were not deprived of their entire estates, a power was taken to substitute for the portion left with them equivalent lands in other parts of Ireland—a power exercised in what is known as the transplantation to Connaught. (See for the statute Scobell's *Acts and Ordinances*.) It is not improbable that this greater severity as to the Catholics had its origin, not so much in political considerations as in resentment for the sufferings of the Protestants in

Appendix. Note R. the rebellion of 1641. Cromwell had, when in Ireland, openly avowed that he 'came to take an account of the innocent blood that had been then shed.' (See *Carlyle's Cromwell*, ed. 1871, vol. ii. p. 210-23.)

NOTE S, PAGE 44.

Note S. Besides the Tobacco Acts, mentioned at page 43 *supra*, the following Acts, passed by the Parliament of England under Charles II., affect Ireland:—12 Car. ii. ch. 18; 15 Car. ii. ch. 7; 13 & 14 Car. ii. ch. 11; 18 Car. ii. ch. 2; 32 Car. ii. ch. 4; 22 & 23 Car. ii. ch. 4, and 26.

Of these the most important were the two first (the Navigation Acts). The earliest (passed in 1660) placed Ireland, but not Scotland, in the same category in respect of access to colonial ports as England. The second (passed in 1663) excluded both Irish and Scotch ships from the colonies. This was followed by other Acts in 1670 and 1696, framed in a similar spirit, until at last there could be no direct trade between either Ireland or Scotland and the colonies, under the Crown of England. One of the provisions of this code was, that the master and three-fourths of the mariners of the ships trading to the Colonies should be English. From all such restrictions Scotland, by its union with England, was freed in 1707. Ireland continued subject to the Acts. A curious illustration of the operation of these laws has been mentioned by Mr. Huskisson. A ship from an English settlement in America, laden with colonial produce, was stranded on the coast of Ireland. The law did not allow the cargo to be landed in Ireland, or to be carried away in an Irish ship. To bring the cargo to England, another English ship had to be sent for it; and although the cargo might be wanted in the Irish market, it could not be delivered there without being unloaded in an English port, and again re-shipped to Ireland. (*Speeches of Huskisson*, vol. iii. p. 9.)

Note T, Page 47.

The Acts of James the Second's Parliament (A.D. 1689), which the English Act of 1690 professed to annul, were thirty-five in number. The most important were 'An Act declaring that the Parliament of England cannot bind Ireland, and against writs of error and appeals into England'; the Act repealing the Acts of Settlement and the Attainder Act, which are mentioned at pages 46 and 47, *supra;* Acts relating to tithes and provisions for ministers in towns: 'An Act for liberty of conscience,' and repealing such Acts or clauses in any Act of Parliament which are inconsistent with the same.' The interference with these Acts—principally on account of the Act repealing the Act of Settlement and of the Attainder Act—was, according to Molyneux (*Case*, ed. 1719, pp. 63-65), at the solicitation of the banished laity—those who had fled to England when James landed in Ireland—of whom Molyneux was himself one.

The Act repealing the Act of Settlement reached back to the day before the rebellion of 1641 broke into action—a period of 48 years. *Prima facie* it would operate on all confiscations made in the interval; but, in consequence of restorations made under the Act of Settlement to a large number of the original Roman Catholic proprietors who had been deprived by the Commonwealth, it practically affected only a part. Sir William Petty's calculation of the entire confiscations of the Commonwealth and of the mode they were dealt with under the Act of Settlement is, that before 1641 the Roman Catholics and sequestered Protestants had 5,200,000 acres (Irish measure). These, he says, were seized by the usurpers, but the Roman Catholics recovered back 2,340,000 like acres. What the new Protestants received, and additions to the property of the Church, he estimates at 2,400,000 like acres. This would leave 460,000, which he describes as of 'a more indifferent nature.'—*Political Anatomy,* pp. 2-4. Nearly, therefore, two millions and a-half acres (Irish measure) would, if the Act repealing the Act of Settlement had been allowed to come into operation, have been taken from those who, in 1689, were their possessors. For the loss to be thus occasioned neither the original grantees, nor persons deriving from them by descent, devise, or marriage, were to receive any compensation; but purchasers were to be, as it was expressed, reprised out of the forfeitures expected to be enforced against the adherents of William and Mary. The Attainder Act apparently inflicted all the penalties of High Treason; but it is probable that its object was the same as that of the 'repealing Act'—to work out forfeitures of landed property, as it was very unlikely that those specified in it as subject to its provisions would return to be tried before the tribunals appointed for the purpose. (See as to the proceedings of this Parliament, Macaulay, *Hist.*, iii. 12; Froude, *English in Ireland*, i., 184; Lecky, *Hist.*, vi. 184; Ingram, *Two Chapters of Irish History*.)

The Parliament of 1689 was composed almost altogether of Roman Catholics. There are said to have been only six Protestants in the House of Commons, and this is not unlikely, since a person attending would thereby in some degree acknowledge James's title, and Protestants almost universally took William's side. The same House has also been spoken of as if its members were almost all of native race; but this seems to me an exaggeration. To judge by the names, less than a third would answer that description: the rest are from Anglo-Irish families, who did not conform to the religion of the State under Henry VIII. and Elizabeth—a class more numerous than is generally supposed.

NOTE U, PAGE 49.

The language of the Irish Act of Supremacy (2 Eliz. ch. i., s. 7), which prescribed by whom the Oath of Supremacy was to be taken, is not applicable to members of Parliament whether Peers or Commoners. And accordingly they took their seats without being required to swear it. Thus, in the House of Commons of 1613 there were 101 Recusants. In 1661, however, that House passed a resolution with the object of obliging the oath to be taken by its members, but this being only a resolution could not bind future Parliaments ; and therefore the English Act (3 W. & M., c. 2, mentioned at p. 48, *supra*) must be regarded as the legal authority which, by imposing the new oaths and declarations contained in it upon members of the Irish Parliament, first permanently excluded persons professing the Roman Catholic religion from both Houses of Parliament in Ireland.

Note V, Page 52.

The Act of the English Parliament (10 & 11 William III., ch. 10) enacted that no person should directly or indirectly export, and ship off from Ireland into any foreign realms, or any place or places whatsoever, other than certain specified ports within the kingdom of England or dominion of Wales, any the wool, wool-fells, &c., cloth, serges, kerseys, &c., or any other drapery stuffs or woollen manufacture whatsoever, made-up or mixed with wool or wool-flocks, &c. From Ireland the export to the permitted ports in England was to be only from six ports which were specified.

The object of this Act was to make wool plenty and therefore cheap in England, by bringing all Irish wool there. For the same purpose all exportation of wool from England was prohibited. It is not surprising, therefore, that Adam Smith should have pronounced the woollen manufacturers of England to have been ' more successful than any other class of workmen, in persuading the Legislature that the prosperity of the nation depended upon the success and extension of their particular business.' (*Wealth of Nations*, book iv., ch. 8.)

Note W, Page 101.

The unpopularity among the people of Scotland outside Parliament of the Union with England seems to me admitted by all historians. Smollett describes their resentment as

Appendix.
Note W.

rising to transports of fury and revenge (*History of England*, A.D. 1706). Burton says, 'the popular preponderance was undoubtedly on the side of the Opposition' (*History of Scotland*, ed. 1873, vol. viii., p. 140); and Sir Walter Scott mentions one fact quite decisive on the point—that while the table of Parliament was loaded with addresses against Union, only one could be procured in its favour from a few persons in the Burgh of Ayr (*Works*, vol. xxv., p. 80). In the Scottish Parliament (which was a convention of estates, Peers and Commoners sitting and debating together) the principal support of the measure came, according to Burnet, from the Peers (*Own Time*, A.D. 1706). There was, however, a majority for it of representatives of counties, and also of representatives of towns.

The general repute among the Scottish people of actual bribery being used to procure support in their Parliament for the Union seems to be also admitted by historians. There was then an actual distribution of money from England that gave a sort of confirmation to rumours, which the prevalent discontent was of itself sufficient to account for. Indeed, Sir Walter Scott does not hesitate to regard this money as 'employed to secure to the measures of the Court the party called the Squadróne Volánte—by which name some Peers and Commoners, who acted together, and were able to turn the scale either way, were designated' (see Scott's *Miscellaneous Works*, vol. xxv., pp. 99-102). Burton, however—and in this he is followed by Earl Stanhope—takes a different view of the use made of this money. According to him the larger part was paid to the Lord High Commissioner for expenses, and what was paid direct to individuals was to satisfy arrears of salaries then due. (See Burton's *History of Scotland*, ed. 1853, vol. viii., ch. 24; and Lord Stanhope's *History until the Peace of Utrecht*, 3rd ed., p. 282.)

Whether well- or ill-founded, the belief that corrupt means were used to carry the Union increased the enmity with which the Act was regarded by the Scotch people. The few may discriminate between the merits of a political measure and the demerits of the means by which it was carried; but the many will view the former through the medium of the indignant feelings excited by the latter, and pronounce on both the same condemnation.

[margin: Appendix. Note W.]

Until 1745 the discontent which the Union excited continued, being fostered by the Jacobites, who held out the hope that in case of their success the national Parliament might be restored. With the establishment, by the events of that time, of the title of the House of Hanover, and of the authority of the United Parliament, in Scotland, commenced the complete devotion of the energy and enterprise of the people to advance its prosperity, undisturbed by any rival attraction or interruption. 'The air,' observes Burton, 'had to be cleared of mischief before men's minds could set freely and heartily to the great function of industrial progress.'

NOTE X, PAGE 106.

The introduction of the system under which the patronage of the Crown was directly used in order to influence votes in the Irish Parliament is attributed to Lord Townsend, Lord Lieutenant from 1767 to 1772. He substituted it for the previous plan of allowing this patronage to be used for the same purpose by a few nobles or other persons who predominated in Irish society, and were, in return, to secure a majority for the measures of Government. Among the papers of Lord Harcourt, the Lord Lieutenant who succeeded Lord Townsend, is preserved a paper containing a list of the Peers and Members of the House of Commons in Ireland, and opposite each is an account of the favours asked by him, the favours conferred upon him, or on his family, friends, or connections, by Government, and of his conduct in Parliament. It will be found in a most interesting collection of the Harcourt Papers, printed for private circulation by Colonel Harcourt, of Nuneham Courtenay, lately M. P. for Oxfordshire (vol. x., p. 429).

[margin: Note X.]

Note Y, Page 128.

In 1780 the number of Volunteers was estimated at 42,000 (see page 110, *supra*). In 1782 they had increased, according to the estimate of one of their most influential officers, to 60,000. The same authority describes them as 'self-raised, self-disciplined, self-clothed, self-paid, and for the most part self-armed.' (See Dobbs' Speech in the Irish House of Commons, Feb. 5, 1800.)

Lord Buckingham has been blamed for not compelling the Volunteers to disband; but he thought that he could not effect this without legislation for the purpose. (See his Letter to Lord Weymouth, Dec. 12, 1778, printed in *Grattan's Life*, vol. i., p. 349.) And such legislation could not have been obtained from the Irish Parliament. The leading Peers and members of the House of Commons were at the head of the Volunteers; and the House of Commons, to mark its approval of their conduct, passed an express vote of thanks to them (October, 1780). The British Parliament might perhaps have been induced to enact whatever measures Ministers suggested. But would its enactment have been obeyed? At that very time, because the Mutiny Act was an English statute, its enforcement in Ireland was resisted. (See p. 125, *supra*.)

Note Z, Page 130.

Grattan's eloquence was admirably suited for the objects upon which he was engaged before 1782. It was eminently calculated to awaken enthusiasm. Even the characteristics which were attributed to it as defects, its point, antithesis, epigram, tended to aid its practical influence by fixing it in the memory of those whom he sought to move to action. The same may be said of the rhythmical arrangement of his sentences, which, as too artificial, has also been objected to. 'Cujus,' says Cicero of Demosthenes, 'non tam vibrarent fulmina illa, nisi numeris contorta ferrentur.'

In the British House of Commons, of which Grattan, after the Union, was a member, his reputation as an orator was not less than it had been in the Irish. His genius triumphed over the difficulties interposed by a tone of thought and sentiment, and a standard of taste in the former assembly, entirely different from what he had experienced in the latter.

Appendix.
Note Z.

A tendency to depreciate Grattan may be observed in some writers who have recently discussed the proceedings of the Irish Parliament. The wisdom of the measures he supported is of course a fair subject for difference of opinion; but can there justly be other than the highest estimate of his intellectual and moral excellence? He entered Parliament in 1775, and although without fortune, rank, or any other influence than what his abilities and character might create, he had, before the close of 1782, obtained—for to his advocacy it was due—freedom for the commerce and Parliament of Ireland; and he had achieved this success without using any unworthy means whatever.

On questions of general policy, Grattan belonged to the school of political thought which found favour in England with the Whig party; but, after the French Revolution, he leaned to the opinions rather of Burke than of Fox. Thus, in 1794, he supported the policy of war with France; and about the same time he accompanied moderate proposals for reform of the Irish House of Commons with warnings against the democratical views encouraged by the example of France. 'We have not,' he observed, 'to seek for a constitution. . . . We have a monarchy, the best form of government for rational and durable liberty. . . . We have to advise and limit monarchy, and to exercise legislative power, a Parliament, consisting of a senate, without which no country was ever temperately or serenely conducted; and a Commons, without which the people cannot be free.' (*Irish Debates*, vol. xiii., p. 14.) 'Transfer,' he said, 'the power of the State to those who have nothing in the country, they will afterwards transfer the property, and annex it once more to the power in their own persons. Give them your power, and they will give themselves your property.' (Speech, 4th March, 1794.)

Appendix.

Note A A.

NOTE AA, PAGE 113.

John Hely Hutchinson, Provost of Trinity College, was in 1782 Secretary to the Lord Lieutenant. Although he was the head of a great educational institution, he had not pursued an academic career; on the contrary, he had previously been a successful practising barrister, and had attained the high rank of Prime Sergeant. He was a most able speaker, described as always having something to say which gratified the House of Commons. But, insatiable in his demands for offices and places, he is now, perhaps, best known by the description which Lord North gave of him to George III., when, seeing him at his levee, the King inquired who he was ... 'That is a man on whom, if your Majesty were pleased to bestow England and Ireland, he would ask the Isle of Man for a potato garden.'

NOTE BB, PAGE 139.

Note B B.

The provision in the statute, passed in 1783 to modify Poynings' Act, which required that a Bill introduced in the Irish Parliament should, in order to become law, be transmitted to the King in England, and be thence returned under the Great Seal of Great Britain (see p. 136, *supra*), was afterwards, in some instances, used to compel alterations in Bills before the Irish Parliament. (See *Edinburgh Review*, April, 1866, p. 579.) But this could not have been often, or on important questions, since Foster, in 1800, was able to describe this restraint as 'theoretic dependence, but practical independence.' (*Speech*, Feb. 17, 1800.)

It will be observed that the Bill, when transmitted, did not come before the British Parliament or the British Privy Council. Whether it was or was not to be returned under the British Great Seal depended upon the decision of the Minister in England who had the charge of Irish affairs, generally the Secretary of State at the Home Office. Thus the legislation of one country was under the control of the Minister of another. The beneficial working of such a system too much rested upon the moral courage of a single individual. To veto what is presented as the demand of a nation through their authorised legislative representatives involves an amount of responsibility from which most public men are certain to shrink. In general they will yield to whatever is so demanded, and, when they have yielded, the interference of the Parliament of their own country would be late.

Of this the history of the Security Act in Scotland affords a striking illustration (see page 81, *supra*). Its provisions were (and deservedly) most unpopular in England. Instead of following the English limitations of the Crown, they asserted for the Scottish Parliament the right to choose a different sovereign: nay, unless certain commercial advantages were conceded, they compelled such a choice. As a menace to England, they directed that the Scotch people should be universally drilled and trained to the use of arms. Anne, under the advice of Godolphin, gave her assent. When it was given, the Act was safe beyond the power of the British Parliament. Of what use would it then have been to put the Lord Treasurer's head in a basket, as Wharton is said to have suggested?

Note CC, Page 173.

Before the Act of Union there had been two statutes of the Irish Parliament relating to the Crown—(1) 33 Henry VIII. ch. 1 (see p. 13, *supra*), which provided that the King, his heirs, and successors, kings of England, should always be kings of Ireland. It recited that the King and his progenitors had always been lords of this land of Ireland, with all manner kingly jurisdiction, &c.; (2) 4 William and Mary, ch. 1, which, reciting that the kingdom of Ireland was annexed and united to the Imperial Crown of England, and that after the accession of William and Mary to the Crown of

Appendix.
Note CC.
England they had delivered Ireland from an intestine war, declared that the Lords Spiritual and Temporal, and the Commons of Ireland in Parliament assembled, did recognise and acknowledge that the kingdom of Ireland, and all royalties, &c., were vested in William and Mary.

NOTE DD, PAGE 177.

Note DD. A protectionist policy was adopted by the Irish Parliament from the time when it obtained freedom of action. Its legislation aimed at stimulating both manufactures and agriculture, by bounties to reward exports from, and by duties to discourage imports into, Ireland. And, at the time when the question of the Union began to be agitated, this was not only the policy in operation, but the policy almost universally approved in Ireland. That, after an union with Great Britain, the existing system could not be maintained, without at least extensive modifications, was foreseen: and, accordingly, the probability that the protective statutes would be repealed by an Imperial Parliament was strongly urged by opponents of the Union. And this continued even when the Government had introduced into the Articles of Union a special provision to continue a number of duties, designed to serve the local manufactures, at a reduced rate of 10½ per cent. for twenty years. 'All the policy,' said Grattan, 'of nursing our growing fabrics, and thereby of improving the industry of the country, employing her children, and expending her wealth upon her own labour, is now abandoned; and the language of the Union is buy where you can, and as cheap as you can, and if the English market be cheaper, resort to that market in preference to your own' (*Speech*, March 19, 1800, and compare Foster's *Speech*, April 11, 1799, at page 92 of the pamphlet in which it was published: Dublin, 1799).

How far experience justified the favourable estimates entertained by Irish statesmen of a protectionist policy may be doubted. Grattan, indeed, in the speech I have referred to, says that 'manufactures had flourished under the high duties then in force'; but reasons for at least not implicitly adopting his statement have been adduced by a high financial authority, Spring Rice (*Speech* in the House of Commons, April 22, 1834). And with respect to the Corn Laws—notwithstanding that an Act of 1784, granting bounties on its exports, had been followed by a considerable corn trade, and, as a consequence, by extensive conversion of pasture into tillage, and, after a short time, by a rise in rents and in the wages of agricultural labourers—it may be doubted whether Ireland then presented any exception to the ordinary rule that the benefit derived from a stimulus of this character is more apparent than real—temporary, not permanent. (See a memorandum of Richard Burke, dated December, 1792, in *Edmund Burke's Correspondence*, vol. iv., p. 48.)

That, however, there was, during the period when this policy was in operation, increased general prosperity in Ireland, there is the testimony not merely of Grattan and Foster but of Lord Clare. (See his *Speech*, Feb. 19, 1798, in which, assuming the fact of prosperity, he uses it to show that Ireland could not be conciliated by concession, her 'discontent keeping pace with her prosperity.') But if there was this prosperity other causes beside the protectionist policy contributed to it. Before that policy was introduced, before the Irish Parliament had, in 1782, obtained the constitution which enabled its introduction, the British Parliament had conceded to Ireland free trade with the colonies. To illustrate the effect of this, the import of sugar in 1781 was 7000 cwt., but in 1782, 18,000 cwt. Also, previously, hindrances to trade with Great Britain had been removed. In 1781 the exports from Ireland to Great Britain were estimated at £2,180,215, and in 1782 at £2,699,825. (See *Grattan's Life*, vol. iii., p. 275.) Moreover, nothing contributed more to Irish prosperity than a rise in the price of agricultural produce; and this was taking place quite irrespective of any special legislation; wheat, having been in Great Britain, in 1780, 4s. 5½d. a bushel; in 1794 6s.; and being in 1800 14s. 1d. (See *Annual Register* for these years.)

Appendix.
Note DD.

Appendix. Note DD. The growth of prosperity among the people in Ireland did not, however, prevent the financial depression of the kingdom. Speaking in 1800, Lord Clare did not hesitate to assert that they had not 'redemption for three years from public bankruptcy, or a burthen of taxation which will sink every gentleman of property in the country.' He attributed this to the amount borrowed in the previous seven years. The National Debt in 1793 was £2,440,390; in 1800 it was £25,662,640. (*Speech* of Lord Clare, Feb. 10, 1800.)

NOTE EE, PAGE 178.

Note EE. The towns in which, according to Plowden, there were free seats were, Dublin, Cork, Carrickfergus, Drogheda, Dungannon, Dungarvan, Downpatrick, Lisburn, Londonderry, Newry, and Swords. Ross, the editor of the *Cornwallis Correspondence*, seems not to regard Dungarvan, Downpatrick, Lisburn, or Swords, as deserving this character, and to think that Limerick did.

The compensation given at the Union to the persons who were found to be the owners of disfranchised boroughs enables us to estimate by how small a number of persons the seats in them were owned. 164 seats were compensated for. All these, with the exception of one (Swords), were shown to belong to not more in any instance than four owners. The Marquis of Downshire owned seven; Lord Ely six; eight others thirty-two seats; thirty-nine more (including three bishops) had seventy-eight seats. The whole number of compensated owners was less than 150: these returned 162 members. Besides, there were the close boroughs, not wholly disfranchised, for which no compensation was paid, and they each belonged to just as small a number of owners as did those which received compensation. There is some reason to think that previously the number of owners was even smaller. According to Lord Bolton's MSS. (cited by Massy, *History*, vol. iii., p. 264), 126 seats were, in 1784, commanded by twenty-five persons; and, according to Grattan, in 1794 less than ninety persons (he said he believed about forty) returned a majority of the House of Commons. (*Speech,* March 4, 1794.)

NOTE FF, PAGE 185.

There is preserved a letter, written by Lord Clare while he was in London conferring with the English ministers respecting the legislation to be proposed in connexion with the Union, which very clearly shows that he opposed any introduction in it of relief for the Catholics. At the conclusion he says, . . . 'If I have been in any manner instrumental in persuading ministers to bring forward this very important measure, unincumbered with a proposition (*i. e.* what he before calls "the doctrine of emancipation"), which must have swamped it, I shall rejoice very much in the pilgrimage which I have made.' (Lord Clare to Lord Castlereagh, Oct. 16, 1798, *Castlereagh Correspondence,* vol. i., p. 393.) It appears from a letter written, about a week later than this letter from Lord Clare, by Elliott, Under-secretary in the Irish military department, from London to Lord Castlereagh, that the leaning of the opinion of the Cabinet was then against 'extending the privileges of the Catholic body at the present conjuncture.' This he attributed partly to a fear of embarrassment, which it was supposed might accrue from a proposition to alter the test laws in England, and partly to apprehension that the government would experience difficulty from the prejudices of its Protestant friends in Ireland. The latter, he says, he believed to be the argument which Lord Clare used, and which, he adds, he perceived operated most powerfully on Mr. Pitt's mind. (*Castlereagh Correspondence,* vol. i., p. 404.) How far Lord Clare's assertion was well founded, that the measures of Government would have been swamped in the Irish Parliament, if Pitt, having overcome such difficulties as either the disinclination of some of his own colleagues or the conscientious scruples of the King might have interposed in

Appendix.
Note FF.

England, had accompanied Union with Emancipation, it is difficult to pronounce. Even without this additional difficulty the measures of Government, when first brought forward, were defeated in the Commons. And in the Lords, where their majority in 1799 was only thirty-five, their success very much depended on the conduct of the Spiritual Lords (twenty-two in number), who (with two exceptions) favoured or acquiesced in Union by itself, but would probably (if we may judge by their conduct after Union) not have done so if it involved admission of the Catholics into Parliament.

NOTE GG, PAGE 201.

Note GG. The following are the testimonies to Lord Castlereagh's capacity for public affairs, referred to in the note on page 201 *supra*, as having been given by Sir Robert Peel and Thiers: ... 'You well know,' Sir Robert Peel writes to the third Marquis of Londonderry, 'that no vindication of your brother's memory was necessary for my satisfaction; that my admiration of his character is too firmly rooted to be shaken by criticisms or phrases, and cavils at particular acts selected from a long political career. I doubt whether any public man (except the Duke of Wellington) who has appeared within the last half century possessed that combination of qualities, intellectual and moral, which would have enabled him to effect, under the same circumstances, what Lord Londonderry (the title to which Lord Castlereagh succeeded in 1821) did effect in regard to the Union with Ireland, and to the great political transactions of 1813, 1814, and 1815.' (*Castlereagh Correspondence*, vol. i., p. 130.)

Thiers' reference to Lord Castlereagh is in his *History of the Consulate and Empire*, vol. xvii., p. 199: ... ' Lord Castlereagh issu d'une famille irlandaise ardente et energique, portait en lui cette disposition héréditaire, mais tempérée par une reason supérieure. Esprit droit et pénétrant, caractère prudent et ferme, capable tout à la fois de vigueur et de ménagement, ayant dans ses manières la simplicité fière des Anglais, il était appelé a exercer, et il exerca en effet la plus grande influence.'

Note HH, Page 209.

In speaking upon the question of compensation for disfranchised boroughs in 1785, Pitt observed that there was a sort of squeamish and maiden coyness about the House in talking upon the subject. They were not, he said, ready to talk on what, at the same time, it was pretty well understood out of doors they had no great objection to negotiate—the purchase and sale of seats. (*Speeches*, vol. i., p. 232.)

It was not until some time had elapsed after the Union that the sale of seats was made illegal. At first in the Imperial Parliament they were sold and bought just as they had been in the separate Parliaments. In 1807 the Ministry and the Opposition competed for such seats as were then in the market; the prices consequently were extremely high. Romilly states that Tierney in vain offered £10,000 for two seats for that Parliament, of which trustees for creditors were then disposing (see *Romilly's Diary*, vol. ii., p. 206). Some transactions, which about that time occurred, attracted attention, and about two years after (1809) Curwen's Act was passed (49 Geo. iii. c. 118), which imposed penalties for corrupt agreements for the return of members, whether for money, office, or other consideration. Notwithstanding this Act, the traffic in seats seems to have continued, but necessarily secretly. If it was detected, the parties concerned were liable (as was pointed out by Lord Campbell in his speech on the Reform Bill of 1832) to punishment. Whether obeyed or not, the Act altered the position of the owners of boroughs. If they derived a revenue from nominating to seats, it was an illegal revenue. It was, therefore, from that time impossible for them to claim, in case there should be a Reform Bill depriving them of their power, compensation for the loss of a such revenue. And accordingly the Reform

Appendix.
Note HH.
Bill of 1832 was carried without giving compensation to the owners of disfranchised close boroughs.

The price of a seat for a Parliament in Ireland was, in 1775, calculated by Sir John Blaquiere, secretary to the Lord Lieutenant, at from 2000 guineas to £2500 (see *Harcourt Correspondence*, vol. x., p. 20); in 1795 by Grattan at £3000 (*Irish Parl. Debates*, xiii., p. 162); in the Parliament of 1797 by Lord Castlereagh at £1500, seats being then, he says, less dear from the number in the market (*Castlereagh Correspondence*, vol. ii., p. 151). The price of a borough was in 1797 estimated by Grattan at from £14,000 to £16,000. (See Dr. Dunbar Ingram's *Legislative Union*, p. 179.)

In the first plan of Union it seems to have been intended to give but one member to a county, and to have kept a larger number of boroughs than were afterwards retained. Lord Castlereagh then thought that the pecuniary loss to owners of disfranchised boroughs would amount to £756,000. The loss to persons who had paid for their seats for the existing Parliament he estimated at £75,000. The loss to Dublin, by the non-residence of the gentry, and consequent depreciation of house property, he rated at about £200,000. (*Castlereagh Correspondence*, vol. ii., p. 151.)

NOTE II, PAGE 211.

Note II.
In a speech in the House of Commons (Feb. 1, 1790), Grattan stated—and he was not in the debate on that occasion contradicted—that the number of placemen and pensioners then sitting in the Irish House of Commons equalled over one-half of the whole efficient body. He also then stated that besides conferring peerages to reward parliamentary support, ministers caused peerages to be in some instances granted in return for money contributed to purchase seats in the House of Commons for persons recommended by the Government. (See also his *Speech*, Feb. 26, 1790.)

The habitual use of the patronage of the Crown, for the purpose of obtaining a majority of votes in Parliament, is admitted by Lord Clare (*Speech*, Feb. 10, 1800); but, while admitting the fact, he derived from it an argument against the separate existence of an Irish Parliament. So long as that continued, the Government of Great Britain, he urged, must, for its own safety, secure 'a permanent and commanding influence of the English Executive, or rather of the English Cabinet, in the councils of Ireland.' 'A majority,' he proceeded, ' in the Parliament of Great Britain will defeat the Minister of the day, but a majority in the Parliament of Ireland against the King's Government goes directly to separate this kingdom from the British Crown: if it continues, separation or war is the inevitable issue, and therefore it is that the general Executive of the empire, so far as is essential to retain Ireland as a member of it, is completely at the mercy of the Irish Parliament; and it is vain,' he says, 'to expect, so long as man continues to be a creature of passion and interest, that he will not avail himself of the critical and difficult situation in which the Executive Government of this kingdom must ever remain under its present constitution, to demand the favours of the Crown, not as the reward of loyalty and service, but as the stipulated price to be paid in advance for the discharge of a public duty.'

Note KK, Page 214.

In the letter of Lord Castlereagh to Pitt (Jan. 1, 1801), referred to at page 212 *supra*, he says that he, in 1799, represented to the Cabinet 'that the resistance of the Catholics to the Union would be unanimous and zealous, if they had reason to suppose that the sentiments of Ministers would remain unchanged in respect of their exclusion.'

A statement in the same letter which is cited in the foregoing reference to it—that the efforts of the Irish Government were very generally successful in calling forth the Catholics in favour of the Union—seems to me to be strongly corroborated by other evidence. There is no doubt that some of the

Appendix.
Note KK.

most influential of the Roman Catholic Bishops were decidedly advocates for the Union. Thus, Dr. Dillon, Archbishop of Tuam, expressed his opinion that 'this measure alone can restore harmony and happiness to our native country.' (Letter to Archbishop Troy, Sept. 1, 1799, *Castlereagh Correspondence*, vol. ii., p. 387); and Dr. Moylan, Bishop of Cork, wrote that 'nothing will more effectually tend to lay party feuds and dissensions, and restore peace and harmony among us, than the great measure in contemplation of the legislative Union and incorporation of this kingdom with Great Britain.' (Letter to Sir J. Hippesley, Sept. 14, 1799, *Castlereagh Correspondence*, vol. ii., p. 399.) The latter prelate considered that at that time 'the measure was working its way and daily gaining ground on the public opinion,' and he spoke of 'the Roman Catholics as in general avowedly favourable to the measure, the South,' he says, 'declaring for it.' So also Dr. Troy, Archbishop of Dublin, observed that 'the question of the Union was daily gaining ground.' 'The Catholics,' he added, 'were coming forward in different parts in favour of the measure, which the generality of them consider as their only protection against a faction seemingly intent on their defamation and destruction.' (Letter of Archbishop Troy to Mr. Marshall, Oct. 12, 1799, *Castlereagh Correspondence*, vol. ii., p. 420.) With these expressions of opinion may be compared addresses from meetings of Roman Catholics favourable to the measure. (See Dr. Dunbar Ingram's *History of the Legislative Union*, chap. vi., where the question of Catholic support of the Union is investigated with much research.)

With respect to the project of making provision for the Roman Catholic clergy, the Irish Ministers seem actually to have opened negotiations with the Bishops; for in January, 1799, a meeting of Bishops was held 'to deliberate on a proposal from Government of an independent provision for the Roman Catholic clergy,' and a Paper was then drawn up, signed by the four Archbishops and by six Bishops, in which 'it was admitted that a provision for the Roman Catholic clergy of this kingdom, competent and secured, ought to be thankfully accepted,' and the regulations, which it was thought proper should accompany it were laid down. (See *Grattan's Life*, vol. v., p. 57.) Indeed, the Knight of Kerry, who was in 1801 employed to reconcile these Bishops to delay of a measure of relief, holds that what passed between the Irish department and the Bishops amounted to a compact. (See letter of Right Hon. Maurice Fitzgerald to Sir Robert Peel, cited in the *Quarterly Review*, vol. lxxvii., p. 247.)

^{Note KK.}

NOTE LL, PAGE 224.

Upon the motion in the British House of Commons (April 21, 1800, see p. 222, *supra*) to induce delay in proceeding with the Resolutions for Union until the opinion of the Irish people could be ascertained, the great numerical preponderance on the side of the opponents of the Union was strongly insisted upon, and this was said to appear clearly from the petitions to the Irish Parliament against the measure. In the speech of Mr. Grey (afterwards Earl Grey), as it is given in the *Parliamentary History*, he is reported to have stated that 707,000 signed petitions against it; but Dr. Dunbar Ingram has ascertained from the contemporaneous newspapers in the British Museum, that although two newspapers report the figure stated as 707,000; fourteen others (including the *Times* and the *Dublin Saunders' Newsletter*) report the figure as 107,000. (See Dr. Dunbar Ingram's Review of Two Centuries of Irish History in the *Fortnightly Review* for February, 1889, p. 242.) The latter is more probably the correct report, for 707,000 is difficult to reconcile with Lord Castlereagh's assertion in his letter to Pitt of the amount of Catholic support called forth (see Note KK), or with the degree of support generally which he claimed in a speech in the Irish House of Commons (February 5, 1800).

In connection with this subject it deserves to be noted that when, for the first time after the Act of Union was passed, the Irish county constituencies were enabled to express their

Appendix.
Note LL.
opinions as to the conduct of their members, the following persons who, in the red and black lists in which the names of those who voted for and against Union were published, were held up for condemnation as having voted for the Union, and some also, as being placemen and pensioners, were yet returned again: M'Naghten for Antrim, Burton for Clare, Lord Boyle for Cork, Lord Castlereagh for Down, Hon. Richard Trench and Richard Martin for Galway, Knight of Kerry and Crosbie for Kerry, O'Dell for Limerick, Newcomen for Longford, Hon. D. Browne for Mayo, Bagwell for Tipperary, Rt. Hon. J. Stewart for Tyrone, Rt. Hon. J. Beresford for Waterford, Rochfort for Westmeath, and Lord Loftus and Ram for Wexford.

NOTE MM, PAGE 227.

Note MM.
The objections of George III. to permitting Roman Catholics to sit in Parliament being founded on the supposition that he could not, consistently with the engagements he had entered into under the sanction of an oath at his coronation, give his assent to this concession, were insuperable. 'The oath,' he said—in reply to a letter from Pitt, which laid before him reasons for concession—'bound him to maintain (what he described as) the fundamental maxims on which the Constitution was placed, namely, "that the Church of England was the established one, and that those who held employment in the State must be members of it." He seems to have been under the idea that if he violated the oath, such as he interpreted it, the condition 'on which the Crown had been conferred upon the House of Hanover was broken. 'If,' he said—after reading the Coronation Oath to his family—'I violate it, I am no longer Sovereign of this country, but it falls to the House of Savoy.'* (See

---

* The House of Savoy was prior in the line of descent to the House of Hanover. The former was descended from Henrietta, Duchess of Orleans, daughter of Charles I.; the latter from Elizabeth, daughter of James I., married to Frederick, Elector Palatine. (See Hallam, *Const. Hist.* ch. xv.)

Diaries of Lord Malmesbury, vol. iv., p. 21; and the letter of the King to Pitt, February 1, 1801, printed in the Appendix to Lord Stanhope's *Life of Pitt*, vol iii., p. 28.) Unfortunately the King was encouraged in his scruples by one whose office gave especial weight to his advice, Lord Loughborough, then the Chancellor of England. It, however, appears that others in Pitt's Cabinet beside Lord Loughborough took the same line in 1801, although before Union they, as well as Lord Loughborough, had made no objection to Lord Cornwallis and Lord Castlereagh negotiating with the Irish Catholics on the assumption that the Cabinet were favourable to their claims (see p. 212, *supra*). The other dissentients in the Cabinet from Pitt's policy were Lord Westmoreland, who had been Lord Lieutenant of Ireland from 1790 to 1795; Lord Liverpool, Lord Chatham, and, it is said, even the Duke of Portland; the three first acting in conformity with their real sentiments on the question, the last on temporary considerations, he himself being, like Wyndham, Earl Spencer, and other Whigs, who, with him, had joined Pitt, an advocate for yielding to the claims of the Catholics. As neither Castlereagh nor Canning were in the Cabinet, Pitt's support seems to have been from Lord Grenville and Dundas, Earl Spencer, and Wyndham. (See as to the proceedings in 1801, which led to Pitt's resignation of office, Lord Stanhope's *Life of Pitt*, vol. iii., chap. xxix.)

Appendix. Note MM.

Note NN, Page 229.

In 1799 it was looked upon as a great feat for a messenger to go to London and return to Dublin in four days and a half (*Cornwallis Correspondence*, vol. iii., p. 100 n.). And this seems to have been a then recent improvement in expedition; for Lord Cornwallis, writing on 20th of May in that year, says our communication with the Secretary of State is *now* so expeditious, that I last night (Sunday) at ten o'clock received an acknowledgment of a letter dated from this lodge at twelve o'clock on Wednesday.

Note NN.

Appendix.
Note NN.

For this, however, favourable weather was required, for either storms, or contrary winds, or calms prevented the packets crossing to or from Holyhead. A letter from Lord Castlereagh of 19th November, 1798, took six days to reach London (*Castlereagh Correspondence*, vol. ii., p. 27). On 15th December, same year, Cooke writes: 'No packets have sailed hence this week, and none have been received these five days' (*Cas. Cor.* ii., p. 44). A letter, written 29th January, 1799, did not reach London until 4th February, owing, Elliot says, to the desperate state of the roads (*Cas. Cor.* ii., p. 161). On one occasion Lord Castlereagh was detained eight days at Holyhead before he could cross the sea—'no small penance,' he says, describing his detention. (Letter to Rt. Hon. J. Beresford, October 17, 1800; *Beresford Correspondence*, vol. ii., p. 251.)

It is, however, not merely in connection with arrangements at the time of the Union, but at all times when considering the mode in which the Executive Government of Ireland before the Union was administered, that the imperfect nature of the communication, whether by letter or in person, between London (the seat of Government in England) and Ireland is to be kept in mind. In 1685, it was a four days' journey from London to Chester. If the traveller, not finding a ship at Park-gate ready to take him to Ireland, or for any other reason, went on to Holyhead, he had to encounter one of the worst roads then in the kingdom. According to the editor of Dorothy Osborne's Letters, a Lord Lieutenant going to Ireland had taken five hours to go from St. Asaph to Conway; then from that to Beaumaris he had to walk, his lady being carried in a litter. The same authority also mentions that on some occasions carriages had been taken to pieces at Conway and carried to the Menai Straits on the peasants' shoulders round the dangerous cliff of Penmaenmaur (see the recent edition of these Letters, p. 258).

In Swift's Journals we have recorded the actual journeys which he himself made, going from Dublin to London and returning from London to Dublin, in 1710 and 1713 (see the Journal to Stella under these dates). On the first occasion, the voyage to Park-gate took fifteen hours. He rode from Park-gate to Chester, meeting with a fall but no hurt, 'the horse,' he says 'understanding falls, and lying quietly till I got up.' In riding from Chester to London he took five days, ' weary,' he says, 'the first, almost dead the second, tolerable the third, and well enough the rest.' On the second occasion he found that the boat from Park-gate had gone, and, having no prospect for some time of another ship, he determined to proceed from Chester to Holyhead, which he calculated would require three days.

In 1783, Mrs. Delany, writing to induce an English friend to pay her a visit in Ireland, described the passage at sea (probably from Park-gate) as 'seldom more than 40 hours, and often not much more than half that time.' (Letter to Mrs. D'Ewes, 28th April, 1753, *Life and Correspondence* of Mrs. Delany, 1st ser., vol. iii. 225.)

Note OO, Page 233.

In the interval between the Scotch Union and the proposal of an Irish Union, and a few years before the latter, Blackstone's *Commentaries* had been published. He referred to the Union of Scotland with Great Britain, and the jurisdiction of Parliament to enact it in the following terms: ... 'Parliament hath sovereign and uncontrollable authority, and is the place where that absolute despotic power, which must reside somewhere, is entrusted by the Constitution of this kingdom: it can alter the Constitution of the kingdom, and of Parliament itself, as was done by the Act of Union.' The same high view of the authority of an English Parliament was taken so far back as the time of Lord Coke: ... 'The power and jurisdiction of Parliament,' he says, 'is so transcendent and absolute, as it cannot be confined within any bounds' (4th Inst. f. 36).

So far, indeed, as legal authority, none was cited to cast doubt on the Scotch Act of Union, or against the power of Parliament. What those who denied its capacity relied on was, that in some philosophic writings abstract principles

Appendix.
Note OO.

were laid down inconsistent with it; while those who argued for it cited the *dicta* of legal authorities as to the English Parliament, of which the effect was expressed (as it appears to me correctly) by Grant, afterwards Master of the Rolls in England, in the following words: '... Parliament is morally incompetent to do anything wrong; but it is legally competent to do anything: it may do that which the people at large may do for themselves.'

The precedent of the Scottish Act of Union was entitled to the greatest weight, for, as was pointed out by William Smith, afterwards Baron of the Irish Court of Exchequer, in the argument for the Irish Union which he published as an expansion of his speech in the House of Commons (Dublin, 1799), more consequences of importance than the junction of the kingdoms were to depend upon it, and the question of its validity necessarily came before the eminent legal persons concerned in the proceedings connected with it. On this Act was to depend the title of the House of Hanover to rule in Scotland. This it was which constituted the heirs of the Princess Sophia sovereigns of the new United Kingdom of Great Britain; but no Act had conferred on them the Crown of Scotland as a separate kingdom. Under the Security Act this could have been done upon Anne's death, but a Scotch Parliament did not then exist. In the line of descent the House of Hanover was not next to the Pretender and his issue (note, p. 290, *supra*); and the legislation which, in England, disqualified those prior, if Roman Catholic, had not been enacted in Scotland. The legal persons engaged with the Scotch Act of Union were Lord Somers, who, according to Burnet (*Own Time*, vol. iv., p. 137-144), had the chief hand in projecting the scheme, and was its advocate in the British House of Lords, Chief Justice Holt, and Sir Simon Harcourt (afterwards Lord Chancellor), who were both among the Commissioners appointed to settle the terms of Union on the part of England; the Scotch Lord President, two Lords of Session, and the Lord Justice Clerk, who, on the other hand, acted as such Commissioners on the part of Scotland.

In favour of the capacity of Parliament there were, at the

time of the Union, the following judicial personages :—The English Chancellor (Lord Loughborough); the Irish (Lord Clare); Chief Justice of Ireland (Lord Kilwarden); Chief of the Common Pleas in Ireland (Lord Carlton); Chief Baron of the Exchequer in Ireland (Lord Yelverton).

NOTE PP, PAGE 237.

The observations of Canning, referred to at p. 237, *supra*, are the only notice in debate of the subject to which they relate that I have found. They were as follows :— . . . ' What, sir, is the point the most essential to the character of a House of Commons ? What is the power and the function without which it may, indeed, be a senate, it may be a grave and respectable council, it may be an assembly of representatives of the people, if you will, but it would cease to be a House of Commons according to the genuine spirit of the British Constitution ? Is it not the power of the purse—the control preserved over the conduct of the executive Ministers of the Crown, by the right of giving or withholding the supplies necessary for carrying on the business of the Government ? Let us see how the exercise of this characteristic and most important right would be secured to the Irish House of Commons by a device which, it seems, is one of the main expedients proposed as a substitute for an Union—a settled scale of proportional contribution. I confess I should like to see the first meeting of an Irish House of Commons after this ingenious security for its independence had been provided, and to hear the explanation which must be given by some great patriot, who might pique himself upon having invented so saving a substitute, to any country Member of Parliament who might very reasonably be at a loss to comprehend its operation. Suppose a message from the Throne communicating a declaration of war, and supplies to be voted in consequence. The country gentleman, conscious of his duty as a member of the House of Commons, proud of the additional means of discharging it which he might presume himself to have acquired by the defeat of the Union,

Appendix.
Note PP.

and the consequent vindication of Irish independence, would very naturally propose to consider of the causes of the war in order to judge of the propriety of granting supplies. He would be stopped, however, by the patriotic member, who would tell him, "Sir, your independence does not allow this latitude. The Parliament of Great Britain have already voted the supplies. We have nothing to do but to follow them." "Good" (would the country gentleman answer): "let us proceed to consider the *quantum* of the supplies which we are to raise." "You may save yourself that trouble, sir" (would be the reply of the great patriot). "In the act of last year, intituled 'An Act for Vindicating the Independence of the Irish Parliament,' you will find that we are bound by the vote of the British Parliament not only as to the general question of supplies, but as to the *quantum*. When England votes so much, Ireland is understood to have voted so much. This was my substitute for the slavish dependence of an Union; this is what we mean by proportional contribution!" The country gentleman would, perhaps, be somewhat surprised at this explanation, and would inquire rather anxiously what function then it might be that he was come there to exercise. "What" (says the patriot): "why, since the establishment of our independence our business is to devise the means by which the money already voted for us by the Parliament of that country, from whose domination we have so happily rescued ourselves, is to be raised." Is this, then, the notable contrivance by which the dignity and effective power of the Parliament of Ireland are to be maintained? And is it for a victory over Union purchased at this price that the Irish Parliament would crown with laurel the brows of the champion of its independence? And yet, sir, I defy any man to point out to me any other meaning than that which I have ascribed to the phrase "proportional contribution"; and I equally defy him to show that there would be in the accomplishment of an Union anything a thousandth part so degrading and destructive to the importance and character and constitution of the House of Commons.' (*Collected Speeches of Canning*, vol. i., pp. 220-2.)

INDEX.

A.

Act of 6 George I., 88; repeal of, 133.

Acts of Union, 224; accompanied in Ireland by an Act compensating owners of disfranchised boroughs, 224; provisions of Acts of Union, 225.

Authors favourable to Union—Molyneux, 83; Petty, 84; Adam Smith, 158; Decker, Child, 158; Montesquieu, 159.

B.

Bolton, Sir Richard, Chancellor of Ireland, his treatise against jurisdiction claimed by English Parliament over Ireland, 37, 54.

Boroughs disfranchised at Union, compensation for, 224; £7500 allowed for each seat suppressed, 224; total amount, £1,260,000, 224; Pitt intended similar compensation in his English Reform Bill, 209; his reasons for, 224; Act of Imperial Parliament, (A.D. 1809) making sale of seats illegal, App. n. H H; value of Irish boroughs, App. n. H H.

C.

Calvin's Case, judgment in, favours right of English Parliament to make laws for Ireland, 31; considered, 67.

Canning, Right Hon. George, comments on suggestion of Parliament with limited powers for Ireland, 237, and App. n. P P; his objections to it, 237, 295.

Clare, Earl of, Chancellor of Ireland, advocates Union from about 1793, 166; his influence, 183; opposes any relief to the Catholics in the Act of Union, 150, 183, and App. n. F F; his speech in support of the Union, 10th Feb., 1800, 219.

Cashel, Synod of, 12, and App. A.

Castlereagh, Viscount, afterwards Marquis of Londonderry, his conduct of Bill for Union in Irish House of Commons, 200; his character, 200, and App. n. G G.

Catholic question, 98; comes into prominence in 1792, 164; difficulties attending it suggest Union, 164, 177.

Commercial Propositions, proposed by Pitt in 1785, 150; originated with Pim, a Dublin merchant, 151; first set, 150; objected to in England, 152; second set, 153; objected to in Ireland, and withdrawn, 154.

Commons, House of, mode in which at first constituted, 11, 12; under Queen Elizabeth, 13, 15; under James I., 17; from 1692, 97.

Constitution of 1782, 137; Duke of Portland suggests that provisions restrictive of jurisdiction should be added to it, 139; found that it was impossible to carry them, 140; and that, if carried, they might not be permanent, 141.

Convocation, 20, 89.

Councils were the first legislative assemblies in Ireland, 3; copied from the English, 4; whether Councils under Henry II., 3, and App. n. B.

Council, Privy, 7, and App. E and Q.

Councils along with Parliaments, 10.

Counties, 12, 15; of Pale, 263.

Cox, Sir Richard, Lord Chancellor of Ireland in Anne's reign; his reasons for advising Union, 85 n.

Cornwallis, Marquis, comes to Ireland as Lord Lieutenant, 181; speech to Irish Parliament, 197.

Crosses, parts of counties so called, 8.

Crown, Irish statutes relating to, App. C C.

D.

Disagreement of British and Irish Parliaments on commercial propositions, 154; on the Regency, 160.

Dissolution, motion for, 220.

Dundas, Right Hon. Henry, refers to the Scottish Union as affording an argument for Irish Union, 157 n.

E.

English law introduced in Ireland, 5, 260.

Executive continued at Union as before, 228, 292.

F.

Flood, eminence of, 107.

Foster, Right Hon. John, Speaker of the Irish House of Commons, opposes Union, 199; speech against, 202.

G.

George III. prevents Catholic Emancipation, App. M M.

Grattan, Right Hon. Henry, advocates commercial freedom, 111; resolution in favour of free trade carried, 112; takes up question of legislative independence, 115; moves resolution asserting it in Irish House of Commons, 19th April, 1780, 116; failure of motion, 117; speech on that occasion, 117–123; renews the subject, 22nd February, 1782, 130; speaks again, 16th April, 1782, 131; his terms for Ireland, 132; success, 133; eloquence and eminence, App. n. Z.

H.

Heads of Bills, 38, and App. Q.

Henry II., whether Councils held by, 3, and App. n. B; gave royal authority in Ireland to John, 55; whether conquered Ireland, 68.

Henry III. confirmed English law in Ireland, 6, and App. n. D.

Hutchinson, Hely, n. A A of Appendix.

J.

James I., his Parliament, 1613, 17, 266.
James II. convened Parliament in Ireland, 1689, 46; Acts of, 46, and App. n. T; annulled by English Parliament, 46.
Jebb, Richard, afterwards Justice, writes pamphlet on Union question, 234; suggests retention of Irish Parliament with restrictions, 234.
John, Council of, 3; Acts of, 6, 260.

L.

Legislative system with restrictions, suggested by Duke of Portland in 1782, 139; found could not be carried, 140; see also 'Parliament with limited powers.'
Lismore, Council of, 12, 258.
London, difficulty of communicating with, App. n. N N.
Lords, House of, consisted of Lords Spiritual and Temporal, 11; some Abbots and Priors in, 11, 12.
Lucas, Charles, M.P., of medical profession, agitates against right of English Parliament to legislate for Ireland, 100.

M.

Mayart, Serjeant-at-Law and second Justice of Common Pleas, his treatise in support of the legislative authority over Ireland of the English Parliament, 54, 62.
Molyneux, William, M.P., his treatise, published in 1698, against the right claimed by the English Parliament to make laws for Ireland, 50, 59; his treatise condemned by English House of Commons, 51.

P.

Parliament (English) makes laws for Ireland, 25; its right not admitted by Irish Parliament, 26; questioned in legal cases, 28-32; affirmed in *Calvin's Case*, 31; attended by Irish representatives, 23; makes laws for Ireland under Commonwealth, 40; includes in 1654 Irish representatives, 41; under Charles II. makes laws for Ireland, 43; also under William and Mary, 46, 48, 52; right denied in 1641 by Irish Parliament, 36; arguments against it by Bolton, 55; by Molyneux, 59; arguments for the right, by Mayart, 63; united with Scottish Parliament, 83; statute asserting the right of British Parliament to legislate for Ireland, 6 George I., 88; comment of Swift, 94; the right questioned by Lucas, 99; by Grattan, 116; resolution proposed against it in 1780 in Irish House of Commons fails, 117; Grattan's speech, 117; resolution of Volunteers in 1782 against the right, 117; statute of George I. repealed, 133; united with Irish Parliament, 224.

Parliament (Irish) preceded by Councils, 3, 5; elective representation introduced by Wogan in 1295, 7; thenceforward the legislative assemblies justly called Parliaments, 7; Wogan's Parliament and Kilkenny, 1367, App. n. F; character of early Parliaments, 9, and App. n. G; natives did not attend them, 10; Councils held along with Parliaments, 10; two Houses, 11; counties returning members down to Queen Elizabeth's time, 12; number at this time, 12; Irish admitted to sit in Parliament, 33 Henry VIII., 13; where Parliaments met, 13; new counties formed under Elizabeth, 15; Perrot's Parliament, 1585, 15, and App. n. M; Parliament of James I., 1613, 17; under Henry IV. and VI. claims exclusive right to legislate for Ireland, 25, 26; Parliament, 1634, 34; Parliament, 1640, 35; renews claim of exclusive jurisdiction, 36; Bolton's treatise on the question before House of Lords, 37; Poynings' law requires consent of English and Irish Privy Councils for legislation, 38; held not to prevent discussion of 'Heads of Bills,' 39; no Parliament in Ireland under Commonwealth, 40; Parliament of the Restoration, 1660, 42; Parliament of James II., 1689, 45; its acts, 46, and App. n. T; nullified by English Parliament, 46; Parliaments under William and Mary (1692, 1695), 48, 49; Molyneux asserts exclusive jurisdiction of Irish Parliament, 50; Parliament under Queen Anne, 84; Lords and Commons then suggest Union of Ireland with England, 84; suggestion discouraged, 85; Parliament under George I., 97: under George II., 98; Parliament managed through the great nobles, 98; acts independently as to finance, 99; Opposition formed in House of Commons, 103; Parliament of George III., 1760, 104; octennial Act, 104; Parliament of 1768, 106; patronage directly used to influence Parliament, 106, and App. n. X; improvement in House of Commons, 107; its discontent, 109; Parliament and the Volunteers, 111; unite to demand free trade, 111; resolution for carried in House of Commons, 112; motion by Grattan to declare exclusive jurisdiction of the Irish Parliament in Ireland, 19th April, 1780, 116; fails, 117; renewed 22nd February, 1782, 130; ultimately conceded, 133; constitution of 1782, 137; Parliament of 1785, 146; disagreements of Irish Parliament with British (1785 and 1789), 154, 160; constitution of, defects in, 177, 178; use of patronage to manage, 211, and n. II of Appendix; Parliament of 1799, 197; Lord Lieutenant's speech to, 197; debate on Union, 198; majority against Government on the Address, 198; use of patronage, 211; proceedings in 1800, 212; majority in commons for Union, 216; Union enacted, 224; Act of, 225; whether Parliament competent to enact, 229.

Parliament with limited powers, suggested for Ireland by Duke of Portland in 1782, 139; idea abandoned, 140; again suggested by Jebb, afterwards Justice Jebb, in 1798, 234.

Parliament for Ireland, merely for internal affairs, disapproved by Sheridan, 234; scheme not without precedent at that time, 236; objections made to, 237.

Patronage, used to manage the Irish Parliament, 98, 106, 211, notes X and II of Appendix.

Perrot, Sir John, Deputy under Elizabeth, his Parliament, A.D. 1585, 15; of whom composed, 15, and App. n. M.

Pilkington's Case, judgment in, decided against jurisdiction of English Parliament to tax Ireland, 28.

Pitt, Right Hon. Wm., First Lord of the Treasury, 147; his opinion as to position before 1782 of Irish Parliament, 148; has commercial propositions prepared, 150; letter explaining them to Duke of Rutland, January 6, 1785, 151; in 1792 first begins to favour Union, 164; letter to Lord Westmoreland referring to Union, 165; not until 1798 engaged with any measure for Union, 182; speech for Union, 23rd January, 1799, 182; second speech, 31st January, 1799, 131.
Portland, Duke of, appointed, in 1782, Lord Lieutenant, 131; his suggestion of restriction on the jurisdiction of the Irish Parliament under the Constitution of 1782, 139; unable to procure assent to it, 140.
Portugal, dispute with, in 1782, 162.
Poynings, Deputy under Henry VII., his law as to Irish Parliament, 14; enacts that Irish Bills must be submitted to and approved by the English and Irish Privy Councils, 14; this provision when enacted desired by Irish Parliament, 14; another law of Poynings makes the English statutes to its date law in Ireland, 31; his first law repealed and new provisions substituted in 1783, 136.
Protectionist policy of Irish Parliament, 176, 280.

R.

Regency, question of, 1789, 160; disagreement of Irish and British Parliaments on, 160.
Reform of House of Commons, difficulties hindering, 178.

S.

Scotland had Parliament of its own, 77; Union with England, 83; circumstances out of which Union arose, 80; Union at first unpopular, App. n. W; prosperity after Union, 157.
Sheridan, leads the opposition to the Irish Union in the English House of Commons, 186; speech against, 187; opposed to having an Irish Parliament merely for internal affairs, 235.

Swift, comes forward against English commercial laws, 92; publishes, in 1724, the Drapier's Letters against Wood's coinage, 24; writes against general ascendency of England, 94; his letters prosecuted, 95; failure of the prosecution, 96.

U

Union of Ireland with England, in 1672, approved by Sir Wm. Petty, 83; in 1698 by Molyneux, 83; with Great Britain, suggested in 1707 by Irish Parliament, 84; not encouraged in England, 85; unpopular then in Ireland outside Parliament, 86; again suggested about 1785, 155; reasons which, after that time, began to recommend Union, 136–166; hindrances and aids to, 171–180; in 1798 this policy adopted by Ministers, 182; Bill for prepared in 1798, 182; proceedings for in 1799, 185; in 1800, 215; carried, 224.

V.

Volunteers, in 1778, organized, 109; progress of the organization, 128; number of, &c., App. n. Y; meeting and resolutions of at Dungannon, 129.

W.

Waterford Merchants, Case of, decisions in, as to jurisdiction of English Parliament in Ireland, 28, 30.

Wool, export of, except to England, prohibited, 52, 273.

Wogan, Sir John, Deputy, Parliament convened by, A.D. 1295, 7, and App. n. F: in his Parliaments members first elected from the counties and towns, 7; sent from outside Pale, 263; Pale in 1515, 263.

THE END.